DISTURBING THE PEACE?

In memory of my dad and grandad

Disturbing the Peace?

Politics, television news and the
Northern Ireland peace process

GRAHAM SPENCER
School of Social and Historical Studies,
University of Portsmouth, UK

Ashgate

Aldershot • Burlington USA • Singapore • Sydney

© Graham Spencer 2000

Published by
Ashgate Publishing Ltd
Gower House
Croft Road
Aldershot
Hants GU11 3HR
England

Ashgate Publishing Company
131 Main Street
Burlington, VT 05401-5600 USA

Ashgate website: http://www.ashgate.com

British Library Cataloguing in Publication Data
Spencer, Graham
  Disturbing the Peace? : politics, television news and the
  Northern Ireland peace process
  1.Television and politics - Northern Ireland 2.Northern
  Ireland - Politics and government - 1994 -
  I.Title
  384.5'54'09416

Library of Congress Control Number: 00-134842

ISBN 0 7546 1522 7

Printed and bound by Athenaeum Press, Ltd.,
Gateshead, Tyne & Wear

Contents

Acknowledgements

This project owes thanks to many people, especially the politicians, journalists and editors who gave time and thought to my questions. I am also indebted to Keith Tester and Chris Shilling at the University of Portsmouth who provided support and advice throughout, and to my family and friends for providing encouragement and humour when it was needed. Most of all, this work is dedicated to the many people who have suffered and endured the conflict in Northern Ireland.

Introduction

The Problem and the Purpose of the Research

This study is concerned with how the national television news media has covered the Northern Ireland peace process and its role within the politics of that process. It examines how news constructed the peace process during the formative years of peace negotiations (1994–98) and how politicians tried to use news as a mechanism for contesting and promoting the shape of peace.

The peace process, which took the form of an expansive political process more specifically from 1993, signalled a marked change in the political complexion of Northern Ireland by offering the possibility of moving from a situation of conflict to one of conflict resolution. It represented, to put it another way, a fundamental shift away from the politics of terrorism which had dominated the conflict in Northern Ireland since 1969, towards a politics of peace.

Central to explaining and describing this transition has been the news media, who now refer to developments and events by way of their impact on the peace process as a matter of convention. The peace process, it would appear, now provides us with a framework for understanding the political developments of Northern Ireland and to the extent where it is less Northern Ireland which is now in crisis, or on the verge of a breakthrough, but the peace process itself.

Television news coverage of the emerging peace process signalled a fundamental break with some of the conventions of reporting which previously dominated much of the conflict. Once established as a credible political process, news was no longer able to rely on images of terrorist violence to represent the conflict as being inherently about warring factions or sectarian hatreds as before. Instead, the peace process replaced the politics of terrorism with negotiations about peace, and for news this meant applying a different set of references and codes by which to make sense of what was going on in Northern Ireland.

This book sets out to examine the function of news within the political transition which became commonly referred to as the peace process. In particular, it is concerned with how news and politics interacted and how this interaction affected the promotion and development of peace. It is concerned with how politics was contested through news and how patterns of reporting about peace (referred to as the peace process paradigm in this study) impacted on that contestation.

This research addresses a number of questions surrounding the problem of the role of news within peace negotiations. To start with, although there has been much written on the role of the news media within the conflict in Northern Ireland from 1969 until the peace process in 1993 (Curtis 1986; Schlesinger 1987; Miller 1994; Butler 1995), there is far less material available about the role of the news media within the resolution of that conflict from 1993 onwards (Tangen Page and Schwarz 1994; Miller and McLaughlin 1996). There is plenty of material available about the media's tendency to adopt dominant explanations of the conflict and to play a supportive role in relation to state propaganda in the war against terrorism (Curtis 1986; Schlesinger 1987; Miller 1994), but less is known about whether the media played a similarly supportive role in relation to dominant explanations about the emerging peace. One of the key concerns of this book is to address this deficiency and to examine whether the news media acted in a similarly supportive way towards dominant articulations of the peace process as they did before, during the war against terrorism. To put it another way, I aim to examine how the peace process emerged as a news paradigm (pattern of reporting) and how that paradigm affected the representation of elite positions and political discourse.

In conducting this study, I obtained interview data from those involved in the politics of peace and those involved in the selection and presentation of news reports about that peace. Indeed, the central importance of this study resides in the interview material, which has been gathered through a series of in-depth interviews with politicians, journalists and editors involved in the politics and the reporting of the peace process from 1994–98 (see Appendix 1 for research methodology and interview techniques). Through this material I have been able to establish a picture of how politicians perceived the role of news in relation to their objectives, as well as how those working in news production came to understand those objectives in news terms. This has helped to create a comprehensive picture about how news functioned in relation to political objectives and introduces relevant new material with which to consider the role of news in relation to dominant political intentions.

If politicians are not assisted by news in the promotion of their respective positions in relation to peace, then this raises questions about the importance of news for political control and suggests a need to re-examine theories which emphasise the role of news for the legitimisation of political direction and policy. This study is not therefore only about news and the peace process (although its primary intention is to examine that relationship), but has implications which impact on theories which assert the necessity of news for the legitimisation of political power. If politicians experience problems in their efforts to develop peace which are exacerbated or even caused by news coverage, then there is clearly a need to question perspectives which stress the centrality of supportive news coverage for the effective conduct and exercise of political objectives. Because of this and in the light of the empirical material which is foregrounded in this study, it becomes pertinent to examine key theoretical debates which prioritise the reproductive tendencies of news in relation to political elites and conflict and which view news in terms of being an essential arena for the communication and contestation of political aims.

Another important consideration this book addresses is how the promotion of peace sits in relation to news imperatives which thrive on conflict. During the war on terrorism, television news was well placed to serve the moral condemnations of politicians and represent responses to the Northern Ireland situation in conflictual terms. The antagonisms and the contended nature of responses towards acts of terrorism (particularly between state agencies and republicans) were invariably used in news to simplistically reinforce and entrench positions with regard to terrorism and rarely moved beyond stereo-types (Butler 1995). However, the peace process signified the need for a very different approach. Reconciliation, dialogue and agreement become the main stated political goals, but are especially difficult when news prefers to communicate oppositions and obstructions. My intention is to enquire into how politicians tried to promote peace through television news given this emphasis and to see how journalists and editors understood this problem.

Notably, although this study is concerned with national television news, it includes interviews conducted with individuals working within news and politics in Northern Ireland who tend to comment on how news impacts at a local level. This can be seen as creating a problem for this study because it brings into question whether this analysis is concerned with a homogeneous or heterogeneous treatment of news. I want to make it clear here, that although this book brings out some effects of coverage specific to Northern Ireland, these effects also impact and intersect with national coverage and have relevance for the peace process. Many issues and concerns covered by reports in Northern Ireland also become covered by national news networks and reflect important political debates at a national level. Moreover, although some of the interview comments suggest differences in the type of coverage being discussed, most of those comments are based on a local interpretation of national reporting and indicate problems and perceptions about coverage which this study benefits from enormously. Differences in news coverage are taken into account into this study, but their use is to primarily demonstrate problems with the homogeneous approach provided by the mainstream news networks. Since coverage of the peace process has itself tended to be homogeneous, it seems pertinent to look at news in those terms.

To summarise then, this study is important because it: (1) outlines the emergence of a new paradigm used in the coverage of Northern Ireland; (2) addresses how that paradigm impacts on the politics of peace and negotiations; (3) considers whether dominant political objectives received the same kind of ideological support from the news media as during the war against terrorism; (4) introduces new considerations about the interaction between news and politics and the role of reporting within the political process; and (5) considers efforts to develop reconciliation through news imperatives which emphasise conflict and simplification.

Structure and Content of the Research

This study is composed of seven chapters which collectively aim to examine and interrogate the role of television in peace negotiations.

Chapter 1 provides historical background to the media's role in Northern Ireland and focuses on the representations of terrorism which dominated coverage throughout much of the contemporary period. In particular, this chapter is designed to establish how the media conventionally constructed the Northern Ireland problem throughout 'The Troubles' (a term used to refer to the period from 1969 until 1993) and how representations of violence maintained the enduring perception that the conflict was sustained by tribal hatreds and the inherently evil nature of terrorists. This impression was furthered reinforced by government propaganda and news management which sought to maintain public support for counterinsurgency campaigns against terrorism by constructing it as an essentially pathological, morally repulsive activity, without legitimate foundation. Not only did this entail defining those who carried out terrorism through the language of condemnation (by labelling them as 'gunmen', 'bombers', 'killers', 'murderers', 'men of violence' etc.) and involve coercive measures being imposed on the media by the state, but it also deterred examination of the political and social context within which the violence was situated. As with many media representations of violence and war, much coverage of Northern Ireland failed to go beyond simplistic stereotypes about those who commit violence and sustained mythologies about the conflict deriving from groups with atavistic mentalities who are locked into sectarian loyalties (Allen and Seaton 1999). After summarising the main arguments of the background literature which examines media coverage of Northern Ireland, this chapter then goes on to look at two prominent themes which underpin the literature: definitions of terrorism and the struggle for political control of coverage. The debates and contentions over representations of terrorism are considered in depth before I then look at the Broadcasting Ban as an example of how controls were imposed on the broadcasters by the British government in an attempt to obstruct political spokesmen of paramilitary groups appearing on television. The ban offers a clear indication of how politically sensitive the Northern Ireland has conventionally been for successive British governments and demonstrates how far politicians were prepared to go to try and manage the flow of reporting.

This section of the study not only aims to establish the historical background to news coverage of Northern Ireland, but also to inform the reader about the limitations of such analysis for understanding a new climate concerned with the development of peace. This chapter concludes by calling for a rethink about the role of television news in the changing political landscape of Northern Ireland and brings to attention a need to consider the affects of news on the politics of peace rather than the politics of conflict.

Chapter 2 outlines how the peace process emerged and represented a new phase of political relations in Northern Ireland. It highlights how political emphasis moved from conflict to conflict resolution and begins by explaining the background which influenced the shape of peace negotiations. It then goes on to evaluate how news entered into that process and adopted a paradigmatic response to peace negotiations, by representing developments in repetitive, conflictual and simplistic terms. Raising critical questions about the ability of politicians to promote peace through news given these conventions of coverage, the chapter concludes by highlighting significant problems which politicians came to face when communicating peace and brings into view key differences about the media's role in peace as compared to its role in conflict. The identification of possible problems associated with promoting peace through news then brings to light the need for a more intensive interrogation of those problems, which is given through interview material in the next three chapters.

Having described how a peace process paradigm emerged in news and highlighted some of the difficulties which this may have created for political efforts at building trust and confidence, chapter three draws on interviews with politicians to assess political perceptions of news and the role of news in peace negotiations. It does this by discussing material from interviews with fifteen political representatives from a cross-section of parties involved in the peace process. Representatives from Unionist and Loyalist parties, Nationalist and Republican parties, British and Irish governments, as well as American peace delegation members, were interviewed on how they dealt with the television media during the formative stages of the peace process and questioned on what they saw as the main concerns and problems associated with this interaction. They spoke about how they tried to use news as a communicative device and gave examples of how they tried to use reports as a facilitative mechanism for trying to develop peace. Importantly, this chapter also looks at how politicians tried to keep certain communications away from the media. Issues of confidence and privacy play a key function in the development of peace, but clearly also pose problems for dealing with the media who rely on a constant flow of information. The fact that at times politicians have deliberately tried to avoid talking to the media about what was going on in the peace process, clearly raises questions about the media's centrality within the political process and indicates that in particular situations and under particular circumstances, it may be more desirable for politicians to avoid the media, or, at least to assign the media a peripheral role in political affairs. The promotion of peace negotiations is an example where at times, the media can be a disadvantage or obstruction to political objectives and the interview material in this chapter addresses that problem.

Chapter 4 is based on interviews with eleven journalists who reported the peace process on national television news. Although similar questions about communicating peace and the importance of television within that process were also put to journalists, this chapter is more concerned with how they perceived the politics of peace and how they came to construct news in association with that perception. Since most journalists who were interviewed emphasised similar things and similar patterns of reporting the peace process, it seemed appropriate to section this chapter into areas which address the relationship of journalists to sources, the affect of political pressures, how reporters decided to represent peace negotiations, and the routines and constraints they worked under. This not only made the material easier to organise, but provides a narrative which is easier for the reader to make sense of. This part of the study provides a useful comparison to the political interviews by allowing journalists to explain how they see their role with regard to political discourse. It will also provide valuable information about whether journalists see their work as having a political role to play in peace negotiations, how the reporting of peace compares to the reporting of conflict and how they see their work in relation to the promotion of dominant political objectives.

Chapter 5 attempts to elicit the attitudes and perspectives of editors who managed news coverage of the peace process during its early and tentative stages. It aims to identify the priorities which influence the content of reports, how editorial decisions are made, and how news is seen in terms of its potential impact on the politics of peace. Based on interviews with seven editors from the mainstream news networks, this chapter is particularly concerned with how editors manage coverage of the peace process and how they view that coverage in relation to political talks and negotiations. Like the previous two chapters, this section of the study organises the empirical material into sections which broadly address the problems of broadcasting Northern Ireland and the search for balance. These include how the conflict has been covered, the transition from war to peace and how that shift was handled by editors, the nature of politics and its influences, and routines and responsibilities. This chapter is concerned with the management of news production and how editors conceive the internal politics of newsgathering in comparison to the political process which they are interpreting, emphasising and articulating.

Having outlined the main themes which arise through the interviews and having established a picture of the interaction between politicians, journalists and editors, chapter 6 presents a case study of how news reported and covered the Provisional IRA ceasefire of August 1994. Although the main point of this analysis is to see if the perceptions and attitudes of the three groups have a basis which is grounded in the actuality of reporting, it is also concerned with highlighting how those involved in news production came to understand the developing peace, and how they came to understand it in relation to dominant political discourse and objectives. Looking at the speculation of a forthcoming IRA ceasefire which emerged in coverage more than a month beforehand, this analysis will draw out the main representational features of reporting and question what those features signified in terms of journalistic understanding about the developing peace. One indication that journalists found it difficult to break free from the previous representations of conflict can be found in the way they speculated about a possible ceasefire leading to an increase, rather than decrease, in violence. Not only does this also indicate problems for politicians who were working for peace, by interpreting a major gesture of peace as a ploy which could exacerbate tensions and violence, but it raises questions about the news media supporting dominant political aims and how journalists conceived the emerging peace process paradigm. This main aim of this chapter is to examine how the perceptions and views of politicians, journalists and editors compare in relation to actual news reports and the reporting of a key event in the peace process.

The empirical material used in this study highlights a number of key points about the interaction between news and politics which has implications for theorisations about the relationship between news, politics and conflict. In chapter seven, I consider the work of Stuart Hall, Daniel Hallin and Gadi Wolfsfeld as examples of theorisations about this relationship. The studies which these writers have produced, provide a framework for interrogating the role of political sources within news, the impact of news on political policy, political contestation in the media and the influence of news on the promotion of peace and these are all issues which affect this study. Apart from some recognition by Wolfsfeld in his work about the role of news in the Middle East peace process (which is used here because it is one of the few studies which highlights how news can obstruct peace), these theories argue that the media is essential to the political process and the conduct of policy. However, what my research reveals is that there can be times and circumstances when media involvement can undermine the work of politicians and that political success may be enhanced by excluding the news from developments.

Although the media were important at particular moments in the peace process (helping to sell the Good Friday Agreement for example), it also emerges that communicating to the media was actively discouraged by lead players in the negotiations. The probability that reporting can obstruct political aims poses new questions about the impact of news on policy and indicates that totalising theories about the relations between news and politics are inadequate for understanding just how complex and even contradictory this interaction can be. Rather, the importance of news for political legitimisation depends on particular policies, goals and circumstances, as well as how each of these complement news values. At the centre of this analysis, is the argument that on occasions (in this case, moments in a peace process) it may be more politically desirable for the media to be kept out of political affairs than to be involved in them. Chapter 7, then, contextualises the theoretical implications of my research within debates about the media's role in conflict and raises issues and concerns which have consequences for thinking about that relationship.

The main concern of this research is to investigate how news and politics operate both independently and interdependently in the context of political objectives concerned with the promotion and development of peace and negotiations. Or, to put it another way, to examine how politics and news interact and consider that interaction in terms of how it impacts on the development and promotion of peace in Northern Ireland. What is important to bear in mind throughout, is that this study is not meant to be a definitive theoretical account of news processes and values, even though it creates questions and has implications for such accounts. It is primarily about the dynamic which exists between news and peace negotiations and how that dynamic shaped those negotiations.

1 Reporting Northern Ireland: Terrorism and News Management

Introduction

This chapter provides an overview of how the news media has constructed the Northern Ireland situation during the contemporary period. This means looking at the portrayal of conflict and at how dominant elites have managed the flow of news in order to affect such portrayal. To put it simply, this part of the study is concerned with how the news media reported Northern Ireland as a war of terrorism and how the British government influenced the flow of news in order to wage an effective propaganda war against those seen as terrorists. It therefore also serves as an historical account of the conventions of news coverage and the political restraints which influenced that coverage.

Along with the main political factors which have affected reporting of the conflict in Northern Ireland, I will provide a detailed examination of the background literature about news coverage and pick up on the central themes of that literature. Notably, those themes are concerned with representations of terrorism and the political control of reporting. Consideration of those areas will constitute the bulk of this chapter and will involve dealing with key debates about terrorism. A tendency for news to report political violence within a 'terrorism paradigm' which dominated coverage throughout much of 'The Troubles' (1969–93) is prioritised in many of the available studies about coverage and needs to be understood if we are to get a sense of how far coverage has changed during the new climate of peace.

Once the conventions of the terrorism paradigm have been established, this chapter then goes on to examine how political forces have shaped and affected those conventions. In particular, this involves highlighting how political constraints were placed on the news networks in an attempt to avoid potentially damaging publicity about state policy in Northern Ireland. The Broadcasting Ban of 1988 is used here as an example of political control which has been imposed on broadcasters in an effort to close off propaganda opportunities for the political representatives of paramilitary groups, and underlines the importance of definitional control over stories about the conflict and the struggle for dominance over representations.

Finally, this chapter concludes by calling for a need to rethink the existing literature about news coverage of Northern Ireland given the changing political climate. As the politics of peace takes precedence over the politics of conflict, so new questions are raised about the role of news which the existing literature is unable to address. This highlights the relevance of this study and the importance of conducting an enquiry which addresses the role of news as part of the peace process.

In short, the intentions of this chapter are to: (1) look at the arguments which have focused on the media's propaganda function in relation to the Northern Ireland conflict; (2) explain how news has tended to adopt a supportive role towards dominant articulations of the conflict; (3) assess how debates about political violence have affected its coverage; (4) look at how political control has been exerted on the news media; and (5) suggest a need for rethinking relations between news and politics in Northern Ireland given the emergence of a new political climate concerned with peace rather than conflict.

The Background

Historically speaking, news coverage has tended to emphasise the Northern Ireland problem as being about two conflicting forces; the Provisional IRA and British state forces. This tendency became particularly apparent after 1969, when the Provisional IRA became a serious force and took to violence in order to resist the presence of the British government in Northern Ireland. The civil rights movement (from which the Provisional IRA of the modern period effectively grew (Farrell 1988)) and the issues of discrimination which it highlighted, became increasingly excluded in reports as a context for understanding tensions between Unionists and Nationalists when the civil rights marches of 1969 erupted into violence and provided news organisations with the dramatic images which resulted from that violence. Developing into what became perceived as a war between republicans and the British state (Schlesinger 1987: 223), measures and propaganda campaigns were staged by the British government in order to win the hearts and minds of the British people in their battle against terrorism and those who supported it (Curtis 1986; Miller 1994). A confidential Downing Street memorandum about the killings of Bloody Sunday in 1972, detailed an exchange between Sir Edward Heath and Lord Widgery who had been given the task of investigating the deaths of 14 civil rights marchers by the Parachute Regiment, with Heath explaining 'it had to be remembered 'we were in Northern Ireland fighting not only a military war but a propaganda war' ('Memo reveals "propaganda war" in Ulster', *The Guardian*, 10 November 1995).

From 1970 on, propaganda became key to government intentions in Northern Ireland and the potential success of such propaganda was augmented by 'voluntary' arrangements made between government and the media for determining how organisations like the Provisional IRA would be represented (Schlesinger et al. 1983: 113). This arrangement, according to Schlesinger, led to a construction of events and situations which excluded the Provisional IRA from the realms of conventional discourse and reinforced interpretations and articulations 'predicated upon notions of consensus and legitimacy'. This development, continues Schlesinger, was achieved by depicting groups such as the Provisional IRA 'as outside the bounds of tolerance', where 'broadcasting reproduces decisions and definitions which are initiated by the state' and then subsequently reproduced within the news media (Schlesinger 1987: 229). Dealing with terrorist groups who defied the parameters of legitimate dissent posed problems for the broadcasters in their efforts to uphold the image of objective and balanced reporting, bringing changes to reporting which challenged the assumptions of the early broadcasters who saw most areas of coverage as fairly noncontroversial and unproblematic (Curran and Seaton 1995: 300–1).

The problems were essentially political in orientation and were concerned with how to portray terrorists in their actions against the state. Coverage of the state in a critical light was minimalised by a tightening of editorial controls (Cathcart 1984: 225), and from early 1971, permission to interview IRA members was practically always with withheld, with similar guidelines later attached to loyalist paramilitaries (Article 19: 55). The tightening of editorial control was exemplified by the 'reference-upwards system' which was introduced in 1971 and transferred the decision making power about programming on Northern Ireland to the highest editorial levels for clearing, effectively curtailing journalistic autonomy and contributing to a process of self-censorship as contentious programme ideas were obstructed, or blocked (Curtis 1984: 173–96). Many programmes on Northern Ireland have been blocked over the years (Curtis and Jempson 1993) but the fact that they were made at all, also indicates how programme makers also challenged dominant articulations within the restrictive climate.

The fall of the Stormont parliament in 1972 led to a further tightening of editorial control however, where reflecting the shift of political power to Westminster the BBC also transferred editorial control from Northern Ireland to London (Cathcart 1984: 226). According to Butler (1991), this shift also corresponded with a change in coverage which increasingly favoured representations of state policy. Butler argues that throughout the early 1970s there was an 'institutional bias against analysis', which left journalism 'progressively diluted to a descriptive function'. He further contends that because of this transition the surge of sectarian murder and destruction could therefore only be depicted as a 'continual procession of unique and inexplicable events and that ithout a wider frame of reference, an interpretation was perpetuated that a 'few extremists on either side' were the cause rather than a symptom of deep division'. This encouraged the (mis)perception that if 'the British could negotiate a 'reasonable' settlement between the parties, the good sense of the vast majority would prevail, isolating the tiny minority of malcontents (Butler 1991: 111). This diminution of reporting to what Butler views as a 'descriptive function' is seen by Schlesinger to have resulted from the reference- upwards system, which created 'a cautious 'factual' approach to coverage and a wholesale absence of investigative journalism because journalists are unwilling to pursue controversial topics, and tend to engage in self-censorship' (Schlesinger 1979).

Although, Schlesinger was unable to predict the making of such programmes as *Real Lives*, *Creggan* and *Death on the Rock* and the political controversy they sparked precisely because they pursued controversial topics (*The Information War*, BBC2, 16 August 1994), his assertion is supported by much of the literature which has since considered the role of news reporting in Northern Ireland. Concerned ostensibly with the political pressures exerted by elite information agencies in general and governmental controls in particular, the academic orientation towards media coverage of Northern Ireland highlights the inability of the news media to convey the complex ideological differences which exist within the respective communities there. Resorting to a misleading consensual interpretation of events which has been largely shaped by the moral and political dilemmas of reporting terrorism, the news media have provided a role which has been more supportive than critical of British state policy in Northern Ireland.

News Coverage of Northern Ireland: A Review of the Background Literature

Much of the available literature produced before the peace process depicts news as playing a predominantly reproductive role in relation to elite political discourse, constructing the Northern Ireland conflict through official interpretations and an emphasis on political violence. The more comprehensive accounts of how terrorism became a context for understanding conflict and how reporting was influenced by state agencies are *Ireland: The Propaganda War* by Liz Curtis (1984), *Putting Reality Together* by Philip Schlesinger (1987), *Don't Mention The War* by David Miller (1994), *The Most Contrary Region* by Rex Cathcart (1984), *The Trouble With Reporting Northern Ireland* by David Butler (1995), and more recently, *War and Words: The Northern Ireland Media Reader*, edited by Bill Rolston and David Miller (1996).

In the works of Curtis, Schlesinger and Miller, the thrust of analysis is concerned with how the discourse of terrorism became absorbed into news as a matter of convention and how reporting was shaped and managed by way of political power and effective state propaganda strategies. Cathcart's analysis, on the other hand, looks at changes in BBC reporting from 1924–84 and how those changes were introduced to meet the information needs of a divided community. More currently, David Butler's thesis argues that the fundamental underlying causes of conflict are misrepresented by the broadcast media, and that this results from institutional structures and objectives which are ill-equipped to make sense of the complexities, contradictions and the dissensual nature of Northern Ireland politics. Together, these works provide useful background for understanding how the news media dealt with coverage of Northern Ireland prior to the peace process and in so doing they help to establish the conventions of the conflict paradigm which the peace process was to later represent a shift away from.

Central to consideration of how news has represented Northern Ireland, is the work of Liz Curtis, who highlights the importance of state propaganda in the British state's war against terrorism, and where 'For over a decade, Ireland has been the most closely controlled issue on British television' (Curtis 1984: 276). This control, according to Curtis, derives from powerful state institutions which obstruct interpretations and articulations that challenge or undermine the dominant perception that terrorism underpins conflict. As Curtis puts it:

> Those in positions of power, both in government and in the media, have proved most reluctant to provide a full picture of events in the North, or their context,

and have made considerable efforts to prevent journalists, dramatists and filmmakers from exploring the situation from any angle other than that favoured by the British establishment (ibid.: 275).

For Curtis, the capacity of the British government to wage a successful propaganda war against organisations like the Provisional IRA, derived from extensive resources which enabled a comprehensive distribution and control of information and greatly increased the possibilities for managing news. The implications of this influence were such she argues, that 'Republicans cannot, in any case, hope to match the facilities available to the Northern Ireland Office, RUC and press offices. Even if they could, it is doubtful whether this would win them a good press in Britain: the ties between the media and the authorities are too strong' (ibid.: 274).

However, though the media's fixation with terrorism is a valid subject for analysis, Curtis does tend to convey both press and television coverage as equally sympathetic to the dominant political line. This tendency creates a rather generalising evaluation of media coverage and is indicative of further weaknesses. Firstly, there is little differentiation between local, national and international coverage of the conflict and so negligible examination of how reporting may vary through these different contexts. Secondly, although the assertion about republican groups being unable to compete in propaganda terms with the state is fair enough, Curtis does not consider propaganda successes for republicans; a good example being the hunger strikes of 1980, which drew considerable media attention towards the republican movement, highlighted the profile of Sinn Fein and internationalised the conflict. Thirdly, Curtis does not examine why propaganda was more or less successful, nor address media resistance to the official line. Failure to recognise these factors is reflective of the author's own nationalist sympathies, which are evident through remarks such as 'given the way television coverage hangs on the coat-tails of the establishment, substantial change can only be expected when British policy towards the North shifts radically, or when there is a major split in the political arena over what policy should be pursued' (ibid.: 278). This perception supports a continuing dual theme throughout the book, which is that the state operates repressive and effective propaganda strategies and that the news media oblige in reproducing the dominant official line. Although she emphasises the hegemonic function of news reporting and points to the subordination of journalism to elite power, Curtis does nevertheless tend to neglect consideration of alternative discourses in news and how sources compete for control of the news agenda.

In contrast to the picture expressed by Curtis of a repressive state and a tightly controlled media, Schlesinger suggests a more consensual relationship between the two. He argues:

> In recent years, the social and political conflict in Northern Ireland has illustrated the power to circumscribe the broadcast media's coverage of the events, issues and points of view there. This has been handled, not through overt censorship, but rather through a mediated intervention, in which spokesmen in the sphere of politics have defined the permissible limits, and these conceptual orientations have been picked up and reproduced within the media. The internal mediation of the boundaries of the permissible has taken place preeminently through a tightening of editorial controls within the broadcasting organisations (Schlesinger 1987: 205).

In adopting a consensual relationship with the mainstream British political parties and utilising the parliamentary system of debate to contest developments and events in Northern Ireland, Schlesinger identifies a significant problem with the representations of news production. This problem (later elaborated by Butler) is that since 'Northern Ireland's crisis is not one which can anyway be handled in terms of consensus politics' (ibid.: 206), the values of consensual news cannot therefore get to grips with the causes of conflict there. In using a frame of interpretation which draws on the conventions of parliamentary discourse, Schlesinger views coverage as sympathetic to state responses, which creates a paradigm whereby the 'entire approach to illegal organisations is predicated upon notions of consensus and legitimacy. By identifying them as outside the bounds of tolerance, broadcasting reproduces decisions and definitions which are initiated by the state' (ibid.: 229). Continuing, he observes, 'The celebration of consensus brings with it a depreciation of radical forms of action, their characterisation as violent and irrational, and, moreover, obscures any understanding of why these should occur' (ibid.: 168). In comparison to Curtis, Schlesinger argues less about the repressive nature of state controls which operate to censor particular types of coverage, and more towards an acceptance of dominant interpretive forms within news production. He thus appears to be talking about a reproduction of the official line as a convention of news discourse, rather than it being directly imposed from above.

Miller's account of coverage of Northern Ireland has more similarities with the work of Curtis than Schlesinger, and is an attempt to unravel the use of propaganda tactics and public relations strategies by state agencies engaged in the conflict. This analysis makes a valuable contribution to the literature on news management and highlights the effectiveness of official agencies in promoting representations of the conflict. However, like Curtis, Miller tends to ignore propaganda strategies used by groups who oppose official interpretations. Although he acknowledges that the news media can exert pressures on propaganda sources ('the media themselves played a prominent role in spurring the search by the government for more "legitimate" ways of describing the conflict' (Miller 1994: 82)), Miller fails to elaborate on the complexities of this dynamic, or give attention to the political pressures which coverage itself generates. Moreover, although Miller highlights propaganda opportunities for groups who do not support dominant articulations and on this point writes:

> The success of a particular media strategy may not mean, and in fact tends not to mean, the domination of news agendas or the reproduction of frameworks of understanding. In general, media strategies focus on more limited goals. Some of the major successes in the media strategies of non- official sources have still operated within parameters set by official sources. It is not always necessary for the media to become oppositional for non-official sources to succeed (ibid.: 159),

it is not evident from his analysis how and why this occurs, or with what frequency. Like Curtis, Miller's focus on the effectiveness of state propaganda overlooks how the media have been used by groups who oppose dominant interpretations of the conflict. There is also a propensity to look at media coverage in general terms, and not differentiate between the conventions of print and television, or, assess differences between local, national and international coverage.

The problem of differentiation between media forms and their particular usage does not arise in Cathcart's work, *The Most Contrary Region: The BBC in Northern Ireland 1924–1984*. This historical overview of how the BBC operated in and conveyed Northern Ireland, describes how from the early fifties, the BBC sought 'to win recognition for broadcasting as an agency for improving relations between the communities', and that 'their conviction was that this dialogue would help the communities discover what they had in common' (Cathcart 1984: 170–71). But, by concentrating on universal problems and ignoring issues of discrimination, the broadcasters were seen to be creating a false consensus which became especially evident when civil disorder erupted in the mid-sixties. At this time, the BBC faced criticism about failing to inform, or examine that which divided the communities and in response, began to focus on divisions (ibid.: 201). The problems of broadcasting to a divided community stimulated three main changes of strategy over the sixty year period which Cathcart explores. Summarising how reporting responded to changes in the political context, Cathcart concludes:

> In the pre-war period, the BBC ignored the division and sought to prevent any of its manifestations from impinging on programmes. This was an abdication of social responsibility. In the post-war world, the pursuit of such a strategy proved impossible. The BBC then sought to be the means of bringing both sides of society together. The feeling that this should be done without provoking vociferous and possibly violent reaction from the unionist majority meant that the positive aspects of community relations were emphasised and the negative downplayed. A consensus emerged which had a false basis. When the civil rights movement attempted to give it a real basis, the BBC's strategy became irrelevant. Broadcasting House, Belfast, threw over the incubus of having to always placate local unionist feelings and there then emerged the third and current strategy which requires the broadcasters to reflect the whole of society in Northern Ireland as it is, in its negative and positive aspects. Within the constraints imposed by the law, BBC Belfast is increasingly endeavouring to do this. The price of the strategy is that neither community is satisfied, for each manifests exclusive political and cultural attitudes, and harbours the ultimate determination that the other side will not be seen or heard. If there is middle ground, then that is where the BBC in Northern Ireland endeavours to stand (ibid.: 262–3).

Two points arise here which are critically addressed by Butler in his book, *The Trouble With Reporting Northern Ireland*. Firstly, Butler (1995: 10) highlights how coverage changes in the wake of political changes and developments (i.e. 'the limits, or to use a photographic metaphor, the aperture of 'consensus' will tend to open and shut according to the constantly shifting power relations within the polity and economy in each epoch'). Secondly, he contends that the use of a consensual middle ground politics for explaining the conflict, provides an inappropriate context of interpretation given that a political middle ground is notably absent in Northern Ireland itself. Highlighting how a consensual paradigm is unable to adequately interpret or dissect the Northern Ireland problem, Butler elaborates on an argument made earlier by Schlesinger, when he stresses that an 'appearance of oneness has ever always been a feature of the public service model. Based as it is on the production of consent (or at least common assent) for its integrative worldview, the inclination to unify is endemic to the system. In this way, British broadcasting blithely purports to replicate the middle ground of politics and society' (ibid.: 72). The difficulty for applying this value system argues Butler, is that 'The conflict in Northern Ireland is about and between irreconcilable interests. Founded on a harmony model of consensual left/right politics. British reporting habitually interprets the dispute along centrist/extreme lines where in fact no such simple dichotomy appertains' (ibid.: 85). Thus, 'In general, the routinized institutional procedures of orthodox journalistic understanding – news values – are cerebrally ill-equipped to make coherent sense of the double-codedness of political language and political violence in Northern Ireland' (ibid.: 90).

The argument that consensus politics is unable to articulate the political complexities and nuances of Northern Ireland is reflective of how conflict causes are perceived and contested. For some, the conflict is religiously based along Protestant and Catholic lines, whilst for others it arises through the antagonistic political philosophies of unionism and nationalism (Whyte 1990: 18–22). Butler's emphasis on the shortcomings of consensus broadcasting largely supports the work of Martin McCloone, who also takes issue with the interpretive framework applied by broadcasting and argues:

> The thrust of broadcasting's role in Britain and Ireland, has been towards a denial of the complexities and dynamics of cultural identity. It has attempted, through its own ransacking of the rag-and-bone shop of history, to fix and to freeze a certain notion of identity. It has selected and discarded, remembered and forgotten, invented and imagined in ways which have coincided with, if not always been directed by, the needs of the nation-state. In the process it has evolved as a central cultural agency for the promotion of collective consciousness (McCloone 1991: 9).

As a result of this process, public service broadcasting is 'antithetical to the authoritarian impulses of either nationalism or unionism', and in turn 'leads from the front, promoting and supporting a sense of identity which commands no ready consensus in either society' (ibid.: 16). Whether broadcasting to antagonistic cultures and identities in Northern Ireland impacts on communities in ways comparable to broader social, economic and political factors remains questionable (O'Connor 1993; Porter 1996; Whyte 1990), however, much of the available literature underlines the consensual nature of news coverage and its tendency to focus on terrorism as the main underlying cause of the Northern Ireland conflict. Here, the media created representations which criminalised rather than politicised the conflict. The historical context to understanding the reporting of Northern Ireland is thus concerned with how the discourse of terrorism and state responses to it overwhelmingly dominated news, relying on specific articulations and interpretations.

For the broadcasters who pride themselves on being impartial and unbiased, there are dilemmas in referring to certain actions as terrorism. The idea that journalist's operate in an objective fashion which refrains from promoting certain political values is clearly not the case when those who carry out political violence are constructed in relation to dominant political reactions and articulations. The ideal of impartiality is indeed rendered mythical by use of the very terms 'terrorist' and 'terrorism', which reinforce moral positions and conjure responses of condemnation. In using the language of terrorism therefore, journalists tend to ignore or downplay background causes which may influence violence, preferring to concentrate on its moral consequences. Or as Gearty puts it

> The point about deployment of the language of terrorism is that the mere use of the word implies that the judgment has already been made. To call an act of violence a terrorist act is not so much to describe it as to condemn it, subjugating all questions of context and circumstance to the reality of its immorality (Gearty 1997: 11).

Constructing Terrorism: Issues of Convention and Articulation

Writing about the semantics of political violence and Northern Ireland in 1986, television journalist Peter Taylor observed:

> There is no doubt that the IRA poses a threat to the existence of the state because its campaign is directed at the severance of one part of it from the main body. Government has to counter the threat not only by taking direct measures against those who seek to subvert it but by enlisting the support of the media in what it calls 'the battle against terrorism'. In its language and interpretation of events, the media helps to condition the way the 'battle' is perceived. This leads in turn to the synthesis of the political and public perception of the state's enemy. This is why words are so crucial in describing and defining the contemporary phenomenon of political violence not just in Northern Ireland but worldwide. These words can be an aid to understanding or a distortion of it. They not only reflect the journalist's perception of a particular situation but condition the way his report is received. The problem remains one of definition (Taylor 1986: 211–12).

This definition of terrorism which Taylor uses, draws construction from how the terrorist act relates to the state and how it stands in oppositional terms to the democratic values espoused by the state. This tension and how it influences representations and definitions of political violence is also addressed by Schlesinger et al. who observe

> Contests over definitions are not just word games. Real political outcomes are at stake. If the public, or sufficient sections of it, can be persuaded that the state's perspective on a given 'war against terrorism' is questionable, this might imply a weakening of support. On the other hand, if the public can be persuaded that the state is right, this helps mobilise support for transferring resources from welfare to security. Language matters, and how the media uses language matters (Schlesinger et al. 1983: 1).

What the arguments of Taylor and Schlesinger et al. appear to emphasize, is that an act of political violence is terrorism when it is primarily an action conducted against the state and that therefore attributions of terrorism depend more on the direction of violence rather then questions about motivation or legitimacy. One of the consequences of constructing terrorism in this way (that is what violence is targeted at rather than its motivations) is that the background causes for violence become excluded from consideration of the event itself, creating the perspective that conflict is self-perpetuating, self-fulfilling and largely enclosed. In other words, the actions and effects of terrorism become the context by which to understand and react to it.

With regard to Northern Ireland, the assertion that news coverage has focused on acts of political violence and not the motivations (political, religious, social, ethnic) which lay behind them, has been consistently argued by those who have written on the subject. Writing in 1977, Philip Elliott noted that acts of violence were 'the main focus of attention in the news coverage' which he analysed (Elliott 1977: 268). He also noticed that 'the tendency of the British media was to report violent events as simply irrational and horrid' (ibid.: 295) and that in Northern Ireland, 'political comment on violence tended to become a source of tension in itself, with arguments developing over who was prepared to condemn what sort of violence' (ibid.: 319). This concentration on the emotive and sensationalist aspects of political violence arises not only because of efforts to delegitimise it, but importantly because news organisations support the nation state. As Schlesinger et al. observe, 'since terrorism, particularly that which makes its presence felt on the domestic scene, is seen as threatening the social order, this is one field of coverage where broadcast journalism cannot remain impartial' (Schlesinger et al. 1983: 35). Particular definitions and explanations attributed to acts of terrorism in news coverage do not, therefore, exist because they constitute some objective articulation of what terrorism is in itself, but because of what it means in relation to the state.

This relationship is a crucial determining factor in the construction of news representations and gives us a means to understand the ideological positions adopted by news organisations when they represent political violence.

If terrorism is a symbolic form derived from the conventions of news production does it therefore follow that if it is not reported it does not exist? This viewpoint was given some appeal by Margaret Thatcher with her remark that the media should deny terrorists 'the oxygen of publicity'; a comment which paved the way for the Broadcasting Ban imposed on Sinn Fein in 1988 (itself an example of direct political control over the news process). But, the assertion that news coverage acts as a contagion of terrorism because reporting draws attention to the terrorist's perspective and in so doing helps the motivating cause, is highly questionable. Clawson, for example has argued that 'the more the public knows about a terrorist group, the less likely it is to support that group' (Clawson 1990: 242), adding that efforts to remove terrorism from coverage 'is likely to force terrorists to escalate the level of violence in order to attract more attention' (ibid.: 243); a conclusion similarly drawn by Paletz and Boiney (1992: 22).

The proposition that coverage of terrorism automatically amounts to effective exploitation of the media by terrorist groups for propaganda purposes may serve the interests of governments or military advisors (Picard 1991;52), but also reinforces the view that since terrorism lay outside of rational liberal-democratic structures of action and discourse, it should therefore not be afforded publicity. The justification for this thinking derives from the belief that terrorism is foremost irrational, pathological and criminal, so beyond the pale of acceptable and consensual liberal-democratic political discourse (Schlesinger 1991: 18). Such reasoning adopts an official perspective of interpretation which depoliticises terrorism by emphasising its criminality (Schlesinger et al. 1983: 2) and concentrates on its potential to wreak continued havoc through an innate capacity for violence; a consideration which entwines with populist arguments that terrorism can only be solved militarily (Schlesinger et al. 1983: 24). However although the contagion effect has been largely discredited within media analysis ('no causal link has been established, using any acceptable social science research methods, between media coverage and the spread of terrorism' (Picard 1991: 56)), the question of media access to terrorists is contentious. On this problem, former BBC General Advisory Council member Richard Clutterbuck argued:

Some journalists and politicians have put a strong case for giving the terrorists themselves access to the media in the form of personal television interviews.

Their main arguments are that the public need to see terrorists for what they are, and that denial of such access will lead them to grab the news with more spectacular violence. These arguments are outweighed by the arguments against giving publicity and a propaganda platform to criminals ... television interviews with terrorists, operating in the UK, or with spokesmen for illegal and criminal organisations, whether facing or back to camera, should never be given (Clutterbuck 1983: 160).

Although Clutterbuck does not appear to be arguing for a total censorship of terrorism, he is clearly arguing for censorship in some form and appears to stress that news reporting should function primarily to delegitimise and criminalise the protagonists. This position also received support by former BBC Controller of Northern Ireland Colin Morris, who similarly underlined how this critical representation of the terrorist act should be applied as a matter of convention in news discourse, i.e.:

Organised violence, especially terrorism, is able to persist from one generation to the next only if it can find genuine grievances to feed on, to exploit in however demonic and twisted a way. Terrorism is sometimes mindless, motiveless and pathologically destructive; at other times it m ay be a suppurating sore, a revolting symptom that some part of the body politic is really hurting. And democracy has got to find out, it has got to scrutinise its life to see whether there are areas of rottenness which might harbour parasitic organisms. To change the metaphor – society must be made aware of the nature of its enemies and what intellectual force their ideas possess. How can you fight an enemy whose strength you are unable or willing to assess? (Morris 1988: 7).

Morris describes a representation of terrorism which is indicative of the rhetorical tradition in that he prioritises the criminal rather than the political motivations of terrorists. But, in doing so he also highlights the myth of impartiality when reporting terrorism in this way. From an editorial perspective, terrorists should it seems, be represented in binary opposition to democratic structures, outside of the consensual framework which determines social order for rational analysis and consistent with Clutterbuck's recommendation that 'Consideration for the community includes a moral obligation on those who wish to retain freedom of the media to preserve the parliamentary democracy and rule of law upon which that freedom depends' (Clutterbuck 1983: 163). The myth of impartiality which may be explained by an over-reliance on official sources and centres of power may thus also be understood as deriving from the cultural values of editorial judgment.

On this matter, Paletz and Schmid are quite right to point out how 'The art of responsible news judgment on the part of an editor consists of finding a suitable balance among the public's need to know, its mere desire to know, the terrorists' wish to intimidate and/or to propagandize the public or sectors thereof' (1992: 128), but this does not take account of a tendency for editors to sanction a representation of the terrorist which is fundamentally short-sighted (as Peter Taylor's BBC documentary series *Provos* in 1997 and *Loyalists* in 1999 illustrated) and misrepresentative of the motivations and imperatives of terrorist actions.

Highlighting the highly partial and distorting nature of this representation, the work of Taylor and Quayle is particularly instructive. In their examination of the psychology of those who conduct political violence and based on a series of interviews with members of paramilitary organisations, the authors conclude:

> A popular image of the terrorist is that he or she is abnormal in some way, and that the violence associated with terrorism can only be understood by reference to madness, psychopathology, or deviance of some form. Yet perhaps the most striking feature of those discussed here is the lack of signs of psychopathology, at least in any overt clinical sense. With rare exceptions, and contrary to popular misconceptions, the Irish terrorists are neither madmen or blind bigots. They have considerable insight into their own actions, and often show a striking awareness of how others view them ... What strongly emerges from them is a sense of understanding and order in what they do, a claim to rationality and intention which lies behind their acts when seen from their perspective (Taylor and Quayle 1994: 103).

To understand why such a recognition of terrorists is absent from television news reports, one must also understand the constraints imposed on news production whereas Schlesinger observes 'The televising of "terrorism" in Northern Ireland is subject to the limitations imposed by the double mechanism of continual political pressure and routine internal self-censorship' (Schlesinger et al. 1983: 121). Importantly, the pressures shaped by political forces both internal and external to news organisations has also lead to a rather narrow field of view by which to understand the actions of political violence. This field of view notably involves the use of recurring explanations and classifications of terrorist events, both containing and restraining contextual analysis and routinely derived from official sources, which helps to keep reporting within a predominantly rhetorical framework. That is, the focus tends to be oriented towards emphasising that terrorists are 'evil', 'criminal', 'men of violence', 'killers', 'gunmen', 'bombers', etc., who will not dent British efforts to contain or defeat them. As Elliott notes, this practice leads to a situation where 'repetition of the same treatment of similar events amounts to an implicit explanation of the situation' (Elliott 1977: 268), and contributes to what Butler terms the 'aperture of consensus' (Butler 1995: 10), which frames public knowledge of such events.

An example of this can be seen from news coverage given to the Provisional IRA bomb warning which lead to the postponement of the 1997 Grand National. As news focused on the misery caused to thousands of race-goers forced to leave Aintree, as well as riders and trainers who were 'unable to take in what had happened', the coverage prioritised rhetorical responses. Prime minister John Major was quoted as saying 'I am appalled that the IRA seem to be threatening hundreds and thousands of people and causing such disruption. This is further demonstration of their contempt and disregard for the lives and interests of ordinary people.' This was promptly followed by Shadow Home Secretary Jack Straw's response: 'These tactics simply stiffen our resolve against terrorism. Their gratuitous decision to secure the abandonment of the 150th Grand National is contemptible.' Concluding the condemnation, Liberal Democrat leader Paddy Ashdown added 'This is a stupid, futile and idiotic policy that will achieve absolutely nothing except make people in Britain more angry and more determined to make sure that there's no action the IRA can take which will either disturb the process of the election, or give them any chance of participating in the peace process' (BBC1, 17.20: 5 April 1997). This report highlights the inability of television news to examine the broader context of why actions of political violence take place, or their relevance to current political circumstances. Writing in *The Independent* about the Aintree incident, David McKittrick noted how recent events such as railway and motorway disruptions had 'opened up a whole new vista of headaches for the security authorities', and how based on interview with a republican source, the Aintree incident was part of 'a strategy aimed at maximum disruption and maximum publicity coverage with a minimum of threat to the lives of the civilian population'. Moreover, it was devised to remind 'the incoming government that the IRA's campaign can be effective and can hurt them economically'. McKittrick also noted how the goal was to get Sinn Fein into negotiations and went on:

> It is clear enough that a second IRA cessation will be on offer; it is also clear that it will not happen unless the next government gives a guarantee that it will lead automatically to Sinn Fein's entry into multiparty talks. In other words, all

this chaos is aimed at securing Sinn Fein's place at the conference table under the best terms possible. They [republicans] forecast that the ill-will generated by the wrecking of the Grand National will, post-election, have evolved into a sober realisation that the only way to cope with republicans is to sit down with them (McKittrick, 'The IRA's grand strategy', *The Independent*, 7 April 1997).

This tendency to ignore significant changes in motivation and strategy is reflective of the repetitive nature of news production which maintains conventional stereotypes and frames of discourse. Although the repetitive nature of reports is reinforced by the time restraints imposed on the production process which demand immediacy and simplistic articulations, there is also a propensity to normalise representations by simplifying and explaining them in a cyclical fashion. This point is drawn out by Taylor, who in his book on war photography notes how terror becomes similarly 'naturalised' through a recurring use of images of death and misery, by which we are offered 'the correlatives of disorder, the proof of madness and mayhem' (Taylor 1991: 135). Moreover, coverage which focuses on the terrorist event as an atrocity detached from the context which lead to its occurrence, leads to a structured recycling of images which mark boundaries between 'us' as viewers and 'them' as murderers. This perception and the consensual picture it creates (i.e. we are all be invited to be imaginary victims of terrorism but not invited to be imaginary terrorists) is also nicely addressed in the work of photographer Paul Graham, whose book of photographs of Northern Ireland called *Troubled Land*, integrates the effects of war into landscape photography, and by so doing illustrates the potential distortions that arise from a dramatic documentary approach which reinforces the emotive misery of killing by removing it from social, or political contexts. What Graham's work perhaps reveals most, is how the effects of political conflict are absorbed into the everyday lives of those living in Northern Ireland and that indeed political violence is not some entity divorced from social background, but is actually of it and embedded within it. Highlighting the possible misrepresentative nature of conventional photographic depictions of events which relate to, or are of Northern Ireland, Andrew Wilson observes:

> In the archetypal newspaper photograph the conflict is presented as a spiralling succession of incidents and their aftermath. These images can only provide an illustration and cannot explain what has happened in front of the lens; divisions, questions of identity and history are conflated by unitary presentation. Given such a stage, the eye of the camera can only present a carefully constructed, and allegorical, illusion (Wilson 1996: 70).

This unitary presentation which Wilson talks of, is not only a convention peculiar to press photography, but also television news, which represents political violence in a similarly one-dimensional way. Furthermore, though this unitary picture contains internal contradictions (i.e. that violence perpetrated by forces in defence of the state are reflexive measures to counter terrorist groups and so acceptable – consider consecutive British government justifications for the killings of civil rights protesters on Bloody Sunday and the refusal to apologise in the light of comprehensive eye witness accounts (Mullen 1997)), it provides us with a highly selective and restricted perspective which clouds analysis of terrorist motivations. This perspective removes the possibility of examining political violence in the same way as state violence, which is seen as reflexive, responsible and legitimate (that is to uphold the law and maintain the peace), or consideration that there is any credible reason for its existence, i.e. 'Extremism is testimony to provocation' (Apter 1997: 4).

That terrorism exists as action opposed to the continuation of social order as it exists and that its chief motivation is to change that order, is a point strongly made by Apter, who notes:

> Political violence disorders for a designated and reordering purpose: to overthrow a tyrannical regime, to redefine and realise justice and equity, to achieve independence or territorial autonomy, to impose one's religious or doctrinal beliefs. Boundary smashing goes together with boundary resetting. Just as there are reasons of state, so there are reasons of anti-state. Indeed, it is as an anti-state which gives a social movement its rationale as a 'discourse community'. The key to political violence is its legitimacy (Apter 1997: 5).

Terrorist organisations like the Provisional IRA clearly believe that actions of political violence are driven by grievances and causes, which are rarely extrapolated within the confines of news discourse. Different perceptions emerge however, when we address the representations of pro-state terrorist organisations. In part, this may be because as Elliott argues:

> Such groups like the loyalist extremists, in Northern Ireland, pose special problems for the dominant ideology. Starting from the premise that all violence is bad, all types have to be condemned. But to carry that through beyond a token opposition to 'violence on both sides' or 'wherever it may be found', to present 'ugly' violence in the same way as 'bad' violence would be to direct the opposition of the state and its people against those whose interests it has decided to protect (Elliott 1977: 366).

This also highlights the inappropriateness of a unified analysis towards terrorist activity within Northern Ireland since pro-state and anti-state terrorist activity, as Bruce suggests, has to contend with very different restraining forces:

> The appeal of any terrorist organization will depend in part on the existence of alternative expressions of the values which that organization purports to embody. An east Antrim Protestant who feels moved to 'do something about the IRA' can join the UDR or RUC; a west Belfast Catholic who wishes to drive out the colonial oppressors has only republican terrorism. The pro-state terror group has to compete with legitimate state agencies, the anti-state terror group does not (Bruce 1992: 273).

The relations with state agencies also has a significant impact on the possible organisation and effectiveness of loyalist groups. As Bruce continues,

> because the pro-state terror group recruits from the same population as the state's security forces, it sometimes has the advantage of being able to 'tap' the expertise and resources of the state (as in the case of UDA-UVF men who join the UDR). The cost is that the security forces have the pro-state terror groups well penetrated and are able, when they wish, to police the pro-state groups much more easily than the anti-state groups (Bruce 1992: 279).

These complexities are hardly extrapolated within the confines of news reports which tend to construct different terrorist groups by how they 'fit' within the broader conventions of discourse; a position which also suggests that terrorists and the terrorist act are received and conceptualised in predictable and predetermined ways by news personnel in advance of the terrorist event itself. As Cohen et al. observe:

> The dramatic form of social conflict rests on the juxtaposition of forces that are dramatugically portrayed in opposition. Such conflictual presentation of forces has long been used in characterizing television news. The nature of the actors – their appeal, their appearance, their time 'on stage,' and their position in societal structures – affects their viability as characters in the drama of conflict (Cohen et al. 1990: 114).

As Gilbert notes, this dramatic construction of conflict is also developed in relation to underlying social norms and conceptions of the modern state (Gilbert 1994: 54). Characterisations of the terrorist and of terrorism, depend on how both stand in connection to present structures of social order and the public's 'natural desire for social stability', which 'is translated into loyalty to the existing state' (Gilbert 1994: 160); a loyalty which is supported and reinforced in news reports.

We can see the implications of this if we consider the reactions of journalists to the Provisional IRA ceasefire called on 31 August 1994. Caught unawares by the announcement of a 'complete cessation of military operations' by the Provisional IRA, the news networks adopted a reflexive approach which relied heavily on responses from the mainstream political parties. No news report on ITN, the BBC or Channel 4 asked the fundamental question of what had brought the republican movement to reach agreement on a peace strategy? That there had been an obvious and major shift in Republican thinking was something overlooked, as news reports focused on the inflections of the language used in the ceasefire statement and the fact that the ceasefire had not been expressed as 'permanent'. Both the BBC and ITN broadcast 'live' interviews with John Major, who reinforced that the ceasefire announcement had not gone far enough and that only 'once we have a permanent renunciation of violence' would a 'large number of options' become available (BBC1 18.00: 31 August 1994). The bipartisan line taken by the other mainstream parties echoed Major's sentiments, as the ceasefire was defined by what it was not (i.e. permanent), and so negatively (see chapter 7).

These conventional frames tend to ignore that Provisional IRA terrorism may be read as a social and civil disorder phenomenon underpinned by a nationalistic philosophy with particular social and political intentions. Provisional IRA violence is conducted to ultimately rid Northern Ireland of British jurisdiction and contribute to a unified Irish state. Loyalist political violence on the other hand, aims to prevent this and secure existing relations with the British state. Both forms of violence are therefore supported by oppositional notions of identity and self-determination which are politically entrenched and strongly influenced by nationalistic philosophies. However, the fundamental conflict of interests and the dissensual nature of political life bounded within the confines and complexities of unionist/loyalist and nationalist/republican thinking, is less evident within the frames of news discourse. The consensual nature of television news broadcasting is unable to properly articulate the problems of Northern Ireland precisely because it is unable to break out of interpretive frames which are drawn from parliamentary style contestations. And since in parliamentary terms, there is little discussion or dissension on the circumstances of terrorism (supported by a bipartisan approach to Northern Ireland), there is a corresponding lack of debate within news.

Political Control – The Broadcasting Ban

One of the more obvious examples of where the British government attempted to secure direct control over news representations of those seen to be connected to terrorism was introduced in 1988. The Broadcasting Ban as it became known, aimed to exclude political representatives of paramilitary organisations from using their own voices in news reports, which would be replaced by those of an actor and screened slightly out of synchronisation with lip movements. The Broadcasting Ban represented an act of censorship (since it prevented real voices from being heard) on the broadcasters and challenged the notion that they worked independently of political authority. However, this dilemma also contributed to an erosion of the ban's potential effectiveness since although broadcasters were obliged to adhere to the ban by law, they also felt obliged at times to challenge its repressive nature and its propensity to undermine the credibility of broadcasters as autonomous and politically neutral agents.

That the ban both succeeded and failed to some extent indicates the contradictory nature of relations between broadcasting and the state. On the one hand, broadcasting operates within a political environment, yet on the other it is obliged to be seen as critical of those who determine this environment and this conflict weakened rather than strengthened the legitimacy of the ban. The ban succeeded from the government's point of view in that it led to a dramatic 63 per cent reduction in the number of appearances by Sinn Fein in reports in its first year of enforcement (Miller 1995: 56), yet it failed because of efforts made by broadcasters to find loopholes in the regulations of the ban, exposing both its infringement of free speech and the absurdity of its design. This contrast of outcomes highlights the conflictive nature of interaction between broadcasting and the state which is neatly expressed by McCloone when he writes:

> Consensus broadcasting has ... been an intensely contradictory phenomenon. On the one hand, in its pursuit of hegemony, it has operated as a rather blunt instrument, legitimising (and marginalising) forms of public discourse by patrolling the boundaries of accepted, social, political and cultural behaviour. And yet since its formative days under Reith's guidance, it has always striven to maintain its autonomy from government interference and from the influences of the market place. Thus in its commitment to impartiality and its obligation to represent all sections of society it has also provided a space for the kinds of dissent or minority opinion which in its hegemonic role, it sought to disavow (McCloone 1991: 11).

The Broadcasting Ban itself, which was introduced on 19th October 1988, prevented a number of 'paramilitary and associated political organisations' from being heard via a representative of that organisation and was primarly designed to exclude articulations which did not condemn those who conducted violence. In attempting to provide some justification for the ban, the then Home Secretary Douglas Hurd made the following announcement to Parliament:

> For some time broadcast coverage of events in Northern Ireland has included the occasional appearance of representatives of paramilitary organisations and their political wings, who have used these opportunities as an attempt to justify their criminal activities. Such appearances have caused widespread offence to viewers and listeners throughout the United Kingdom, particularly just after a terrorist outrage. The terrorists themselves draw support and sustenance from access to radio and television – from addressing their views more directly to the population at large than is possible through the press. The Government have decided that the time has come to deny this easy platform to those who propagate terrorism. Accordingly, I have today issued to the chairman of the BBC and the IBA a notice ... The restrictions will not apply to the broadcast of proceedings in Parliament, and in order not to impair the obligation on the broadcasters to provide impartial coverage of elections the notices will have a more limited effect during election periods ... These restrictions follow very closely the lines of similar provisions which have been operating in the Republic of Ireland for some years ... Broadcasters have a dangerous and unenviable task in reporting events in Northern Ireland. This step is no criticism of them. What concerns us is the use made of broadcasting facilities by supporters of terrorism. This is not a restriction on reporting. It is a restriction on direct appearances by those who use or support violence (reproduced in European Commission of Human Rights report, 'Decision of the Commission', submitted to the NUJ, 1994).

Though the BBC contested the ban and questioned the meaning of certain words such as 'represents' and though this contestation resulted in a process of dialogue between the BBC and the Home Office, it soon emerged that the BBC would adhere to the ban even if the broadcasters opposed its repressive nature. The BBC's handbook for journalists, 'Producer Guidelines' (1994 edition) which was produced just before the ban was lifted, took the following position:

> The BBC opposes the continuation of the Notice because it believes that the ban deprives audiences of the right to hear and judge the representatives of organisations which have a profound effect on life in Northern Ireland, and because it enables those organisations more easily to avoid taking responsibility for the consequences of their actions.

While the notice remains in force it is necessary to observe its provisions but it is also vital that we do not extend its scope unnecessarily. BBC journalists must ensure that they continue to seek, question and report the views of all significant parties and organisations in accordance with providing full, responsible coverage of the Northern Ireland situation and in accordance with the other provisions of these Guidelines (BBC Publications 1994: 67).

In attempting to challenge the premise of the ban, the Deputy Director of the BBC at the time, John Birt wrote in the national press

We have been told that broadcast reporting remains unrestricted, that we are free to use the plain words like our colleagues in print. But the Notice denies broadcast journalists the tools of their trade: the captured moment, the cross-examination in interview, the penetrating unblinking eye of the camera which notes the pause or uncertainty when answering difficult questions, the conviction or lack of it. All tell a tale. From that we learn ('Gagging the Messenger', *The Independent*, 21 November 1988).

Continuing with the contention some four years later, Birt used the press again to argue that the ban had effectively compelled broadcasters 'to deliver to their audiences an incomplete version of the politics of Northern Ireland'. Exposing how the ban was inconsistent with political reality, Birt went on, 'In 1991, the High Court in Belfast upheld the rights of Sinn Fein councillors in Belfast to speak openly in council debates; but those same councillors could not speak on television about the court's ruling', concluding 'this perverseness is an inevitable consequence of a government setting down, in a tangled legal directive, matters that are properly for the editorial discretion of independent broadcasters'. However, though Birt was critical of the ban (an opportunity made more relevant by the developing peace process and a shifting political climate in Northern Ireland), he was also careful to reinforce the argument that in particular, it interfered with the potential for journalists to be critical of Sinn Fein or their relationship with the IRA:

Sinn Fein has close links with the IRA – indeed, some suggest Sinn Fein is, in effect, the IRA's subsidiary. One impact of the notice is to reduce coverage and discussion of this dimension. Before the ban, Sinn Fein's links with terrorism were more evident. Broadcasters were, for example, able to carry testing interviews with Sinn Fein representatives after IRA atrocities. Now, Sinn Fein members often evade interviews after such incidents on the grounds that their voices will not be heard ('Let us Hear their Apologies', *The Independent*, 19 October 1992).

The association with questioning Sinn Fein in relation to violence was hardly accidental. According to a Glasgow Media Group report, 'Of the 93 republican appearances in the year prior to the ban a total of 84 were in items dealing with violence or law enforcement news, for example in commentaries deploring the killings at Enniskillen' (Henderson and Miller and Reilly 1990: 31). Furthermore, 'Sinn Fein representatives mainly appeared following deaths caused by the IRA, the British Army or sectarian killings of Catholics by Loyalist groups' (ibid.: 35). Noting that in news appearances in the year prior to the ban, Sinn Fein dealt with 'political issues' in less than 10 per cent of cases, the report concludes that given this bias 'It is difficult to see from references like these how British news viewers could come to an informed decision about what the 'republican position' actually was' (ibid.: 37).

Tony Hall, Managing Director of BBC News and Current Affairs took a similar attitude to the Broadcasting Ban as Birt in that he also argued how it had obstructed critical examination of Sinn Fein (rather than loyalist organisations). For Hall, the legislation affected not just how viewers might understand Northern Ireland, but more importantly, allowed Sinn Fein to 'avoid being cross-questioned about the terrorist atrocities that it condones'. Given this position, Hall continued: 'There's a real danger that the ban has made it possible for it to take part only on the stories that suit it' ('A gag that Hides the Truth', *The Sunday Times*, 17 October 1993). Reiterating a similar claim some months later, Hall once more used the press to assert how 'the terrorists' spokesmen have used the notice as an excuse not to be interviewed on difficult issues, claiming that the ban on their voices means they will not be properly represented. Far from depriving the men of violence of the oxygen of publicity, the ban is being used by them and for their ends ('A gag that Chokes Freedom', *The Independent,* 12 September 1994).

For republicans, the ban cultivated the opposite of that argued by Hall and Birt. Rather then hindering the examination of IRA responses for particular atrocities, 'It also encouraged a climate in which the assassination of republicans and sympathisers could be explained away by the media as understandable, if not completely deserved.' The ban was also seen as part of a political strategy to set the Northern Ireland conflict in an essentially British frame of interpretation which sought to remove 'the question of national reunification from the popular consciousness of the Irish people' and reduce the unification issue to 'a minority aspiration', with the SDLP promoted as the only legitimate voice of Irish nationalism ('Censorship – A Weapon in the Arsenal of State Terrorism', *An Phoblacht*, 22 October 1992).

To understand what prompted the Thatcher government to implement the ban, it is also important to consider a number of political events which brought about critical examination of state policy in Northern Ireland. The Gibraltar killings of March 1988 where British SAS soldiers shot dead three IRA members, raised a number of questions about the operations of state security forces which the Thames documentary *Death on the Rock* did little to allay and which Foreign Secretary Geoffrey Howe called to have banned. Further, efforts by Margaret Thatcher herself to prevent a BBC Northern Ireland documentary about the Gibraltar inquests which like Howe's attempts were unsuccessful, merely stoked the tensions and outrage (Bew and Gillespie 1993: 214). Against this growing antagonism between broadcasters and the government, two army corporals were murdered by IRA members at a republican funeral in front of television cameras and a number of successful bombing campaigns by the IRA, such as the killing of six soldiers on a fun run at Lisburn and eight others by a bus bomb, had combined to depict the government in a position of weakness and the IRA in a position of strength. Moreover, pressure by Amnesty International to bring about a judicial inquiry into disputed killings by the police and army since 1982, which had been brought to light by 20 RUC men being made subject to disciplinary proceedings as a result of the Stalker – Sampson investigations into collusions between security forces and loyalist paramilitary groups in July (Flackes and Elliott 1994: 41–6), had alongside the Gibraltar case contributed to a flow of analysis which cast the government and its involvement in Northern Ireland in a critical light.

It was against this backdrop of unfavourable coverage that the Thatcher government imposed the censorship ban, using a moral tone of condemnation as justification for its necessity. Such was the effectiveness of this condemnation that the media were unable to offer a credible resistance to it, thus Thatcher's comment that 'To beat off your enemy in a war you have to suspend some of your civil liberties for a time' (*The Times*, 26 October 1988) received negligible interrogation within the broader press and set the debate for other political allies to follow that censorship was an essential step for somehow addressing the terrorist threat. Supporting the position fully, Northern Ireland Secretary Tom King underlined the need for the ban when a few days previous to Thatcher's response to the press he stated:

> Anyone who knows Northern Ireland will know how deeply offensive it is to see terrorists, the paramilitaries and their allies on both sides of the community appearing on radio and television and being treated with the same courtesies afforded to constitutional politicians. They will also be aware of the

encouragement and support that organisations such as Sinn Fein and the UDA draw from being able to be projected directly into people's homes and having their message of violence broadcast by the national media (*The Irish Independent*, 20 October 1988).

That terrorists and paramilitaries had not been treated 'with the same courtesies afforded to politicians' and had rarely appeared on television was an incidental point against the onslaught of government propaganda clearly designed to interfere and minimise coverage of the republican movement, eroding its own propaganda efforts and access to news in the process (Mallie and McKittrick 1996: 95).

The main impact of the ban on broadcasters was that it effectively ended the live interview with those who were prescribed by it (Baker 1996: 123). However, to some extent, it also removed the problem of who could be covered in news and how, which had in the past resulted in self – censorship and moral dilemmas. As one pressure group noted on this point:

> The ban systematised the censorship and set out its legal, administrative and ideological basis. Before the ban, programme-makers never knew at what level, or on what grounds, their approach would cause offence and bring in the censors: now at least they can be sure that certain types of approach are not permitted, and if they were sufficiently courageous they could use the specificity of the ban as implying a blanket permission to cover topics and individuals not expressly covered by it (Article 19, 1989: 59).

The success of the ban according to Moloney, came about essentially because of a consensus around four main points:

1 it helped to reinforce journalistic trepidation when dealing with terrorism and so deterred investigation;

2 resistance was undermined because the media 'had been demoralised by Thatcher's political and economic attacks;

3 resistance through organisations such as the NUJ was weak because of ineffective leadership and coordination; and

4 because 'the BBC management played an important but not entirely explained role in the whole affair' (Moloney 1991: 37).

Although the NUJ appealed to the Divisional Court, the Court of Appeal, the House of Lords and the European Commission of Human Rights about the legality of the ban and its discriminating powers, it would probably be fair to say that the more successful efforts to destabilise it came from the broadcasters themselves, who made a deliberate effort to read the guidelines as loosely as possible, installing the use of an actor's voice as a circumventing device and exposing the ban as a rather ill thought out and generally absurd piece of legislation.

The tensions between the broadcasters and the government over the ban were significantly reduced when it was withdrawn in 1994. The development of the peace process had shifted articulations and interpretations of the Northern Ireland problem beyond the criminal to the political and moved the bounds of discourse to reflect the emerging politicisation. In recognition that those who represented the paramilitaries needed to be brought into the political arena, so as options could be brought into play which would remove the basis for violence, the Northern Ireland situation became increasingly played out via the conventional communicative channels open to politics; namely through the media.

Conclusion

The purpose of this chapter is to establish an understanding of how the Northern Ireland problem has been conventionally explained by the news media during the modern period and to stress that dominant articulations of the conflict have been characterised by an emphasis on terrorism and terrorist violence. This combined with direct political control over how journalists reported particular groups, provided an ostensibly one dimensional interpretation of the Northern Ireland problem which tended to express criminal activity as the underlying basis of the tensions.

The ideological role of news reporting during 'The Troubles', functioned most prominently as a propaganda device in the British state's war against insurgent groups and although reporting raised questions from time to time about state operations in Northern Ireland, its main function was hegemonic and to perpetuate hostility against the dangerous and pathological terrorist enemy. Given this tendency, news emphasised the effects rather than causes of the violence, reinforcing criminal tendencies and downplaying political motivations. In adopting an interpretive framework for understanding the conflict which magnified deviant and ruthless manifestations of violence, news depoliticised the broader social, political and economic contexts from which it grew, but legitimised state articulations of condemnation and many subsequent legislative measures which flowed from and in response to that condemnation. Importantly, this paradigm which relied on repetitive turns of phrase, imagery and reaction, reinforced the perception that the Northern Ireland situation was sustained by irreconcilable extremes driven by sectarian hatreds and that the state's role was essentially neutral, based on containing the rampant sides and halting what would be an inevitable descent into civil war and mass murder.

However, this 'terrorism-as-cause' paradigm (Butler 1995) became increasingly untenable as the political groups became progressively oriented toward the prospect that a peace agreement might be achievable and a lasting peace a realistic proposition. Suddenly, the notion that the extremes in Northern Ireland were locked into a bloodlust looked grotesquely simplistic, as the dominant discourse shifted from one of violence to one of peace. Though the concept of *the peace process* would also appear to contain contentions and varying articulations in ways similarly restrictive, the new paradigm at least exposed the underlying tenets of conflict as political, not criminal in orientation (the criminal emphasis being a physical manifestation of the political however short-sighted, unrealistic or barbaric). A shift which was reflected by the absorption of representatives into the political process who were previously portrayed as little more than a mouthpiece for killers. A key achievement of the peace process therefore, would be bringing the representatives of paramilitaries into the arena of political discourse; representatives whose very presence had previously violated all that such 'respectable' discourse stood for.

The reporting of Northern Ireland thus underwent a change when the peace process began. The emphasis on terrorism and violence which had provoked government propaganda and repressive counter-terrorist responses, along with direct pressures and controls on the broadcasters, gave way to a more open, ideologically contested and disputed climate. As a consensus emerged about the need for peace (what shape that peace might take nevertheless the subject of considerable disagreement and contention) that would be contested and negotiated broadly in the news, so the frame of interpretation underwent a marked transition. The paradigm of terrorism had given way to the emerging paradigm of peace.

In the light of a changing political climate from conflict to peace in Northern Ireland, there becomes a need to recognise the shortcomings of studies concerned with the media's role in the politics of violence. The peace process poses a challenge to the kind of work carried out by Curtis, Miller and Schlesinger, which deals with reporting in a specific historical and political context. What is called for now, is a re-examination of the role of news reporting and how it operates in relation to a different historical and political context. As valuable though the work of the above authors is, it is no longer so appropriate for understanding the news media's role in the politics of Northern Ireland. A new study which examines how reporting impacts on the politics of conflict resolution rather than conflict is required, and it is to this problem which we now turn.

2 The Peace Process and News as Part of Peace

Introduction

The Northern Ireland peace process marked a significant change in the political landscape of Northern Ireland. The British government under prime minister John Major engaged with the Irish government under prime minister Albert Reynolds, to try and produce in consultation with the respective political parties, a framework for addressing what was seen as the main issues underlying conflict. Put simply, the inception of the peace process signalled the development of a conflict resolution process and a move away from entrenched conflict.

This political (re)orientation toward the Northern Ireland situation established a new context for explaining conflict causes which previously had been represented as little more than a result of criminal tendencies. Notably, the peace process created a shift in how conflict was perceived, moving from the criminal to the political. Or, to put it another way, the peace process moved attention from the politics of violence to the politics of peace, where the discourse of terrorism was overtaken and largely replaced by contestations about peace. What this change also underlined is that the Northern Ireland conflict is ostensibly political in orientation and that a resolution of conflict would require political actions and initiatives in order to succeed. In that sense, the peace process (re)politicised the Northern Ireland problem and highlighted the shortcomings of conventional media representations, which historically had been little more than an expression of the violence and the moral condemnations which surrounded it. In the emerging peace process paradigm, the dimensions of discussion and response would be different and the news media would amplify this difference. Political representatives of paramilitary groups would appear in news reports as voices and indicators of political direction, rather than mouthing empty justifications for bombing and killing. They would engage in the contestations of discourse like mainstream politicians, and respond to news in similar ways, using and exploiting propaganda opportunities which had previously been denied. But, perhaps the real difference of the peace process for news derived from its potential to disrupt dominant articulations (which had conventionally meant the media supporting the British government's line in the war against terrorism) that had previously been largely supported. Such articulations would now be subject to greater contestation and challenge, as other ideological variations were incorporated into news discourse. The promotion and development of peace would involve greater competition between viewpoints, and political dialogue would be more disputed as a result. Because of this development, the politics of negotiation and peace would be more difficult to influence and control than the politics of conflict.

This chapter is concerned with how the peace process emerged, how news became part of this process and some of the potential problems it created for politicians seeking to promote peace. In order to address these questions, it will consist of four sections. Firstly, it will outline how the peace process evolved and will consider the main political players and events which shaped it. Secondly, it will examine the role of news within the developing peace and will highlight examples of the media being used as a communicative conduit between Republicans and the British government. Thirdly, it will examine how the peace process became a paradigm for reading events and some of the problems that this created for communicating the various positions and complexities within it. And fourthly, it will highlight the media's ability to undermine politically objectives because of an emphasis on conflict, disagreement and fragmentation.

Unlike the previous section, which looked at the media's supportive and reproductive role in relation to dominant discourse about conflict, this section highlights how a changing political climate can affect changes in how news deals with political discourse and how such change can pose communicative problems for those in positions of power. Those problems and challenges demonstrate the news media's ability to obstruct and negatively affect power in a certain political and historical moment, and this chapter aims to outline those problems so that they can then be examined in more depth through interview material in the following chapters.

The Northern Ireland Peace Process: The Political Background

The Northern Ireland peace process which began in the late 1980s through a series of dialogues between SDLP politician John Hume and Sinn Fein's Gerry

Adams, signified a considerable change in the development of political relations in Northern Ireland. The dialogues captured broader political interest more particularly from the beginning of the 1990s and inspired a process of communications between British, Irish and American governments which resulted in the former two governments producing the Joint Declaration of December 1993 (Coogan 1995; Duignan 1996; Mallie and McKittrick 1996; O'Brien 1995; O'Clery 1996; Rowan 1995). The document had particular interest for Nationalists and brought the possibility of constitutional change into question:

> The British government agrees that it is for the people of the island of Ireland alone, by agreement between the two parts respectively, to exercise their right of self-determination on the basis of consent, freely and concurrently given, North and South, to bring about a united Ireland, if that is their wish (Bew and Gillespie 1996: 33).

Though the wording of the Joint Declaration held interest for Nationalists it also attempted to satisfy Unionist denominations, stating that any constitutional change would have to 'reflect the principle of consent in Northern Ireland' (ibid.: 34). Appended to the document to appease Protestant fears, the British government also made the commitment to not bring pressure which could facilitate a united Ireland, or affect pressure on the people of Northern Ireland to join a united Ireland against their wishes (Hennessey 1997: 293–4). The Joint Declaration therefore held elements of interest for both Unionists and Nationalists (Taylor 1997: 343).

The main thrust of the document was to develop the concept of 'inclusiveness' and draw paramilitary groupings away from violence into the political process (Bew and Patterson and Teague 1997: 203–15). Its primary intention was to bring the political parties into a talks process which would address the critical issues underlying conflict and confront those issues through political dialogue, thus rendering the ideals of political violence redundant and drawing support away from paramilitary activities. However, political efforts to develop peace would need to be shaped against a historical backdrop where political violence had been institutionalised and constructed through images and representations of 'The Troubles'. As Bowyer Bell reminds us, by the 1990s:

> The Troubles were no longer aberration but so protracted as to be convention. The secondary benefits had become institutionalised and primary. It was not so much that violence had paid in Ireland or was seen to pay but that nothing paid

as many as well as the existing level of persistent violence. There always seemed reasons to persist (Bowyer Bell 1997: 618).

The success of the talks process ultimately rested on the potential to reconcile the ideological extremes of Unionists and Nationalists into agreement over how steps towards a possible resolution of the conflict might be found. For Republicans, the possible success of a lasting peace depends on British withdrawal from Northern Ireland and it is British jurisdiction of the province which underscores the conflict. A Sinn Fein document entitled *Towards a Lasting Peace*, produced in 1992 reinforced this perception, stating that 'British rule in Ireland and conflict have been and are synonymous' and that 'British rule in Ireland and peace are incompatible'. The document also made it clear that 'the creation of conditions in which peace can be made permanent in Ireland must involve at some future date the removal of British interference from the political equation in Ireland' (Sinn Fein 1992: 9). This stands in diametric opposition to the Unionist position, where it is the continuation of British sovereignty and identification with Britishness which remains paramount. Stressing how the Nationalist position sits in conflict with this ethos, the Ulster Unionist Party has argued that:

> For Nationalists the real problem is their inability to accept the legitimacy of the Irish Unionist identity … The Union with Great Britain is a Union in the hearts and minds of the Unionist people, and is something which we cannot change, even if we wanted to. This feeling of Britishness is so deeply ingrained as to be almost genetically encoded. It is not a device or artifice which has been imposed on an unsuspecting people; neither is it something which Unionists wish to impose on those who have different aspirations. But for Unionists their basic political heritage is their Britishness (quoted in Hennessey 1997: 281).

Moreover, 'Because of this fundamental principle of belonging, unity by consent, either now or in the future, is not forthcoming' (ibid.). For Unionists, inherent to Nationalist discourses is a failure to recognise the legitimacy of Northern Ireland as part of the UK, and therefore a denial of the Unionist right to maintain and defend that linkage. Thus, 'All action, and perceived intention, by Nationalists has not convinced Unionists to date that the former are prepared to accept the border and to work within institutions of government which recognise that status of NI as an integral part of the UK' (Nesbitt 1995: 51).

Unionist fears of an erosion of the linkage between the UK and Northern Ireland were stoked further by the 'Frameworks for the Future' document released by the British and Irish governments in 1995. The document outlined a greater role for Dublin in the role of Northern Irish affairs and proposed the creation of:

> North/South institutions – with clear identity and purpose, to enable representatives of democratic institutions, North and South, to enter into new, co-operative and constructive relationships; to promote agreement among the people of the island of Ireland; to carry out on a democratically accountable basis delegated executive, harmonising and consultative functions over a range of designated matters to be agreed; and to serve to acknowledge and reconcile the rights, identities and aspirations of the two traditions ('Frameworks for the Future', 1995: 25).

Though the document established that such changes would only operate on the basis of consent among the people of Northern Ireland, for Unionists it represented a serious attempt from the British government to change the political status of Northern Ireland and indicated steps towards disengagement from the province.

Between publication of 'The Joint Declaration' and the 'Framework' document, the Provisional IRA and Loyalist paramilitary groups announced ceasefires, allowing political options to be explored without the pressures of terrorist violence. A lengthy process of communications and diplomatic manoeuvring had brought about the necessary climatic change which led to the Provisional IRA ceasefire of August 1994 (Coogan 1995; Duignan 1996; Mallie and McKittrick 1996; O'Brien 1995; O'Clery 1996; Rowan 1995), which Republicans saw as meeting the necessary criteria for entrance to talks.

The subsequent collapse of that ceasefire in February 1996, for many Nationalists occurred in direct response to the intransigence of the British government and Unionists who had set preconditions for Sinn Fein's entry into talks (Patterson 1997: 287), such as the decommissioning of Provisional IRA arms (Taylor 1997: 349) and an election process. These preconditions were interpreted more as efforts to block Sinn Fein's inclusion in talks than being within the objectives set by governmental documents (ibid.: 352), and galvanised the Provisional IRA into ending its ceasefire rather than risk a split because of internal dissent (Patterson 1997: 283). However, throughout the period between the collapse of the ceasefire and its reinstatement in July 1997, government officials continued to communicate with Sinn Fein. Sinn Fein had resigned themselves to little change in the political climate before the General Election, when a likely incoming Labour government would be less bound by the Unionist constraints which had dogged the Conservative

Party. And indeed, it was the election of the Labour Party in May 1997 which led to a more favourable environment for Sinn Fein's entry into talks. Sinn Fein's interpretation of the Labour Party as more receptive to the Republican position was reflected by a renewed Provisional IRA ceasefire and a signing up to The Mitchell Principles, which included an absolute commitment 'To democratic and exclusively peaceful means of resolving political issues' ('Report of the International Body', 1996: 7). A reappraisal of the political situation had led Sinn Fein to determine that their main objective of removing British rule from Northern Ireland would be a long term process of perhaps 10 to 15 years (Patterson 1997: 296). With the exception of Ian Paisley's Democratic Unionist Party and Robert McCartney's UK Unionist Party, the respective parties commenced talks in September 1997 and the British and Irish governments decided a time frame of until May 1998 to reach some kind of agreement on substantive issues; principally designed to assuage Republican anxieties about delaying tactics by Unionists (ibid.: 297).

Though the process of talks and communications has been, and continues to be, dogged with obstructions and setbacks, it nevertheless represents a serious attempt by British and Irish governments to facilitate the conditions which might bring a lasting peace. However, this cannot disguise the fact that there have been a number of criticisms about the foundations and direction of the peace process. Some have argued that changes of attitude should precede institutional changes rather than the other way round, and that managing oppositional communities firstly requires reconciling structures which maintain divisions and separations (Darby 1997: 34). Others insist that the peace process places 'more emphasis on conflict management than upon conflict resolution' (Gilligan 1997: 19) and that preoccupation with maintaining its continuation has taken precedent over 'the substance of any future settlement' (McGovern 1997: 67). Furthermore, and perhaps somewhat paradoxically, the concept of inclusion has led to a process of exclusion, since the majority of people in Northern Ireland remain ostracised from developments. Or, as Gilligan puts it, 'The exclusion of ordinary people from the peace process has meant that they are not engaged in it. This stands in stark contrast to the 1960s and 1970s when masses of people were engaged in the 'politics on the streets' (Gilligan 1997: 32). Underlying this view is that the main function of the peace process has not been to develop conflict resolution from networks of public and communal support, but to draw the representatives of paramilitary groups into the political arena and make a return to violence more difficult. Or, more specifically, 'to divert republicans from military strategy towards a seeming cul-de-sac of indeterminant negotiation' (Gilligan and Tonge 1997: 165).

These criticisms should not overlook the huge problems which beset the polarised thinking of the different traditions in Northern Ireland, but it is worth remembering O'Malley's comment that

> The psychology that sets the parameters of conflict is not the psychology of how to manage conflict, but the psychology of how to minimize the anxieties that underlie the possibility of change, and what change entails. In Northern Ireland, the overwhelming imperatives to minimize communal anxieties have led to permanent political paralysis (O'Malley 1997: 477).

Having briefly outlined the political context of the peace process and some of the indicative problems played out within it, the concern now is how the television news media became part of that process and how they reflected the political changes which were emerging.

News as Part of the Peace Process

Political use of the news media to promote the peace process is touched upon at the end of David Miller's book *Don't Mention The War* (1994), where the media are seen as important for 'the presentation of intense diplomatic activity' and used 'as part of the negotiation process, in a sort of megaphone diplomacy' (Miller 1994: 283–4). Taking this point a little further in a paper entitled 'Reporting The Peace in Ireland', presented at the conference 'Turbulent Europe: Conflict, Identity and Culture' in 1994, Miller and McLaughlin continue:

> The British, the republicans, and the Irish government have all used the media to engage in megaphone diplomacy by flying kites, floating suggestions, giving clarifications or issuing threats (Miller and McLaughlin 1996: 435).

To justify this claim, the authors look at the toing and froing of news comment after the announcement of the Joint Declaration, when Sinn Fein asked for clarification of the document. This clarification was initially refused by the government, but eventually given. Highlighting the complexion of signals relayed through the news media at this time, Miller and McLaughlin go on:

> As we heard night after night that the peace initiative was dead or still on track, it became evident that the government was indeed engaged in clarification and negotiation ... It has been exceptionally rare for television journalists to

acknowledge that the briefings they are given are not a transparent reflection of government thinking but actually part of the negotiation process (ibid.: 433–4).

It is true that from time to time the news media have been used as a communicative channel. Former Northern Ireland Secretary Peter Brooke in November 1989 used the news media to send a key message to Republicans which recognised the unlikeliness of British forces defeating the Provisional IRA. Brooke stated:

> … it is difficult to envisage a military defeat [of the IRA]... if, in fact, the terrorists were to decide that the moment had come when they wished to withdraw from their activities, then I think the government would need to be imaginative in those circumstances as to how that process should be managed (quoted in Taylor 1997: 316).

This captured Republican attention and activated a Sinn Fein response which was similarly conveyed through the media, where representatives Gerry Adams, Martin McGuiness and Mitchel McLaughlin admitted that Brooke's comments had sparked some 'partial debate' within the Republican movement (Mallie and McKittrick 1996: 101). But, perhaps the most significant message sent by Brooke through the media occurred in November 1990, when in a speech he made to the British Association of Canned Food Importers and Distributors in London, he said:

> An Irish republicanism seen to have finally renounced violence would be able, like other parties, to seek a role in the peaceful political life of the community. In Northern Ireland, it is not the aspiration to a sovereign, united Ireland against which we set our face, but its violent expression … The British Government has no selfish or strategic or economic interest in Northern Ireland: our role is to help, enable and encourage. Britain's purpose is not to occupy, oppress or exploit but to ensure democratic debate and free democratic choice. Partition is an acknowledgement of reality, not an assertion of self-interest (quoted in Taylor 1997: 318).

This comment represented a significant departure from conventional government articulations about the union with Northern Ireland, and stimulated a process of confidential communications between the government and Sinn Fein until those communications were publicly exposed by *The Observer* in November 1993. During this three year period communications were conducted almost entirely out of the media spotlight, with possible revelations that a communications process was taking place seen as damaging to progress and the development of trust (see Sinn Fein's record of communications with the British government from 1990–93, entitled *Setting The Record Straight,* 1994: 37, 39–40). To help maintain confidentiality, the British government continued to condemn the Republican movement as IRA atrocities went on unabated, yet behind the scenes gave Sinn Fein advanced copies of governmental speeches in order for them to plan responses and carry the momentum of dialogue (*Setting The Record Straight* 1994). In this case, the media were used more to distract attention from the communications going on rather than assist them and a concerted effort was made to keep developments out of the public arena.

What is most evident about this process of communications however, is how the print media were used rather than television news. Allowing for a more considered, less dramatic and more detailed expression of communications, the print media has consistently been studied and used by players in the peace process for signs of progress or resistance, and referred to as a part of the communications process much more than television news (Peter Brooke referred to the *Republican News* for signs of Republican thinking (Mallie and McKittrick 1996: 104); Sinn Fein responded to political initiatives forwarded by the British government through the *Irish Times* (ibid.: 109; Patterson 1997: 296); *The Independent* provided valuable insight for political sources about Republican and Nationalist reactions to the peace process (McKittrick 1994: 228-238, 269-274); and *The Times* was used to leak information which favoured Unionists and undermined momentum (Adams 1997: 125)). In the case of television news it seems that the communicative advantages for developing dialogue on the peace process are more problematical. I would therefore argue, that the main function of television news has been to help develop a communicative space to enable the political negotiation process to proceed, rather than it being an integral part of that process. Details of negotiations can it seems, be more thoughtfully and extensively articulated in print than they can on television.

The proposition that the news media may be used to establish a communicative channel is also addressed by Michael von Tangen Page and Kirsten Schwarz Sparre of the Department of Peace Studies at Bradford University, in a paper they wrote entitled 'Peace in Northern Ireland through the journalist channel?' (1994). In their paper, the authors note that 'there are occasions where the ability to use a media system as a channel of communication can help dialogue between parties who for various reasons can not meet or prefer that an issue is not the subject of formal talks' (ibid.: 2). To support this view they use a number of newspaper stories as evidence of how a communicative channel might operate, where political rivals were able to generate dialogue without having to meet directly. It is clear enough that the case studies used present a form of momentum which has political implications and uses, but how important such exchanges proved to be for the peace process is another matter. Moreover, although the authors did not use television news coverage in their analysis they argue 'it is probably safe to say that television played a decisive role in the peace process' (ibid.: 4).

However, this creates a rather limited picture of communications through the media which fails to take into account other factors which make the effectiveness of communications questionable. Firstly, it has become clear that those groups who do not wish to communicate directly with each other may still do so, but through intermediary parties or individuals. This can be seen from work which has been published on how the peace process came about through behind the scenes communications (Coogan 1995; Duignan 1996; Mallie and McKittrick 1996; O'Brien 1995; O'Clery 1996; O'Malley 1997; Rowan 1995) and from revelations that secret contacts between the British government and Sinn Fein to restore the IRA ceasefire in 1996 took place through the SDLP via John Hume (BBC, ITN News, 3 November 1996). Secondly, the business of political communications is such a minefield of controversies in Northern Ireland, it is just as possible that information carried through news could make situations worse as much as better. Since Northern Ireland is the most politically divided area in the UK, it is highly likely that most of the media is scrutinized by parties in the search for concessions, obstructions and possible sell-outs and that this leads to a hardening of positions rather than conciliatory gestures. Thirdly, as I have said, television and print provide different communicative functions. Newspapers cater for specific audiences which may be broadly demarcated along Protestant and Catholic lines (Bairner 1996), but television news does not operate to sectional interests in this way, broadcasting to all groups simultaneously, and it is because television news tends to interpret within totalising and consensual paradigms that dialogue becomes restrained and stereotyped rather than developed and examined.

Interpreting the Northern Ireland problem through a consensus-based political framework which is inadequate for reading the political dimensions and complexities of Northern Ireland politics (Schlesinger 1987: 205) clearly poses a problem for facilitating dialogue which requires analysis and examination of those dimensions and complexities. The disadvantages and shortcomings of reporting Northern Ireland through the balances of a system consistent with British parliamentary consensus politics is nicely outlined by Butler:

'Twoness', rather than 'oneness' defines political and cultural life in Northern Ireland. Ours is a conflicted, dissensual society. At base, the years of killing were a consequence of conceptual disagreement: the conflict (continued by belligerent and/or passive methods) is about and between opposing meanings of the limits of the political nation. Consequently, we have endless disputes over terms of reference. The absence of definitional authority, of agreed or neutral codes, results in a profound crisis of representation. This is the trouble with reporting Northern Ireland. Prefigured on unitary principles – upon the organisation of consent – public service broadcasting has the gravest difficulty satisfying a fundamentally divided polity. Founded on centrist diagnosis, network coverage, by and large, sees the conflict along moderate-extreme faultlines where, in fact, no such simple cleavage pertains. Particularism is at the root of the conflict in Northern Ireland (Butler 1991: 133).

Since the causes of conflict are heavily contested politically, as well as culturally, through Nationalist and Unionist articulations (McGarry and O'Leary 1995; Ruane and Todd 1996), and since the television news media keeps to a public service ethos of maintaining a consensus view of national identity and preserving a unified picture of the nation-state, it is difficult to see how television news can play a positive role in the negotiation process. Especially, that is, if we take as credible the negotiating process aiming 'to foster agreement and reconciliation, leading to a new political framework founded on consent and encompassing arrangements within Northern Ireland' as outlined in paragraph two of the Joint Declaration.

The array of problems which beset processes of reconciliation and which were addressed in *The Opsahl Report* of 1992 and more recently submissions to the Forum for Peace and Reconciliation, not only demonstrate the inability of news to confront the range of factors which underscore conflict but also place a big question mark over its potential to assist a talks process which must deal with such issues. The conventions of television news are well placed to report a process of conflict where simplistic demarcations of good and bad can be easily established through acts of terrorism and state responses. They may not be so easily or usefully applied within a process of conflict resolution, which requires a more sophisticated explanation of ideological positions and which lacks the visual drama and emotiveness of political violence. Although using the 'terrorist-as-cause' paradigm (Butler 1995: 153) as an explanatory construct had become clearly untenable after the IRA and Loyalist ceasefires of 1994, because terrorism had effectively stopped, the television news media (as other forms but more so) found it hard to accommodate the fact that a fundamental shift had occurred in the thinking of parties like Sinn Fein or the

Progressive Unionist Party. The development of a 'peace strategy' which Sinn Fein had been evolving over a number of years, was given little credence by the news media who generally preferred to focus on the apparent gulf between the communities. Concentration on such division can hardly be accused of misrepresentation with regard to Northern Ireland, but it demonstrates how television news tends to emphasise the polarization of Unionist-Nationalist and Republican-Loyalist groups and illustrates a tendency to ignore the viewpoints and proposals of those who do not fit the Nationalist or Unionist agendas which receive the overwhelming bulk of governmental attention (Porter 1996: 49). Given that such coverage does little to challenge representations which continue to emphasize sectarianism and division, it is hard to see how television news helped to facilitate the early stages of the negotiation process.

If all issues are subject to contention because of the irreconcilable identities of the communities and television news tends to amplify those divisions, then the likelihood is issues are not so much negotiated or constructively debated through reports, but subject to continuing antagonism and dispute. It is precisely because television news is unable to dissect the cultural and political complexities of identity in Northern Ireland (McLoone 1991: 9) that it is unlikely to assist any negotiation or reconciliatory dialogue around those complexities. It is important to remember that the disadvantages of news coverage were apparent during the early stages when communications were kept secret and that this highlights the potentially damaging (not positive) effects which reporting can generate. However, this does not mean that coverage does not have uses for the peace process, particularly as the concept of 'peace process' itself became a paradigm for interpreting and explaining events. It is rather that those uses can be negative as well as positive.

Peace Process as News Paradigm

Taking Butler's proposition that up until the peace process reporting followed a 'terrorism-as-cause' paradigm, we can see that a gradual shift occurred in the pattern of reporting after the emergence of the Joint Declaration and that this was based on a recognition that Northern Ireland was undergoing a transition from conflict to conflict resolution. The paradigm which emerged at this point derived from this change in political orientation and was constructed through a flow of events which became contextualised as the 'peace process'. However, this context was much more than being merely about the 'constitutionalising' of Sinn Fein as Butler insists (Butler 1996: 134). It became a framework for understanding events in general and political relations and movements in particular. Whereas previously events had been reported primarily by their relationship to the process of conflict, they were now reported by their relationship to the process of conflict resolution. In some senses this meant a quite fundamental shift in coverage, but in others it meant sticking with an inability to examine the underlying causes of conflict, and it is because of this inability that we can question the importance of television news as a communicative outlet for peace. If the television news media does not examine what is 'behind' negotiations then what kind of role is it likely to play within them?

Like defining the Northern Ireland problem through the restricting focal points of terrorism and sectarianism, the peace process paradigm offered a relatively narrow series of codes and references by which to read developments. Examples of this narrowness can be seen if we consider the coverage of two important events: the Unionist marches in Northern Ireland during the summer of 1996 (more specifically Drumcree) and the issue of decommissioning paramilitary weapons.

The Unionist marches conducted during the summer of 1996 were witnessed by the mainstream television news networks as a considerable threat to the continuation of peace rather than as a defence of historical tradition and identity. That there may have been a deliberate editorial policy not to report events which might jeopardise the peace process, thus working on the principle 'if they didn't draw our attention to what was happening, we might not realise it was happening at all', was an accusation carried in the more pro-protestant elements of the broadsheet press. They were referring particularly to incidents of violence carried out by Republican groups ('BBC's Good News Is No News', Ireland's *Sunday Independent*, 22 October 1996) but footage of events such as the confrontations at Drumcree in 1996 illustrated that this was not the case and indeed, showed how reporting could inflame tensions. However, by reporting the tensions of Unionist and Nationalist marches (ostensibly Unionist) as a significant problem for the peace process there was also a tendency to ignore their historical and cultural significance. My point here is to suggest that political and cultural traditions such as marches became represented as potential conflict causes when before the peace process they were far less newsworthy. In turn, therefore, the peace process (or conflict resolution process) had created another context for reading threats, and by so doing had evolved new ones.

Moreover, the actual possibility of events like marches derailing the peace process was greatly exaggerated. Marches were given much more coverage than, for example, the issue of political prisoners which carries far greater weight in the eyes of Republican and Loyalist communities ('The Prisoners Who Matter', *The Independent*, 18 October 1996) and is central to a political resolution. But, by reinforcing notions of sectarianism and by highlighting fears through the coverage of disturbances and standoffs in the marches, the apparent irreconcilability of communities was amplified. In this sense, reporting was in keeping with the conventional stereotype of depicting violence – and the potential for violence – as underlying the Northern Ireland problem, and was still failing to address the fundamental causes. In contrast, the prisoners' issue indicates shared concerns and an equal recognition within the two opposing communities, Loyalist and Republican, and thereby challenges this convention. This returns us to an earlier point, which is that television news is unable to extrapolate the complexities which underlie conflict but prefers to depict the outcomes and effects of conflict and thus raises questions about any progressive or constructive role for television news within the conflict resolution process.

The issue of 'decommissioning' similarly highlights the media's inability to facilitate communications on particular issues. As a major sticking point for the talks process, the implications of decommissioning (which has lent considerable weight to the Unionist position) have not been extrapolated within news analysis. Though deliberately chosen by civil servants as a word which downplayed the notion of surrender, decommissioning brought a major obstruction to the talks process which favoured those who felt their interests were under threat, namely the Unionists. The mainstream Unionist parties applied the decommissioning request as a knowing obstruction more than a legitimate argument and posed difficulties for the British government in doing so, especially given its historical condemnations of the IRA and terrorism. Far less examined by the media were (and still are) the problems created by an insistence on decommissioning weaponry before a settlement is reached and the problems this causes for Republican and Loyalist groups (although Loyalist groups were rarely mentioned), or even why decommissioning became the problem it did. Writing in *The Guardian* a few days after the IRA ended its ceasefire with the Wapping bomb in February 1996, former Irish prime minister Albert Reynolds also raised this latter point, stating 'Decommissioning was never a precondition of the Downing Street Declaration and the insistence on it created serious problems. It was made clear from early on that it was unacceptable and unachievable' ('Too Little, Too Late', *The Guardian*, 12 Feburary 1996). This issue, still represents a considerable obstruction to political progress, and is a good example of where the media have failed to initiate discussion or inject momentum.

One possible reason for this is the level of propaganda which has been conventionally levelled against those who conduct political violence, particularly Republicans, which has considerably narrowed the scope for political manoeuvre in a new climate of conflict resolution. Nevertheless, there have been notable shifts in attitude towards the Republican position by the British government as the lifting of the Broadcasting Ban indicates, which has resulted in greater possibilities for journalists to examine political dialogue, creating a space for Republican spokesmen to comment on developments in the process. The reintroduction of Sinn Fein into news discourse did allow broader scope for discussion and inclusion of the Republican perspective and as early coverage of events such as Gerry Adams' visit to the United States illustrated (September 1994), also provided real propaganda opportunities, but whether such coverage contributed to the negotiation process is another question.

Much of the available literature which deals with the developments of the peace process makes little reference to political uses of the media, or addresses its advantages in the communications battle (Coogan 1995; Duignan 1996; Mallie and McKittrick 1996; O'Brien 1995; O'Clery 1996; O'Malley 1997; Rowan 1995). A possible reason why the media should receive such little recognition perhaps relates to the convictions and political allegiances of the communities in Northern Ireland which remain largely unaffected and unmoved by pressures for action expressed within the media. There is a case for claiming that the peace process has led to a considerable reduction in the level of violence which most are relieved about and this has created public expectations which politicians cannot ignore. But, whether these expectations have led to direct pressures to shift ideologically, however, is a different story. For Unionists, the issue of being seen to make concessions to Nationalists is a problem which carries the accusation 'that unionists stop being unionists and admit they were muddled nationalists after all' (Porter 1996: 42).

Indeed, the formation of political identities amongst the various parties in Northern Ireland, which inform subsequent responses to the peace process, are largely ignored in news reports, thus the positions they occupy in relation to questions about the constitution, the economy, religion, education, the law, justice and individual rights are overlooked even through they create a basis for conflict. This is especially evident when one looks at the Opsahl report produced in 1992. Also entitled *A Citizen's Inquiry*, the report was the result of an investigation chaired by an international commission which drew on responses from around three thousand people who comprised a broad cross section of the population within Northern Ireland. They were responding to questions about issues which were seen to underpin conflict and what the report attempted to do was to recommend processes which would help bring conflict to an end. In its conclusions, the report noted

> It is evident from the views submitted to the Commission that a parliamentary system of government based on the Westminster model, with its emphasis on majority rule, is not a suitable model for the governing of this fundamentally divide society (Pollak 1993: 111).

It further went on

> we consider-provided that Irish nationalism is legally recognised in Northern Ireland – a government of Northern Ireland should be put in place, based on the principle that each community has *an equal voice in making and executing the laws or a veto on their execution and equally shares administrative authority.* This government should be free to discuss and negotiate its relationships institutional and other, with the Republic of Ireland (ibid.: 112).

Such conclusions derived from a broad consideration of the complexities and opposing interests which exist in Northern Ireland and provide a highly relevant background not only to make sense of the conflict, but also how to proceed into a conflict resolution process. But, the report's usefulness as a context for reading conflict causes is hardly a basis for news reports. Here, coverage overwhelmingly focuses on the effects of violence and positions taken in relation to those effects whether political or rhetorical, rather than addressing possible ways of removing the grievances which give rise to it.

In relation to the peace process, responses have become conducted largely within parameters of debate determined by the British (and to a lesser extent Irish) government who set the structures and mechanisms for political talks. The news media may have played an important part in creating a context for reading events through the peace process paradigm, but the problem then becomes every issue being interpreted through that paradigm. Or more specifically, what each event means in relation to the peace process. This invariably results in a narrow field of view which neglects analysis of how the peace process impacts on the underlying causes of conflict. Instead, the perception is drawn from how the effects of conflict impact on the peace process rather than the other way round, maintaining a series of representations of the Northern Ireland problem which fail to examine communal differences beyond the physical and irreconcilable extremes of 'sectarianism'. In continuing to apply the consensus model of broadcasting which relies on the structures and conventions of British parliamentary discourse we are still left with a field of interpretation unable to make sense of the conflict beyond a crude caricature of those within it. Given this predicament, how can effective or constructive communications between the respective groups involved in the peace process be carried out?

Although the peace process has created public expectations for change and those expectations have undoubtedly been facilitated by media coverage, it does not therefore transpire that the news media will also ease communal difficulties, or overcome problems of identity, or even help modernise particular cultural formations which act as an expression of that identity. Indeed, there is little if anything that television news can do to help resolve such matters of concern given its emphasis on simplistic, stereotypical and short-sighted readings of conflict in Northern Ireland. It does not appear to have the capacity to examine the complexities of political and cultural structures across the Republican/Nationalist and Loyalist/Unionist divide which invariably fall outside the boundaries of what constitutes 'newsworthy'.

There are thus a number of factors which should be considered when assessing whether television news played an important communicative role during the formative stages of the peace process. Firstly, a consensual model of public service broadcasting is unable to dissect the underlying causes of conflict (Butler 1996: 72), preferring to concentrate on effects of conflict and episodes of confrontation which reinforce rather than help to break down divisions and antagonisms. This makes it unlikely that news can help articulate the constructive intra-communal dialogue necessary for negotiation and ultimately conflict resolution. Secondly, to suggest that the television news media can facilitate negotiation implies it has the power to shape some kind of agreement over that which is negotiated. This does not take into account the highly contentious nature of politics in Northern Ireland, or that consensus politics is basically nonexistent there, reflecting the apparent irreconcilable nature of discourses which exists between unionism and nationalism. Thirdly, the importance of the news media for communicating the peace process is secondary to communications performed in the political arena. It is in the field of politics where movements and developments are made, not television news which attempts to compress complex discussion into soundbites and simplistic positions. Nor is the news media particularly necessary to carry communications between representatives who would not meet directly, since intermediaries and mediating individuals can be used for this and would be preferable when passing on sensitive information which can be misconstrued and misused by the media. Fourthly, communications through the news are just as likely to create obstructions and cause problems as be used constructively, especially given the monitoring of news for signs of threats, concessions, sell-outs and directions by the highly politicised audiences of Northern Ireland. And fifthly, as secret contacts between the British government and Sinn Fein reveal (Sinn Fein 1993), the media can seriously threaten momentum and negotiations by reporting them.

The Problem of Communicating Peace

That news can create obstructions for politicians by reporting sensitive developments and that from time to time it may be more desirable for politicians to avoid the media altogether, indicates how problematic it can be for groups trying to use news as a means of communication .

Miller and McLaughlin make reference to this problem in their paper *Reporting the Peace in Ireland,* where they look at media revelations about the British government holding secret contacts with Sinn Fein and how once leaked, this story developed a momentum of denial and counter-denial by the two sides (Miller and McLaughlin 1996: 426–31). Importantly, the outcome of media coverage endorsed the view that 'Publication of the contacts is held by both sides to severely compromise the chances of success. Keeping the media away from negotiations is seen as a precondition for success' (ibid.: 432) and that 'Republicans in particular were concerned that the British might leak details to the media or that elements within the British hierarchy might try to sabotage the process by doing so' (ibid.: 431).

It seems clear enough that news revelations set back trust between the two sides, but there are as many unresolved questions posed by Miller and McLaughlin's analysis about communications through the news media as there are attempts to address the impact of those communications. One important point is that for the British government in particular it was 'seen as necessary to do some public preparing of the ground for a potential settlement' (ibid.: 432). The authors refer to Peter Brooke's speech about the British having 'no selfish or strategic or economic interest in Northern Ireland' made in 1990, but then make no reference to other incidences of communications through the media by the government until publication of the Downing Street Declaration. If it were the case that the public had been prepared for a settlement as the authors argue, then why the commotion about communications with Sinn Fein, which at some point would have become public anyway? And, if the public had not been adequately prepared for the reception of a peace settlement which would necessitate discussion with all the sides, then why not? Revelations of the contacts strengthened the hand of Sinn Fein in the peace process by bringing pressure on the government to justify its position (the government did not deny contacts but the content of those contacts) and helped to establish a process of public dialogue which at the same time also had the contradictory affect of serving to legitimise communications between the two sides, since the initial subject of contention which had been Sinn Fein and the government engaging in dialogue, required precisely such dialogue in order for the issue to be contested and resolved.

The contestation between Sinn Fein and the British government continued over the contents of the Joint Declaration, where as Miller and McLaughlin observe Sinn Fein calls for clarification of the document were met with a refusal by the government to do so. When however, the government moved to provide the clarification which Sinn Fein was looking for, there was a further process of contestation over whether the government had in fact given clarification, or whether it had provided 'exposition', or 'commentary', or 'explanation', or 'elucidation' (ibid.: 434–5). The importance of obscuring developments by particular forms of language so as they may proceed, is a point which remains largely unaddressed by Miller and McLaughlin. The inference here being that the government was able to use the media to divert problems by effective management and not that Sinn Fein also benefited considerably from this process, by gaining the information and movement which it was seeking. Furthermore, the authors do not acknowledge how 'Ambiguous language is a sign and a facilitator of bargaining' (Elderman: 1988: 25) and particularly important for managing divisions and creating space for momentum. Thus a Provisional IRA ceasefire might be 'permanent', 'lengthy', 'complete', 'prolonged', 'indefinite', 'unequivocal', 'genuine', 'credible', or 'lasting' depending on political persuasion; generating scope for broad interpretation and providing greater room for dealing with a ceasefire, if and when it is called.

The work of Miller/McLaughlin and Page/Sparre, suggests quite strongly that news coverage of the peace process played a prominent role in the development of the talks. As Miller and McLaughlin put it, 'It has been exceptionally rare for television journalists to acknowledge that the briefings they are given are not a transparent reflection of government thinking but actually part of the negotiation process' (Miller and McLaughlin: 434). However, the authors seem unclear about which part of the negotiation process they are talking of. Neither do they indicate how or why the subjects of contention made any real difference to the peace process in terms of direction or policy. Although the inference is that news coverage impacts on political policy, this effect is hardly straightforward. As Strobel argues, 'The news media are rarely, if ever, independent movers of policy' (Strobel 1997:5). Yet, in his analysis of how the news media influence peace operations, and American foreign policy decisions, Strobel also noted:

> under the right conditions, the news media ... can have a powerful effect on process. And those conditions are almost always set by foreign policy makers themselves or by the growing number of policy actors on the international stage. If officials let others dominate the policy debate, if they do not closely monitor the progress and results of their own policies, if they fail to build and maintain popular and congressional support for a course of action, if they step beyond the bounds of their public mandate or fail to anticipate problems, they may suddenly seem driven by the news media and its agenda (ibid.).

The news media and the political process are thus subject to a continual tension where the impact of coverage affects not so much the content of policy, but the climate for how that policy is conducted and developed. As Gowing similarly observed in his examination of real-time television news coverage and the pressures such coverage creates for foreign policy decision makers, 'Television coverage is ... a powerful influence in problem recognition, which in turn helps to shape the foreign policy agenda. But television does not necessarily dictate policy responses' (Gowing 1994: 18). The political advantages and disadvantages to be derived from television news, are discerned more specifically from the expectations and pressures it creates for action. As Gowing puts it, 'Frequently ministers and officials talk resentfully of this "profound" relationship between television and policy making because it creates a clamour that "something must be done"' (ibid.: 16). Yet against this pressure Gowing discovered a corresponding attempt by officials to resist the reactions which news seemed to prescribe, highlighting a 'determination to keep to a policy line and to resist the immediately profound and emotive impact of real-time coverage of a conflict on television' (ibid.). According to an interview which Gowing conducted with the then Under Secretary General for Peacekeeping at the UN, Kofi Annan, the likelihood of news coverage affecting policy arises more because of an uncertainty of policy direction rather than as a result of the power of news. As Annan saw it: 'When governments have a clear policy, they have anticipated a situation and they know what they want to do and where they want to go, then television has little impact. In fact they ride it' (ibid.: 19).

The introduction and recognition of problems which news perpetuates and reinforces has a number of political functions and uses which Miller and McLaughlin fail to look at. The representation of a situation or issue as a problem for some, invariably brings with it particular advantages to others; i.e. 'A problem to some is a benefit to others' (Elderman 1988: 14). Moreover, as Elderman identifies, a problem comes in a number of variations. These variations become part and parcel of the 'political spectacle' and an important feature in the development of political policy and power. Though the various forms of problem which Elderman lists under such headings as 'Problems as Ambiguous Claims', 'The Construction of Reasons for Problems', 'The Construction of Problems to Justify Solutions', 'The Construction of Gestures as Solutions', ' The Perpetuation of Problems through Policies to Ameliorate Them', 'Problems as Negations of Other Problems', etc., have obvious differences, they nevertheless also have a similar intention, which is to assist political control and direction.

The creation and use of problems which news has an inclination to promote and reinforce, make it an important component of political power, more particularly because the representation of subjects/situations/issues/events as problems also become associated with expectations for actions and solutions (ibid.: 15). It is this relationship which makes news such a crucial mechanism for the exercise of political policy and control. As Elderman concludes:

> News accounts therefore reconstruct social worlds, histories and eschatologies, evoking grounds for concern and for hope and assumptions about what should be noticed and what ignored, who are respectable or heroic, and who not respectable. News items displace others and in turn take their meaning from other accounts, always in the context of a perspective about history and ideology. Little wonder, then, that interest groups try to shape the content and form of television and printed news, for to create a world dominated by a particular set of problems is at the same time to create support for specific courses of actions (ibid.: 29).

But from this position, we can also argue how unlikely it is that news may be used for facilitating agreement, reconciliation or intra-commmunal dialogue. Here, it appears more probable that the main political advantage of using news is to introduce problems and reactions to problems which may assist political momentum and the development of policy. This is not to say however, that communications progress in some linear, chronological, or progressive manner. As has been noted, the news media can undermine communications as well as further them, and it is this conflicting tension which raises questions about its role within the negotiations of the peace process. Television news it would seem, is better placed to express and reinforce problems, rather than reduce or help resolve them.

Conclusion

The development of the peace process marked a real change in the political climate of Northern Ireland from a conflict situation towards one of conflict resolution. Although this change became reflected by the codes and references used in television news coverage, it was apparent that there was also a tendency to represent emotive and conflicting positions within the structure of reports. Given this tendency, the potential effectiveness and importance of television news as part of conflict resolution in Northern Ireland becomes problematical.

What has been argued here, is that it is difficult to obtain any clear or definitive picture of television news as a facilitative device for the promotion of peace. Clearly there have been occasions where the news media have been used to help establish or affirm a position, but this has occurred more effectively in the press than on television (see David Broomfield's book, *Political Dialogue in Northern Ireland,* for a comprehensive analysis of how the press were used to develop communications and talks from 1989–92). Television news represents a more uncertain outlet for communications and by keeping to a consensus model of broadcasting, seems unable to grapple with the complexities and diversities of the various political positions. Given this tendency, it is especially difficult to maintain or facilitate dialogue which is representative of the political diversity which exists in Northern Ireland. This indicates that the role of television news is highly limited and homogeneous in its representation of the peace process. Megaphone diplomacy may well take place through television news, but it is very difficult to measure what difference such diplomacy makes when its presentation is structured in conflicting terms. Moreover, although the promotion of problems has political advantages and disadvantages, television news can create unexpected as well as expected political problems and it is this which makes it unpredictable and difficult to control. Since news coverage can make a situation worse as well as better, it can thus be counterproductive to political intentions and destabilising in relation to dominant objectives. Clearly, political elites have greater access to news organisations and extensive communications facilities to maximise the possibilities of news management, but even here, as revelations about the British government contacts with Sinn Fein highlight, occasions arise which can cause political difficulty. Efforts to reduce tensions at Drumcree similarly underline that political access and dominant viewpoints may have negligible impact against the emotive and inflammatory images of news reports.

In the climate of the peace process, where the consensus over terrorism has given way to contestations over how peace should be developed and shaped, it would appear that in the early stages at least, political contestation and a news emphasis on differences and antagonisms, tended to obstruct reconciliation and accommodation rather than assist it. Although its main political use was (as it still is) to maintain the notion of a developing peace so as to incite political actions, which in turn create (or obstruct) developments, the positioning of alternate views in a conflictive setting can disrupt momentum while politicians are forced to deal with trying to acquire definitional advantage over the issue under debate. The news media clearly has a political role to play, facilitating the rules of political engagement and shaping perceptions of problems, but, because politicians are effectively more concerned with winning the debate, it is conflict which is prioritised, not agreement or reconciliation.

The impact of news on peace negotiations is therefore more complex and problematic than it is on conflict. The imagery and language of terrorism tends to locate discussion in a tight moral framework, concerned with condemnation and rhetoric which makes it especially difficult to move outside of, without appearing to lack the moral concerns which the imagery of devastation and emotion seem to demand. In playing a key function in helping to promulgate this situation, the news media tend to reinforce and legitimise dominant articulations and responses about such violence, thus reproducing expected perceptions of those who propagated it.

However, because the peace process was about the eradication of violence, it became much more difficult to maintain this simplistic perception. Since most of the respective parties were, on the face of it, committed to the peace process, reporting was forced to concentrate more on the political differences than the moral ones and increased the scope for political contestation in the process. What is less clear, is how political representatives communicated peace and reconciliation within this emerging paradigm, and how they perceived television news in relation to their prime objective of negotiating and promoting peace.

What I have tried to establish at this point in the study is a picture of television news which provides a different and more complex role in relation to political communications than during the time of conflict. I have outlined why confidentiality can be preferable for politicians involved in negotiations and why they may decide that given the emphasis of news on disagreement, antagonisms and problems, it may be better at times to avoid publicity. I have raised questions about the possibilities of promoting reconciliatory dialogue through reports which prioritise a simplistic, dramatic and conflictual approach to issues, and provided instances of where coverage may have added to political problems rather than helped to resolve them. In all, I have tried to use this chapter to establish some of the potential difficulties which news has created for the development of peace and which compares to its more politically supportive role during the years of conflict. Having suggested that it is unlikely television news made a positive contribution to the early stages of peace, I now turn to interview material gathered from politicians involved in that process to find out if this was the case.

3 Political Perceptions of Reporting and the Peace Process

Introduction

In the previous chapter I set out to explain how the peace process came about, the importance of media coverage within this development, and to raise a number of questions about the ability of news to communicate and facilitate peace negotiations. What I have tried to argue, is that within the emerging peace process paradigm, the conditions of political engagement in news were different from before, and that now, alternative discourses were absorbed into coverage, posing new problems for the flow of dominant discourse. With the transition from war to peace, a broader range of political discourses became included in coverage, each competing to try and gain the initiative and stake out the substantive issues which might determine the direction of peace. This absorption of a wider range of competing viewpoints some of which were previously demonised by the media, created new possibilities for challenging dominant discourse and obstructing elites in their efforts to communicate positions and perspectives.

This chapter is concerned with how politicians perceived this development, how they viewed the role of television news in relation to peace and how they tried to use it as part of negotiations. Based on interviews with 15 political representatives from a cross section of the parties who were involved in the formative stages of the peace process from 1993–97 (see Appendix 1), this section will offer a valuable insight into how representatives interacted with television news and tried to use it for promoting peace.

By interviewing politicians from different parties involved in the peace process, I aim to see how their experiences and perceptions of news differ and to find out if some found news more helpful to their objectives than others. I also intend to look at how politicians reacted to the pressures of television news and communicated their respective positions within the spaces afforded by coverage. In particular, the changing political climate signified a period of uncertainty which heightened conflictions and tensions, and how politicians attempted to communicate and construct their positions within this conflictive context is also of concern here.

This chapter therefore provides original primary research on how politicians dealt with and viewed news as part of the transition from conflict to conflict resolution in Northern Ireland. It identifies the problems they experienced when dealing with news whilst engaged in delicate negotiations, and creates a detailed picture of how the media were seen in the light of political objectives concerned with developing peace. Importantly, it also allows us to see if television news was supportive or obstructive towards peace and highlights the role of news in relation to dominant discourse.

Political Communications and the Problem of Peace

A number of representatives involved in the early stages of the peace process were particularly critical of the ways by which television news coverage had institutionalised 'The Troubles' in Northern Ireland (Bowyer Bell 1997: 618) and reinforced the perception that the situation there is 'an insoluble problem' (Moloney 1988: 143). This critical view of the media also affected similarly negative perceptions about the role of news in the peace process, where early coverage was seen as carrying on the same negative stereotypes about Northern Ireland as before. Highlighting how news coverage had conventionally served to reinforce a negative impression of Northern Ireland, one SDLP politician in Belfast noted:

> Given the nature of the last 25 years where there has been one tragedy or atrocity after another to report on, reporting has always been of the moment and the media have tended to emphasise the 'horror moment' over critical analysis of what was happening in the broader context. This has served to characterise the Northern Ireland conflict in a very simplistic, melodramatic and stereotypical way which reinforces a simplistic public understanding. TV networks all want images of policemen covered in flames, because such images confirm the caricature of Northern Ireland.

According to a prominent American peace delegation member, this preoccupation with violence and terrorism had diverted attention away from the changes which were reshaping the political landscape, and where a conflict resolution process was being forwarded as an alternative to conflict. As the delegate expressed it:

> The overall view I have is that British and Irish coverage has been quite bad. The fact that the IRA ceasefire came as a huge surprise to the media is an indictment not just on the Irish and British media, but on the whole profession of journalism. The prevailing view was that the Northern Ireland situation wouldn't change, even though there was a great shift going on under the surface in terms of where the IRA was going, where Sinn Fein was going and where the entire Irish peace process was going. It all sort of happened as a huge surprise. The media is very lazy, very much addicted to handouts by whoever gives them, whether it be Sinn Fein or the British government.
>
> It's an interesting experience when you see in the media that there's nothing new happening, or that the IRA campaign will never end and then you talk to people who are very much on the inside and they say that yes it's going to end and we're getting ready to do it, but nobody's covering the story. There's been no serious attempt at analysis about what's been going on for the last 10 to 15 years. There have been some profound shifts going on which even I, living in the US have been able to pick up on. I read Gerry Adams's book in 1988 and said there's something going on here. This guy's changing, he's not saying Brits out, he's talking about a political path to peace and that was just not picked up at all.

This problem of recognition and analysis, which required a more sophisticated reading of political articulations and developments, was also highlighted by a former Northern Ireland secretary, who used the media to send a key message to republicans. He outlined his intentions thus:

> As soon as I got there in 1989, I was operating on the basis that we were not going to get peace by any other means than a settlement. There was no way in which the IRA was going to defeat the British army and the RUC, and equally, unless you impose total martial law, you're not going to end it by security force. When the terrorists are as effective as they are, you're not going to stop it by military or police oppression, so the only alternative is agreement. The first objective is a ceasefire, the second objective is a settlement. I took my life in both hands in November 1989, a year before the speech about strategic interest, and I said literally what I've just said. I wanted to send it as a message. If you spend all your time saying 'We are going to defeat you', then there is no incentive whatsoever for the person on the other side of the table to start thinking in any other way. There is evidence that McGuiness and Adams were aiming to extricate the IRA from what they are, from as early as 1986.

For the former Northern Ireland secretary, using the media to send messages to republicans required sanction at the highest political level:

> You don't make comments like that [the strategic interest speech] without getting clearance,

and represented a major shift in terms of the British government's approach towards Northern Ireland:

> Of course, exactly the same words were used in the Downing St Declaration, three years later.

Yet, this highly significant change in orientation towards the Northern Ireland situation from the British government and the possible ramifications of this change at first, failed to register within the journalistic community, which maintained its continuing emphasis on acts of political violence. It was this preoccupation which also obscured consideration of political communications which were developing 'behind the scenes' between republicans and the British government (*Setting The Record Straight* 1994), and which maintained the simplistic representations of groups and individuals as either 'pro'- or 'anti'-terrorist. Commenting on how such representations created problems for political dialogue, one Northern Ireland Committee member said in interview:

> There are problems with seeing representatives of groups like Sinn Fein. I saw Sinn Fein in 1981 and was also speaking to Loyalist paramilitary leaders, so I was careful to take a balanced stance. But, there was this problem of presentation and the worry of being seen by the media as pro-terrorist. Often the media, particularly the press, don't separate factual news from opinion, so news gets reported as opinion and the opinion in 1981 was that the Labour Party supports terror, which is a label every political party wants to avoid.

Associations with groups which carry out political violence, tend to produce predictable responses from the media, largely based on the 'Will you condemn those who carry out violence?' question. For one Sinn Fein politician in Belfast, such questions continue to position groups in relation violence and in so doing categorise those groups within simplistic 'good' or 'bad' boundaries. As the politician noted:

> We're doing press conferences every couple of days, and there's the statutory question of Sinn Fein 'Do you condemn the IRA?', even though that conference may be about housing, street lighting or whatever. The journalist will tell you that the reason he's asking that is because his editor demands he does so. And when we say that we don't speak for the IRA the headline becomes 'Sinn Fein dismisses', or 'Sinn Fein washes its hands', or 'Sinn Fein refuses'.

Constructing the Northern Ireland problem through the conflicting forces of 'good' and 'bad' and applying a 'terrorism-as-cause' paradigm (Butler 1995) to give context to these forces, created problems for those involved in developing the peace process. But, those problems were created not only because of the media's obsession with representations of terrorism, they arose because television news needs a clash of interests in order to construct 'the problem' itself and to give the subject of coverage conflict, so making it a topic worthy of public concern. Or, to put it another way, conflict makes a problem dramatic and so particularly newsworthy (Maltese 1994: 1). As Bantz reminds us, the production of conflict is used 'as a routine, expected and appropriate occurrence' in news discourse (Bantz 1977: 127). Thus, in relation to this technique of construction, television news tends to construct and prioritise positions towards subjects as oppositional poles and within a 'presentation of conflicting possibilities' (Eldridge 1995: 213).

In particular, it was this use of 'conflicting possibilities' which created a number of difficulties for those attempting to promote peace. As one former Irish minister commented:

> Media spins can create the situation where somebody thinks they're losing and somebody thinks they're winning and vice versa. When delicate negotiations are going on, that could do very serious damage to the whole situation. The media can look for an angle of interpretation which itself can be a danger to the whole process. Of course, the media want a good story at all times, but they're coming from a different angle than we're coming from.

Highlighting how media and political imperatives may clash, the same minister stressed how a repetitive and simplistic approach to issues by news organisations hindered the complex possibilities of peacemaking, continuing:

> When sometimes a government takes up a hardline position, it makes it infinitely more difficult to change positions because you're seen as weak, or capitulating or whatever. There are times when the media do create that situation and it makes it very difficult for governments to move because they're constantly painted into a corner which they cannot easily get out of. The news media don't worry about the difficulties they cause for governments or politicians.

One potential reason for why television news tends to reiterate similar responses and frames of reference to situations and events is given by Gans, who observed how journalists are 'reluctant to change conscious stands, fearing they will then be charged with inconsistency, which undermines their credibility'. Changes generally occur 'only in the wake of highly visible and traumatic events, for positions then can be justified without loss of credibility' (Gans 1980: 199–200). Problems for advancing conflict resolution through news arise, therefore, not only because conflict is a convention of journalistic practice, but because the very existence of conflict within reports helps to maintain the image of journalistic integrity and continuity. However, this continuity demands a reinforcement of binary positions in the narratives of news discourse, which obstruct rather than assist possibilities for developing intra-communal dialogue, as well as understanding of the broader political context in which conflict resolution is situated. Acknowledging how this emphasis affects political responses in news, a former Northern Ireland secretary pointed out how:

> By seeking to demand instant reactions and soundbites, the media tends to harden positions and tends not to allow for an explanation for a position. So one gets a conclusion, one doesn't get the reason which is leading towards it, and that reason is rarely ever examined.

This also suggests that political articulations in news are constructed more as responses to developments rather than considerations about why those developments happened, or indeed, where they may be headed. Furthermore, such responses become more newsworthy the more conflicting they are and the more apparently irreconcilable they are. As one Northern Ireland Select Committee MP put it:

> The news media try to get you to get your point over in a soundbite way. But they often keep repeating the question in a slightly different way so it becomes more and more difficult to hang on to what you want to say. And when it gets cut down for the final piece, they take out all the conciliatory tones and put out the more contentious parts of your comments, so you appear much more aggressive. They tend to go for effect which inevitably is confrontational. I've been asked to appear in interviews which have been dropped because they haven't been able to find someone with an opposing view. They're only interested in a 'pro' and an 'anti' view.

This emphasis on oppositional perspectives, for a former Northern Ireland Secretary, created real problems for developing dialogue in the formative stages of the peace process:

> The disadvantage is when you're conducting delicate negotiations the media are a bloody nuisance, because, particularly if it's multilateral negotiations,

you're putting everybody in a position where they don't know if somebody else is leaking and therefore they don't know if they should leak themselves. Negotiations like that just can't be conducted on the basis of all the negotiating positions being out in the open. The whole purpose of difficult negotiations is that, is that they've got to be done privately and confidentially. As we know with the Israeli ones, they were done in somewhere like Norway or Denmark. They were done in Scandinavia, miles away from anywhere.

Conducting negotiations in confidence rather than through the news media was expressed as important by a number of interviewees who saw coverage as more of a hindrance than a help. Officials were especially wary of the media reporting developments in the early phases of the peace process and viewed coverage as a potentially negative force, which could unravel work being done. Political fears and sensibilities were notably pronounced in the early more fragile stages of talks, when efforts were concentrated on establishing political momentum. Since media coverage was seen as a major contributing factor for creating and stoking fears, it was also for this reason viewed as a considerably negative force. It was in order to limit this influence, that politicians also made deliberate efforts to keep communications and developments away from the media. As one former Irish minister explained it:

> You are trying to put people in positions which they don't want to be in and trying to move people from where they have been to where they have not been. In that context, it is far more preferable to do work behind closed doors than in front of the media. People are always very sensitive of their own positions and what they might appear to be accepting through television spins or news in general. That's basically the reason why so much work on The Downing St Declaration for about eighteen months was done behind the scenes in a confidential manner, and in fact, no leak got out until about two weeks before it was published and at that stage it wouldn't do too much damage anyway. I don't think it would have succeeded if we had tried to do it out in the open with the television cameras breathing down our necks every time we wanted to do something. We were always careful about what the media might know during that particular sensitive period.

The importance of confidentiality and attempting to avoid news coverage which amplifies fears by focusing on who is losing and who is winning, was also indicated by a former Northern Ireland minister who stressed that reports often:

> ... cause people to react and overreact in ways which damages the work being done to bring people together.

For the minister, it was precisely because of a propensity to reinforce images of division rather than facilitate constructive dialogue, that the initial stages of negotiations were conducted away from media scrutiny. Stressing how essential it was for the British government to develop 'Strand 2' of the talks process (designed to strengthen the role of the Irish government in negotiations), out of the media spotlight, he said:

> We couldn't have got to 'Strand 2' had we allowed the media into our meetings. We had to do it behind closed doors and we had to do it with agreed communiques to the press. Had we been open, we wouldn't have had negotiations because individuals would have been criticised for whatever they said from one side of the divide or the other. It was also useful having the media completely out of Strand 1 because some politicians do play to the cameras and they play to the journalists and therefore, you don't actually get to the real nitty-gritty discussion unless you're doing it behind closed doors. In the main, we reckoned we'd get much more in negotiations if we didn't make daily comments, daily press releases and say what had happened every day.

Political efforts to keep discussions out of the media clearly derive from an inability to control news output and a realisation that coverage may have a destabilising affect on progress. The media's potential to create this situation, is also addressed by Thompson, who informs us:

> Given the nature of the media, the messages produced by political leaders may be received and understood in ways that cannot be directly monitored and controlled. Hence the visibility created by the media may become the source of a new and distinctive kind of *fragility*. However much political leaders may seek to manage their visibility, they cannot completely control it; the phenomenon of visibility may slip from their grasp and on occasion, work against them (Thompson 1995: 141).

Thus continues Thompson, politicians 'must be on their guard continuously and employ a high degree of reflexivity to monitor their actions-and-utterances, since an indiscreet act or ill-judged remark can, if recorded and relayed to millions of viewers, have disastrous consequences' (ibid.). Furthermore,

> however hard political leaders may try to restrict the visibility of themselves or of particular actions or events, they know they run the risk that they, or the actions or events for which they are responsible, may be shown and seen in ways they did not intend, and hence they must reckon with the permanent possibility of uncontrolled visibility (ibid.: 147).

This suggests that the media exercise notable power over the political process and indeed, as in the case of the peace process, may exercise an influence which is both negative and obstructive.

The attention to conflicting positions and opposing extremes within reports is a convention which remains consistent with overriding news values of drama and negativity (Fowler 1991: 12–16), where responses to issues ostensibly take precedence over examination of why those issues themselves are important. This tendency for news to exclude analysis of broader contextual factors which underpin the political process, is also acknowledged by Zolo, who argues:

> Newsworthiness demands a systematic decontextualisation and fragmentation of events. Background situations simply cannot be established in the very short time-spans allowed by newsmaking, and news items can only be such if they are in fact new, that is, in some measure sudden, unexpected and spectacular. They have to be offered up to the consumer in the most immediate and concise form possible. Each item has to be constructed in the form of a narrative flash which is self-standing and conclusive in itself. Thus the focus of a narration inevitably tends to be upon what has happened, and rarely touches upon any of the deeper reasons for why it has happened (Zolo 1992: 159).

For politicians who articulated their opinions and positions about the peace process within the constraints of the soundbite, or 'narrative flash' as Zolo puts it, facilitating discussion on issues proved especially difficult. According to one Northern Ireland Select Committee member, when communicating within a 30 second time frame it is almost impossible:

> … to do anything other than use or repeat familiar or chosen phraseology in the hope that you are reminding people of what you would be saying if you had longer to say it.

It is also because of such time constraints that news does:

> … little more than report the superficial and the immediate.

For some, this restriction is not entirely negative however, enabling simplistic criticisms and condemnations to be employed, and emotional commentary to be foregrounded, both of which provide a specific and sometimes useful political effect. A former Northern Ireland minister highlighted the relevance of these qualities in news by stating:

I used to do probably more interviews on Northern Ireland than most people and I always tried to say the same things, because I think repetition works. I always used to say that the IRA are killers and that they are a bunch of dastardly incompetent cowards. I'm always aware of how effective emotional language is and that phrases do matter. Repetition does matter.

However, in the main, attempting to develop peace through news is especially problematic given the emphasis on, and need for, dramatic, conflictive and simplistic articulations. Since the activities of peacemaking run counter to journalistic imperatives (Wolfsfeld 1997: 67), so news tends to rely on values which are unable to assess the causes of conflict (Butler 1995: 90), or play a constructive role in the development of conflict resolution. Shirlow and McGovern's analysis of how unionist, protestant and loyalist identities are simplified, could quite reasonably be referring to the conventions of news when they argue:

For certain community representatives, the mobilisation of a binary ideological framework of division sanctions a form of censorship over inter-community dialogue as each side purposely promotes differences over similarities. Dividing the population into two blocks also allows sectarianism to thrive upon the demonisation of the 'other' (Shirlow and McGovern 1997: 3).

Moreover, continue the authors:

For too long, commentators on the conflict in Ireland have carelessly thrown diverse groups into general categories which are wholly inappropriate and insensitive. The end result has been to convince many on the grounds that there is an identifiable and united foe which must be resisted. If a more cautious commentary were produced which indicated that there is significant intra-communal heterogeneity, then it is possible that inter-community similarities would also be exposed. The significance of such alliances would be to undermine the demagogues and political manipulators who mobilise contrived homogeneity and in so doing block alternative syntheses and strategies (ibid.: 9–10).

This concentration on images which amplify the irreconcilability of the communities, was exemplified in a BBC *Newsnight* broadcast on 12 August 1997, which brought together Ulster Unionist MP Ken Maginnis and Sinn Fein MP Martin McGuiness. Introduced as the first live debate between the two sides on British television, the Newsnight programme aimed 'to debate the way forward for peace' and 'to find out if there is any common ground'. What the programme actually provided was a clear representation of how apparently irreconcilable unionist and republican positions are. Ken Maginnis used the interview to insist that Martin McGuiness 'is the godfather of godfathers of the IRA' who 'had presided over killings and sanctioned some of those killings', whilst Martin McGuiness impressed how unionists had discriminated against Catholics and abused their power and that 'the northern state had failed'. Rather than address the options for political development, the broadcast actually amplified the incompatibility of the two positions and suggested that in fact, there is no common ground.

This representation counters any notion that republicans and unionists might be able to liaise with each other, which they do at a local political level. As one Sinn Fein councillor explained:

> I think the whole duplicity of politics in the north of Ireland is left unexposed. We're all going to a series of meetings at local council from 9.00 am until 6.30 pm. All of those meetings will be predominated by the unionists, all of who will allow us our full input into the meeting. They will be extremely friendly before the meeting and will talk about football, alcohol or whatever. In fact, they will be as friendly as possible. And then, we will come out to catch the 5.00 pm news and the same politicians who have just spent two hours being very pleasant and amiable, will be on television saying how they won't talk to Sinn Fein. That is completely known by the media, but is not exposed or challenged.

By ignoring intra-communal political activity between republicans and unionists (Adams 1997: 292), and allowing for a reinforcement of oppositions between the two, television news contributes to 'the perceived threat of the "other"' (Shirlow and McGovern 1997: 5) and reinforces polarised positions. Politicians know what the television news media want and oblige in providing responses which minimise any sign of weakness or concession, so reinforcing an image of irreconcilability and hindering the possibility of reconciliation or accommodation. Nor are political responses in news just communicating to opponents who will be looking for signs of movement or weakness, but constituencies and other interested audiences. In aiming not to inflame tensions or undermine popular support, politicians tend to resort to well established forms of commentary which maintain rather predictable responses and articulations of the Northern Ireland problem. Moving toward a fresh conceptualisation of the Northern Ireland problem is inevitably seized by the parties as lending support to one side or the other, thus making the process of change both contentious and problematic. As one Northern Ireland Select Committee member and Labour MP put it:

You always have in your mind the possible impact of the words you're using in a broadcast, and that's influenced by the people who are likely to be listening. And you're always conscious that your words will be interpreted differently by different groups. Northern Ireland is the one issue where if you get your wording and policies wrong, it costs lives and in a pretty dramatic way, so you think it through very carefully. This is one reason why a lot of British MPs stay away from it. They know it's complicated, they know it's messy and that there's no great credit to be gained by being involved in it. So, if you're worried about getting it wrong, you tend to stay away from it.

Articulations which depart from standard perceptions of organisations, groups, or communities within Northern Ireland, thus carry risks because they indicate the possibilities of change and sympathies toward change. Language is loaded with meanings linked to notions of identity which are both pronounced and threatened during periods of constitutional and political transition. An SDLP politician in Belfast highlighted the importance of language in the resolution of conflict, before underlining that language cannot facilitate change without political actions. The politician went on:

The misuse of language will confuse the nature of conflict and will aggravate parties to the conflict. And yet, language itself will not resolve the conflict. You can use the right language to express the nature of conflict, but finding better words will not resolve the situation. The SDLP would be very careful of its use of language in relation to what our analysis of the problem is, and what the solution to the problem is; 'the accommodation of difference', or 'equality and equity between the traditions', or whatever friendly language you might use. But, it's not just a matter of using the right language, it is the perception of those who hear that language. If what people hear is not what they understand, then it is not just a matter of language, but history and identity. The right language can ease concerns, but cannot completely address them.

A reconceptualisation about the role of the nation-state in relation to Northern Ireland and the conduct of democratic politics within it (Bew, Patterson and Teague 1997), cannot be easily elaborated through television news discourse which concentrates on whether the peace process is 'succeeding' or 'failing', on 'efforts to derail the peace process', or 'a crisis in the peace process', or 'fears for the peace process', or 'those out to destroy the peace process'. For one Ulster Unionist MP, stories which reported that 'the last ever army patrol' had taken place and that the 'war' was over created expectations about the success of the peace process which were misperceived. This led the MP to insist that:

Overall, the television news contribution to the peace process has been negative. It has built up hopes that have been dashed,

indicating that coverage had been obstructive to the process of peacemaking and counterproductive to diplomatic efforts to build peace.

Given its emphasis on polarisation and conflictual scenarios, television news is therefore better placed to represent conflict than peace. Highlighting how political efforts to develop a peace process are hindered rather then helped by the media, Wolfsfeld's work on political uses of the news media to promote the Oslo peace process makes observations about the difficulties politicians faced in their efforts to promote peace which are notably similar to the difficulties faced by politicians working for peace in Northern Ireland. In his analysis, Wolfsfeld argues that the news media serve as obstacles to peace because of: (1) a tendency to focus on events rather than processes; (2) focusing on the unusual, the dramatic, and the conflictual aspects of the process; and (3) by making it difficult to conduct successful negotiations (Wolfsfeld 1997). Highlighting how the imperatives and conventions of journalism are at odds with the imperatives of diplomats working to create peace, Wolfsfeld also concludes that:

> There is an inherent contradiction between the logic of a peace process and the professional demands of journalists. A peace process is complicated; journalists demand simplicity. A peace process takes time to unfold and develop; journalists demand immediate results. Most of the peace process is marked by dull, tedious negotiations; journalists require drama. A successful peace process leads to a reduction in tensions; journalists focus on conflict. Many of the most significant developments within a peace process must take place in secret behind closed doors; journalists demand information and access (ibid.: 67).

Articulating the Peace Process: the News of Politics and the Politics of News

Although during the early stages of the peace process politicians attempted to maintain confidentiality, it became clear that once the existence of a peace process had been formally acknowledged, the media were used to communicate positions in an attempt to gain political initiative. It is also clear that even though television news emphasised conflictive positions, it still held potential to bring pressures on representatives and sound out reactions to developments. According to a former Northern Ireland minister, the news media served a dual function based both on trying to develop trust and confidence and acquire political advantage. On the one hand, a position established in the news was used to affirm a political stance which signified an 'actual' rather than an 'artificial' position known by political players beforehand, and in that sense served to ease tensions. But, on the other hand, news offered possibilities to shape the direction of political momentum by promoting initiatives for change and so acquire political advantage. Indicating this dual communicative function, a former minister firstly stated:

> Basically we wouldn't use the media to communicate with politicians, we would do that directly. Often politicians would criticise us if we said something on the news that we hadn't said to them first, because they wanted to be forewarned so that they could react immediately. If you say something on television without telling the politicians in Northern Ireland, they almost always leap to the conspiracy theory rather than anything else. They think you're doing it deliberately to get at them, or go behind their backs, so openness in Northern Ireland is vital.

But he then went on to say:

> You would never do anything, never begin a day without anticipating what the press and the media are going to say; what will come out. I would never begin a day either without analysing what was in the media that morning and wondering how to counter some of the stories. Anticipating how the press and television will take a particular matter is vital to modern politics. We had a meeting every morning at Stormont at 9.00 am, sometimes earlier, every single day and it would be attended by 15 or 16 people as well as five cabinet ministers. We would analyse the day's media coverage which would be established during the breakfast bulletins, and decide what we thought should be in the developing day's news. We would try to set or determine the agenda as much as possible because it is crucial to not be seen as reacting to events, which makes you appear weaker. We would try to shape the stories as much as possible.

The power to influence the direction of news stories and agendas is easier for those who occupy the most powerful positions and who exert greater political and social control. The demand for news access to powerful political figures also gives those figures greater opportunity to manage news and slant stories in their own interest. A former Northern Ireland secretary emphasised how this access enabled stories to be used, when in interview he said:

> Much of the news not being made by terrorists was being made by the

government. The news media need the government and will make themselves readily available if they think an important announcement is about to be made. One method we used to deploy was one day a week somewhere in the province, I would do a full scale press conference and the only warning that they would get would be about 2.00 pm on the same day, when they would be told that there was a worthwhile press conference. They wouldn't know what the event was about. Since we always set this up in advance we also controlled the environment for interviews. This allowed us effectively to create news.

This ability to shape news also helped to reduce criticisms against the more powerful groups. A former Northern Ireland minister indicated this by explaining how continued access to news after the IRA ended its ceasefire with the Wapping bomb, helped to avoid potential criticisms of Sir Patrick Mayhew for communicating with the IRA the following day:

Within half an hour of the Wapping bomb I was in touch with the radio and television. At that time there had also been a run of communications between the IRA and the British government. I dominated the radio and television news from 8 o'clock until around 12.30 pm. On Monday morning, all the editorials said that the government had been right and was justified. Normally, you would get accusations that the policy hasn't worked etc. As a result, on the communication story, Sir Patrick Mayhew had an easier time on the Monday in the House of Commons. The Prime Minister wasn't criticised and our approach was vindicated.

Attempts to manage the news tend to oscillate around two key themes. Avoiding pressures on one's own political position and bringing pressures on opponents. It is tension between these competing forces which also enables movement to be created through discussion and then action. Efforts to move the peace process along through news thus concentrated on generating pressure which might contribute to movement on a particular problem. Or, as an Irish minister put it:

In an interview you put out an angle on something that might attract a bit of attention and put a bit of pressure on those that might be dragging their feet. Politicians also use the media as a conduit for a message and where they're thinking in relation to where the next move should be, or the next step, or what takes place.

However, pressure may not always result in developing movement. It can also contribute to intransigence. To illustrate this, it is useful to look at reactions towards media speculation of a possible IRA ceasefire in the summer of 1994. The belief by some key players in the peace process was that speculation of a ceasefire in news made little difference in terms of bringing one about, and indeed had the effect of delaying it. One American peace delegate involved in communications between all the groups, said of news pressure:

> It would have made no difference. Unfortunately, the Republican movement has a very tin-ear about the media. They were putting things in motion in 1988 that ended in August 1994. They would be enormously frustrating to some people who would say they should have done this sooner or whatever, but that's their own internal process. In fact, they just dismiss the media as an element of the establishment and they are not swayed by what might be broadcast or written. That's my understanding of it anyway. They might be surprised from time to time with what's broadcast or written, but they won't be swayed by it.

This compares with the view of a key Irish minister who argued that coverage did make a difference to a forthcoming IRA ceasefire by obstructing its announcement. The minister noted:

> I know at one stage where there was speculation in the British media supposed to be coming from a senior republican source. I knew that at that point in time, there was intense debate going on within the republican movement on whether there should be a ceasefire or whether there shouldn't, and that certainly set it back for about two months, because the speculation set back the debate. The debate was just stopped for a period because they didn't want the media to dictate what they should or shouldn't do.

Nevertheless, television news serves as a particularly important communicative outlet for those who feel unable to communicate through the conventional means of direct political contact. A former Northern Ireland secretary hinted at the importance of using outlets like the news media, when in response to the question 'Did politicians make a deliberate effort to talk to opposing groups through the media?', he replied:

> It was necessarily the case that as it was the government's position to not be talking directly to terrorists while terrorist campaigns went on, then by definition some of the communication had to occur by indirect and oblique means.

This was also echoed by another senior former Northern Ireland minister who stressed

If I wanted Sinn Fein to pick up a message, then certainly prior to the peace process one would have used the news media. Another advantage of doing this was that you could be seen to be open. You couldn't be accused of hiding anything.

Though as we now know, government communications with republicans were taking place in secret whilst IRA terrorist campaigns were indeed going on (*Setting The Record Straight* 1994), it should also be noted that the news media offers scope for 'megaphone diplomacy' and managing impressions of developments (Miller and McLaughlin 1996: 423–6). The news media also offers a platform for sounding out reactions and allows for efforts to block momentum through the use of political leaks. Even if the effectiveness of leaks in relation to the peace process remain questionable – 'There have been selected leaks from every side, but it would be hard to say that things wouldn't have happened without those leaks. I think they would have happened anyway' (American peace delegate) – with the possibility that the leak may in fact reduce the scope for discussion, it can also be used to gain some measure of public acceptance of an issue and so provide a realisation of whether that issue can be sold or not to wider audiences. A Northern Ireland Select Committee Labour MP indicated how leaks can have a positive or negative function by stating:

Leaks work essentially in two ways. You can use leaks as a way of sounding out the system, where you let it be known that a particular idea is around in order to gauge the public reaction. But you also run the risk of being painted into a corner by leaks because it often becomes assumed that this is your position for all time. So it can be positive in giving you some idea of public tolerance and scope for further movement. Or, it can be negative by stopping movement and providing a political label which might also have longer term damaging implications. Leaks are a risky business.

Communicating through the news media and the struggle for 'media territory' (as one politician put it) also varies in relation to different political groups. Notably, those groups who for ideological reasons feel unable to talk directly with opponents, will resort to using indirect communicative outlets, of which the news media is one. This process is particularly apparent between loyalists and republicans, where as one senior representative of the Progressive Unionist Party pointed out, the news media provides an important function in helping representatives anticipate political manoeuvres:

Gerry Adams and I communicate by television all the time. Every nuance is analysed, every programme taped and gone over again and again to see whether there is any movement. And there are occasions where we listen very carefully and ask what exactly was said, so we can look for any progression in terms of what the last move was and what the next might be, and I know that they do that with us as well.

According to the PUP representative, efforts to gain political initiative by using news to anticipate movements also correspond with efforts to undermine the support base of political opponents by challenging perceptions inherent to their respective community. As the representative put it:

I can want Adams to pick up things, but mostly, I'm wanting to split him from his constituency. The more I can get the catholic people to trust me, the more I can get catholic people to believe me when I talk about trying to create a wholesome society and constructive negotiations, then the more I can challenge the dogma which affects how the other side see us.

What is clear here, is that the representative also views the news media as a constructive force, which can help to develop trust and conciliation. But, this is not an easy task given the tendency for news to concentrate on conflictive, simplistic and where possible, emotive situations. For those promoting peace, the news media is a necessary component in helping to reform public perceptions, but presenting change is a risky business and reaction cannot always be accurately predetermined. The PUP representative highlighted the problems involved in communicating change by reciting the following example:

Gary McMichael shared a platform on television with a senior member of Sinn Fein; the first time it had ever been done. The first time that a unionist politician of any description had done it in Northern Ireland. We knew that Ken Maginnis had done it in America and that it had provoked serious emotion in Northern Ireland. But Gary's efforts prompted a mixture of reactions. On the one hand, he was bombarded by unionists who were saying that he had lowered himself and was touching the unclean, which is something that comes out of the Presbyterian psyche or the protestant psyche, but he was also overwhelmed by people saying how great it was to see someone step forward and begin the engagement which is necessary if we are going to understand each other. So it tells us that there is much out there that people will tolerate if only we can challenge. The media is a crucial for this process to happen, but it's also fraught with risks. It's dangerous to challenge people and one has to be very careful on which measurement you rely upon. Who do you talk to find out whether you are on safe ground? You need the media, but ultimately you can't rely on them. We're trying to promote peace, but the media are also hounding me to do a head-to-head with Gerry Adams. The media are in competition with each other and looking for the big story or event. It's important to remember they have no responsibility for what happens in the peace process even if they create problems which affect it. One thing is also for sure, if the peace process collapses, people won't see it as being the fault of the media.

The communication of peace and negotiation through television news remains a continuing and complex problem for those politically engaged within the peace process, and is especially prominent when the focus is on events which have the capacity to seriously set back development and understanding. Historically, television news has helped communities to view themselves in stereotypical ways and reinforced images of conflict which have contributed to sectarian ideologies and actions. As one observer of the Troubles in the early years recalled:

Suddenly, we were living inside the reports we saw on the television news, which had the odd, almost Brechtian effect of distancing you from things you might have actually participated in: a riot, for example. The result was a kind of documentary unreality. That, and a sort of vicious glamour which would increasingly loosen moral constraints and permit previously unimaginable behaviour. Men who traditionally read only thrillers, spy novels, war books, and James Bond – like my father – and whose cinematic tastes ran to gangster flicks and the rough justice of the Western, now had the chance to star in their own home-grown, patriotic versions of heroic fantasies. They took their chance (quoted in Stevenson 1996: 19).

The content of news reports may thus have consequences beyond any singular intention to inform. The communication of political tensions and emotive situations through television news can damage steps toward peace by representing identities as under threat and so fuel demands for reactionary measures by those wishing to preserve and defend those identities. This can also lead to repercussions in other areas. For instance, news attention given to Drumcree in 1996, highlighted for many nationalists that the security forces were protecting unionist power and that, come a major test, the peace process meant little had changed. It also undermined the possibility of de-commissioning becoming a credible argument. As a former Irish minister explained it:

Television news coverage of Drumcree certainly didn't help the situation. It showed a capitulation to mob rule where the rights of nationalists were not upheld by the security forces, which gave vent to the same old arguments about nationalists being unable to rely on the security forces in a crunch situation. And it certainly defined the argument in relation to decommissioning as well, because the IRA and loyalist arguments were centred on the attitude that they didn't want to leave their communities defenceless. The images on the television screen pronounced this. It set the whole process back and destroyed trust and confidence; there's no doubt about it.

For others, the stereotypical images of Orange marches and the tensions they bring reinforce representations of cultural identities in conflict which may be emotive, but do not explain the complex differences in Northern Ireland. The Progressive Unionist Party representative was quick to insist that:

British minds fail to understand life in Northern Ireland. They tend to see bowler hatted troublemakers and dogmatists playing drums in bands and marching down streets. Now some of our people do that, but that isn't how we live our lives from day to day; yet news programmes insist on providing that kind of symbolism. It's easy television, but it leads to simplistic and invariably distorted perceptions.

This highlights incongruities between the intentions of journalists and politicians in their efforts to promote peace where, against a context of conflictive, simplistic and event based coverage, politicians attempt to shape definitions and subsequent responses towards problems.

It remains somewhat obvious that if the news media served no tangible importance for the peace process, then politicians would feel no compulsion to use it. But, this in itself does not explain the actual effectiveness of the news media in relation to the peace process. Rather the issue seems to be more about how politicians use news to affect public perceptions of peace than how they use it to develop the nuances and details of peace process policy.

In explaining how relations between politicians and journalists operate in relation to the peace process, most interviewees did not distinguish between communicating to news on Northern Ireland and communicating to news in general. The overriding emphasis was that the relationship between journalists and politicians is a symbiotic one, where each relies upon the other. That is, politicians need the media to justify certain political actions or intentions, and the news media need politicians to inform the public of what those actions and intentions are. But, when interviewees were asked to give actual examples of the media being used to bring about a deliberate political end, most preferred to look at how it facilitated pressures on individuals rather than affect political processes. In appreciating that news is essentially event-centred, politicians tend to use the speculative interests of news to anticipate events, rather than tease out the intricacies of policy formulation which the simplistic emphasis of news is unable to articulate. Highlighting how news is used to create expectations of an event and so give political advantage, a Northern Ireland Select Committee member stressed how:

> The news media is necessary to build up tensions around an issue and will contribute to fears which political responses will expectedly solve. This means that the media are crucial in exacerbating anxieties which politicians may benefit from because they created the anxieties in the first place and so stand to derive political advantage by providing responses which were the aim all along.

In order to secure the maximum possibility of success in managing the news, it is clear that political unity is also a prime factor, since unity reduces the scope for journalists to use conflicting or undermining messages which negatively affect the credibility of a party. A Sinn Fein politician in Belfast said on this point that:

> It is especially important that answers to questions in Belfast are consistent with those given in Derry, otherwise the media emphasise the chances of a split, which interferes negatively with the message you're trying to get across.

It is also for this reason that Sinn Fein (like other political parties) use press offices, where interview opportunities can be planned in advance, so removing the element of surprise and potential negative impact. As the Sinn Fein politician commented:

> If any of us get a request to talk to a journalist today, the automatic reaction would be to refer them back to the press centres, so that by the time that journalist comes back to speak to you, you will know what it will be about, how long it's going to be, what material and research you will need and what the party position is.

This underlines the importance of political groups maintaining coherence and agreed positions in the light of news coverage, which on the one hand restricts discussion, but on the other, keeps it focused and specific. In projecting a unified front, political groups are able to keep discussion within agreed boundaries and so limit possible criticisms. This also forms an important function in managing the image of the party and maintaining a cohesive impression when appearing in news reports. A sophisticated and coherent approach in dealing with news organisations indicates the media's potential to exert destabilising influences on parties and create conflictions in the process. And such conflictions are especially apparent when the political climate changes from one of relative consensus to one which is contested. Or, as in this case, when a political climate is shifting from one of conflict to one of conflict resolution.

Conclusion

The interview material used in this chapter indicates a number of problems for political representatives who communicated the peace process through broadcast news, and raises questions about the news media operating in any straightforwardly reproductive way in relation to dominant discourse. What the interview material indicates, is that reporting tends to reinforce the more conflicting aspects of positions between groups and individuals and that, if anything, emphasises or amplifies those differences. What also emerges, is a recognition of how difficult it then becomes for politicians to promote articulations aimed at building trust and confidence between the respective communities and how difficult it is to control in any meaningful way, news discourse which concentrates on division and difference. Attempting to communicate a politics of reconciliation is, it would appear, particularly difficult given the tendency of news to prioritise the more conflictual aspects of developments.

Generally speaking, the interview material reveals a number of points about why the broadcast media did little to help facilitate the peace process during its early years, which need summarising here. The terrorism paradigm created difficulties for those attempting to hold dialogue with political representatives of terrorist groups, because of the potentially damaging publicity which might be attached to being a 'sympathiser' of terrorism. The news media's fixation with oppositional positions (in this case whether a protagonist was 'pro'- or 'anti'-terrorism) and categories tended to hinder positive or constructive dialogue between the two. This polarisation of positions became a significant problem for those trying to advance peace, since it constructed images of winners and losers and contributed to a hardening of attitudes, as groups sought to avoid being represented in a position of weakness. The news media's emphasis on contentious tones and seemingly irreconcilable viewpoints thus undermined productive and reconciliatory dialogue.

It was particularly because of this tendency to highlight and reinforce divisions and conflictions, that the peace process was conducted away from the news spotlight during its early stages. A number of high level respondents emphasised how confidentiality was important for developing trust between the groups and how coverage could jeopardise trust by creating fears, which consequently stimulated reactions that could unravel work being done. What this point importantly indicates, is that during its early stages at least, the television news media did little to assist dominant political discourse and power in any pronounced sense. Indeed, as interview material suggests, coverage had an obstructive and even damaging impact in connection to the development of peace. What is also highlighted, is that at times, the news media may not legitimise and assist the flow of political actions, but may intervene in those actions and create problems for them. By focusing on the apparent irreconcilability of positions and reinforcing the divisive elements of political debate, the news media negatively rather than positively affect the development of intra-communal dialogue.

However, also evident from the interview material, is that once the peace process had been established as an emerging paradigm in news coverage, it held communicative potential for shaping movement on issues. Just how effective news coverage was in helping to initiate movement rather than obstruct it is questionable, but it is clear that particularly with regard to groups who did not meet directly, the television news media served an important communicative function. As one representative of loyalist paramilitaries highlighted, in the absence of conventional political discussion, the news media becomes particularly significant for reading developments and directions. This process is not indicative of how the more dominant groups operate however, since access to a plethora of communicative agencies enables discussion to be conducted on a wider basis. This ability to access a range of outlets and influence negotiations may result in greater inclusion in news broadcasts, but this does not always correspond with greater propensity to manage concerns and pressures. Political efforts to bring about an IRA ceasefire in 1994 by using news to raise expectations and create subsequent pressure may have had the opposite effect, just as political attempts to avert trouble at Drumcree in 1998 were undermined by media expectations of trouble and speculations about an end to the peace process (see chapter 6).

This inability to control the emphasis of news stories which are themselves slanted towards conflict and antagonisms, was the main reason why television news did little to help accommodation and reconciliation. Even though the dominant position was one of seeking to develop the peace process, news reporting was primarily interested in a breakthrough or a crisis, which represented the process as lurching from success to failure. These extremes were invariably constructed as successes for some and failures for others, that is, positions in conflict, and it was this rather simplified and one-dimensional reading of the peace process which sustained reporting throughout the early years of its development. For many politicians then, television news proved to be rather obstructive to progressive dialogue and unhelpful for the promotion and negotiation of peace. This strongly indicates that a changing political climate can create a new set of problems for political communications and brings to light the considerable political difficulties attached to promoting peace through news.

Having established how politicians experienced difficulties in trying to develop peace through news, and shown that peace negotiations can be undermined or destabilised by news, I now to turn to interview material gathered from journalists who reported the early years of peace. By bringing to light how journalists came to understand the role of television news in the peace process, we can see how they experienced relationships with politicians and the political discourse of Northern Ireland. Furthermore, by allowing journalists to explain how they work when reporting the peace process and how they perceive the implications of what they do on that process, the next chapter will provide a relevant comparison to the perceptions given by politicians. It will provide us with an understanding of what journalists consider the priorities when reporting peace, and will enable us to compare those priorities with those expressed by politicians engaged in that peace.

4   Journalistic Perceptions of Reporting and the Peace Process

Introduction

This chapter intends to examine how journalists perceived their role in reporting the peace process, and to establish what they saw as the main influential factors and pressures when reporting peace (Appendix 1). Journalistic practice notably relies on a range of techniques and conventions which are far too extensive to address in any meaningful way here (Gans 1980; Yorke 1995), but what this part of the study does aim to do, is to examine how journalists saw their role as information-providers of the peace process and how they perceived their interactions with the politics of it. Although is should be said at the outset that when being interviewed many journalists had problems describing the specifics of reporting peace, and tended to comment more on the everyday pressures and routines of making news, they nevertheless did articulate a number of similar concerns and priorities which they saw as influential on reporting the peace process. Those concerns and priorities help determine the shape of this analysis and the issues which arise within it.

Although many of the questions which I asked journalists were similar or at least comparable to those asked of politicians (see Appendix 1), they elicited different responses which tended to cover a broader range of areas and issues. For this reason and for purposes of convenience, the responses of journalists have been sectioned into five categories. Those categories are: (1) sources and environment; (2) language and construction; (3) political pressure; (4) reporting peace and negotiations; and (5) routines, constraints and procedures. In the daily routines of compiling news, each of these areas does not operate as a distinctly separate influence, but moves in relation with others. These areas are indicative of what journalists emphasised as salient features when reporting peace, and each in turn throws light on how news reporting interacted with political negotiations.

By asking journalists if they saw television news as having a role to play in the political development of peace in Northern Ireland, and whether they think it helps to facilitate diplomatic efforts at reconciliation, this interview material highlights how the political consequences of reporting are understood by those who compile those reports, and how news is understood in relation to political discourse and power. This interview material therefore provides valuable information about the interplay between journalists and their sources which will form an interesting comparison to how politicians perceived this relationship. Or, to put it another way, this part of the study will enable us to see how journalists viewed the role of reporting in the peace process, and to consider that role in relation to the objectives and perceptions of politicians outlined in the previous chapter.

Sources and Environment

Much of the interaction which goes on between journalists and sources remains inapparent to the public and is not discernible from the content of news reports. The 'off-the record' interview which journalists use as a conventional technique of information gathering, enables them to gain a comprehension of developments and occurrences which would be unavailable on camera, where the source is identifiable and potentially more vulnerable. Important background information which the journalist uses to support a particular premise, or point of view, is routinely acquired in confidence, thus making confidence an essential component of journalistic practice and indicative of how news is a private, as well as public occupation. As one BBC Ireland correspondent described the process:

> All journalists have their own sources, and a source is a term that can be used to refer to almost anything. A source could be a politician who we all know and see on screen, but who talks more on the basis of 'Look, I didn't say this, but here's a tip-off about which way I see it going.' We all have a close relationship with press officers and we look to them for directions at times. It often suits journalists to go to sources on the quiet and say 'Come on Richard or John, it's not coming from you but for goodness sake give me a "steer", it's not good enough to say you know nothing about it', and often they will say 'alright, but you didn't hear this from me'. Even journalists say to sources 'between you and me so and so said this' in order to get a direction. Sometimes things get whipped around in the wrong way and can get magnified in the wrong manner because you're always trying to stay one step ahead of the opposition and that can lead

to misrepresentations. But, you would rarely fish without a purpose, it would always be in relation to something.

According to a Channel 4 political correspondent, talking to sources in order to form a clearer picture of what is going on, is a process conducted both formally and informally. As the correspondent put it:

> Generally, I stand around in the Westminster lobby and talk to people. I never have to reveal my source, but I will regularly seek out the person who has got a grudge or difficulty, because they will be more forthcoming. You cultivate people by getting them to trust you and that means not divulging their identity. If you don't jeopardise their confidence in you, they will tell you something. Mostly, when something is in confidence you log the information in your brain and maybe use it as a script line, but obviously you can't say who told you. At another level I might lunch with a politician and it's not uncommon to do this two or three times a week. We pay for it on expense accounts. I get to know them a bit better and pick up a feel for what they're thinking about. It's very helpful as opposed to a grabbed conversation on the telephone where you can't see their face. You can ask them questions for the best part of two hours and you get a much better feel for what's going on. The politician might want to get the point across that it's all on track and going to plan. Some are pathetic spinners and insult your intelligence and some are focused on one thing and what to make sure you don't get it wrong.

The interview forms an integral part of the information gathering process and produces different results, depending on the aims and knowledge of the journalist and the location where it is carried out. The informal atmosphere of a restaurant for example, increases the chance to gain a more comprehensive understanding of a political position than on the steps of Downing Street. Politicians have realised that controlling the location of an interview greatly influences the outcome of that interview and that this impacts on the kind of responses and information which journalists receive and use. In outlining location subsequently affects construction, a BBC political correspondent commented:

> The live interview has had quite an impact. Although it can have disadvantages for the politician by showing them as evasive or unconvincing, I would say that it has helped rather than hindered them. It's helped them in that they can go into a live interview having thought through their key answers and their soundbites. They're well prepared and by and large they're not going to be tripped up by a question. Because the interviewer cannot go into the kind of detail required,

politicians generally feel safe. But, having said that unless the politician is skilful he can be made to look a fool. Politicians don't like press conferences where there is a greater difficulty in stopping journalists asking questions. Nowadays the party chairman's job is to be a buffer between journalists and politicians. If he spots a journalist who knows his stuff and is likely to ask difficult questions, he will ignore him and ask somebody else. Doorsteps are easier because they allow for the person being questioned to move away. When he has had enough he can walk away and so bring it to an end when he wants. This is very different to being trapped in a press conference.

A freelance Belfast correspondent also spoke about the importance of politicians controlling news by controlling the interview environment where information is given and used Sinn Fein as an example of how this has become an increasingly important consideration for politicians in their dealings with the media. He went on:

> Prior to the 1994 IRA ceasefire, Sinn Fein would hold press conferences in Conway Mill in Belfast and you could quiz Adams for about half an hour. The day the ceasefire happened [31 August 1994], the press were summoned to a scrum on the street in Andersonstown where we were allowed to watch and film Adams making his speech to the crowd, and then we had to try and ask questions. Sinn Fein were totally in control of the situation. No awkward questions were answered and from there on they have controlled their media performances very cleverly and very tightly. They have realised that when you control the environment in which the media work, then you also largely control the media. If you give the media a press room and sit at a table in front of them, then you're a prisoner of the media. But, if you summons them to a doorstep in West Belfast, then you control the situation.

Language and Construction

The political management of news is a bone of contention for journalists and there are differing views on the extent and range of it. To agree that political management is widespread is, of course, also an admission that journalists are subordinate to political power and control; an admission which understandably few journalists are prepared to make. Yet, the use of particular kinds of political language about the peace process in reports also indicates the reproductive nature of news discourse in relation to political discourse. The interview material gathered on how language has been used to construct the peace process and the Irish conflict, on the one hand, points to the complexity of explaining political developments and on the other, signals how journalists tend to rely on politicians to initiate discourse and terms of reference, illustrating the symbiotic relationship between the two. Commenting on the use of language in reports and its political orientations, a Channel 4 political correspondent argued:

It would be confusing for the public if journalists used one word to describe a situation and politicians were using another word. The jargon such as words like 'decommissioning' does become alienating and inclusive, to the extent where if it becomes so dense, then listeners will give up, or not care. It's also difficult for us to understand what politicians are saying sometimes, but if I thought of a pseudonym for 'decommissioning' which covers all the activities it stands for, it would only be doubly confusing. In a sense, it's part of a clever way of keeping ordinary people out of the process. Brokering a peace is not something which everyone can come in on. In the end, it's a job that's got to be done by clever people on all sides, with subtle brains which can edge the thing forward. Having said that, the use of confusing or dense language is an important part of political bargaining. Politicians will often appear to be rejecting those who they are desperate to keep onside. It's like all sorts of sexual courtships and euphemisms. It's like 'I'm only having a one-night stand, I'm not in a relationship'. But it would be true to say, we do tend to reproduce a lot of the phrases and words.

For a BBC political correspondent, the more commonly used expressions and language forms clearly disseminate from the more politically powerful. Indicating how important language is in the context of reports and how it occupies the attention of journalists, the correspondent went on:

We're always looking for precise wording. The build up to the IRA ceasefire of August 1994 in the media was heavily concerned with the wording and what it was going to say; how it was going to be defined. As I recall, the lack of the word 'permanent' was what the British government seized upon. We go to briefings and it is there that you begin to hear officially or unofficially what the important word is at that time. Decommissioning is a phrase central to the Mitchell Report and we are always chasing to find out what that word actually means, but it is true that decommissioning is a British government word. The British government does tend to be in the strongest position and the media do tend to reinforce that. There is always a tendency to give the government of the day the lead in a story, even if from time to time it goes badly wrong for them. Most of the British media perceived the peace process as moving because of John Major. It was Major who was seen as making most of the running and who has taken the risks, and it is because of this perception that it is seen as incumbent on the republican movement and Sinn Fein to make a move. Since most of the momentum is seen to be coming from John Major, so the story is mostly concerned with what he and the government is doing.

The nuances of language and the origins of particular words clearly represent particular interests, but such interests are often submerged beneath general impressions and postures. Many journalists with a history of working in Northern Ireland are aware of how consensus language, which is so readily promoted by London based journalists engaged daily in the banter of parliamentary discourse, is notably absent from political life there. They know all too well that a neutral political language does not exist and that words gravitate ostensibly towards nationalist or unionist articulations. Highlighting how the nuances of language are linked to political identity and specific interests, the same journalist went on:

> The stock phrase 'Move the situation forward' which came originally from Gerry Adams to stymie Unionists and get as close to a united Ireland as possible, softened the political intentions of Republicans by being apparently concerned with promoting and generating peace. Because they couldn't come out outright and say 'give us a united Ireland' they use language like 'move the situation forward'. But, language is more often used to evade exact explanation. The frequent use of language like 'move the situation forward' maintains the impression that the time is right for political compromises even though it isn't. Unionists want to move the situation to an internal settlement in Northern Ireland and Nationalists want to move the situation to a united Ireland; hardly the basis for compromise even if using the same stock phrase. Having said that, fuzzy language can allow things to happen, it can create a space for examination and development. Peace means different things to different people here, but this is hardly reflected by the media who tend to reproduce rather than examine the language and the political interests served by it.

Also focusing on the intricacies of language and the political intentions which lay behind particular phrases and words, one freelance BBC journalist working in Belfast argued:

> The phrase 'peace process' gained general currency through the media having originated as a phrase by John Hume, Gerry Adams and Albert Reynolds to describe the dialogue they had. It has subsequently become something which is used as shorthand for a whole web of interlocking reactions and the irony of it being used as shorthand and as almost a value free description, is that of course, it is an offensive phrase to unionists who regard what Reynolds, Adams and Hume did as directly dangerous to them. Indeed, there were efforts by unionists

in the early stages to not use it, or to call it 'the so-called peace process'. I do think that the practice of doing that did at least get journalists to consider for a while about the disputed nature of peace, rather than one accepted version, but having said that it still receives common usage without little thought or examination.

The journalist further went on to say:

There has been some analysis of words such as 'decommissioning', 'demilitarisation', 'decontamination period' etc., but not a lot. Examination of such language is not a popular exercise amongst journalists. It's quite hard to make work on air on television and radio, and it's a very textual thing. But also many of the London based journalists do not have the skills to analyse such things and you can see that in the lack of consideration given to the term decommissioning. Decommissioning is another example of a value loaded word which means different things to different people, rather than a word which sums up the whole business. It was introduced by the British government to describe something which was used as a precondition for negotiation. Originally when the question of paramilitary arms was raised between the IRA, the British government and the Irish government the word decommissioning was not used. What they were talking about was the eventual disposition of paramilitary weaponry; the word disarmament was used primarily by republicans. When they first used it, they envisaged that if weapons were to be disposed it would be part of a general disarmament, and that meant optimistically disarmament of the RUC, the removal of the British army and the restriction of arms held by Protestants. So, from the start that was the contention between republicans and the British as to which approach was to be used. The British wanted to talk only about IRA weaponry and the IRA wanted to talk about everybody else's weaponry. However, this contention about wording resolved itself in much the same way as the peace process phrase, it too has gained common usage in the media and become a word used to describe a whole web of arguments, though it is largely a British word and subsequently a unionist word. The problem is though that such words tend to bury the range of political arguments which they evoke. The British government when it talks about decommissioning is talking purely about paramilitary decommissioning and not the demilitarisation of its own arms. And if the word decommissioning was introduced to mean not the surrender of arms, it has come to mean exactly the opposite because of the progressive qualifications added to it in different ways at different times.

For a Channel 4 political correspondent, there was contention over use of the term 'peace process' and the correspondent was quick to point out how phrases and inflexions of language used by journalists show variation (if slight), suggesting a degree of autonomy in the choice and application of language itself. As the correspondent expressed it:

> I don't use the phrase 'peace process' because I think it's an instant turn off which gives the impression that actually the process isn't going anywhere. When journalists talk for instance about the Middle East peace process, invariably they are talking out it having stalled. The words 'peace process' and 'stalling' almost go hand in hand. I tend to go for another form of wording and might say for example 'negotiations to continue the ceasefire' or, 'the peace', because to intents and purposes there is peace in Northern Ireland, since there aren't bombs going off.

Although there appears to exist some room for variation in the uses of language, there nevertheless also exists an overwhelming tendency for journalists to use the same kind of language and thus a tendency to articulate the process of conflict resolution in Northern Ireland in a similar and repetitive fashion. This is admitted by a number of journalists themselves, but especially by journalists based in Northern Ireland. Since such journalists invariably demonstrate a more extensive knowledge of political events and positions there, perhaps it is not surprising that they also exhibit a more comprehensive knowledge of the terms and references used and how such terms and references occupy conventional news frames. It is worth quoting at length how one freelance BBC journalist viewed this practice. He said:

> One of the things that I've often been struck by is the question of language and the repetition which takes place through language. Language has a constitutive effect and has been both ignored and taken for granted by the media, who parrot certain phrases with impunity. Take for example the phrase 'the Nationalist community'. In fact, within the Catholic community there are a whole range of political views and it's actually more pluralistic than the Protestant community. Indeed, within that community the Social Attitudes survey conducted a couple of years ago highlighted that 60 per cent saw themselves as Irish and about 40 per cent as Nationalist. The problem with phrases like 'the Nationalist community', or 'the Unionist community' is that diversity and differences get flattened out and that tends to confirm enemy images that people have about each other. Much as in the former Yugoslavia where reference is made to 'the warring factions', 'Bosnian Serbs' or 'the Croats', as if they were this homogeneous collective that all thought and acted in the same way. The effect of this is to shut out those who have thought in multi-cultural, multi-religious, multi-ethnic ways. Journalists working here have some concern about this but don't have it in their heads to change it. So we have 'The Troubles', which

makes it sound like a natural disaster and that there is really nothing anyone can do about it until it passes. 'The Troubles' implies a kind of fatalism and hardly incites a demand to take responsibility to try and resolve it. And now we have 'peace process' a generally accepted term by the media, but highly contested here in terms of what it is, or what peace means, or what it will possess. It's used by the media as if it were a neutral expression and this is because essentially that's how the British government have presented it. The way that 'peace process' has become an accepted phrase is a good example of how the media lack a questioning or critical attitude, and how they tend to adopt an agenda without even thinking about why. The notion of 'peace process' is a good example of the media's reproductive role in relation to government language.

This criticism was echoed by another freelance journalist working in Northern Ireland, who also adopted a critical tone towards the unquestioning stance taken by the news media in connection to certain phrases and events used during the peace process. The journalist argued:

> The type of questioning which might have addressed the heart of the peace process didn't seem to be there as strongly as it might have been. The conviction that the peace process existed seemed to effectively rule out a lot of questioning which might have been possible for probing at the basis of it. Some elements of the media took a critical line but invariably this was not typical of television. In engaging with the peace process (which is an area requiring complex political analysis), as a journalist you're only dealing with questions and political responses, so the prospect of critical evaluation is effectively ruled out. The use of repetitive questions also gets in the way because most of those questions never get unanswered. You get the obsessive 'do you talk with the IRA?', or 'will you condemn the IRA?' questions given to Sinn Fein and they just sidestep them.

For one other freelance journalist, the media clearly display a bias in how they describe particular groups and in the process of doing so, articulate those groups through their relationship to terrorism and violence. As the journalist saw it:

> The use of certain terminology bestows a quality to the subject you're talking about, an approval or disapproval. For example, how is the Progressive Unionist Party described in the media as a whole? Mostly, as 'having an insight into the UVF' when in fact, they are the political wing of the UVF and that is the reality. But for some reason, and in order to distance the PUP from those who kill people, the media have adopted the same terminology. So they talk about the UDP (Ulster Democratic Party) or the PUP as 'having an insight into loyalist

paramilitary thinking'. Yet no journalist would ever dream of saying that Sinn Fein has an insight into the thinking of the IRA. Everyone says that they are the political wing of the IRA.

The orientation of groups and representatives towards political violence has a considerable bearing on how those groups and representatives are articulated through television news and has conventionally played a prominent role in the construction of Northern Ireland as a problem. References and codes about the relationship of groups to terrorism is, to an extent, integral to the process of conflict resolution, where certain types become seen as obstructive to peace, whilst others are seen as trying to advance it. In other words, groups are invariably constructed as progressive or regressive factions. However, such representations do pose a dilemma for some journalists and a number interviewed did recognise that news reports produce moral judgments about groups, who are then simplistically categorised as supportive of, or opposed to terrorism. An Ireland correspondent for the BBC indicated how the use of language changes in relation to different audiences and how articulations about those engaged in violence shift in relation to different news contexts:

> As Ireland correspondent, I would use different terminology when filing the home news than I would when filing for the world service where 'terrorist' is a banned word. This is because as a global service they have to be seen as not supportive of anybody, so they don't define anyone as a 'freedom fighter', 'guerrilla', or 'terrorist'. I prefer to keep to descriptive terms, so a 'gunman' is a man with a gun and a 'bomber' is somebody with a bomb, but inevitably there are certain times when you are dealing with incidents, particularly when they are on the doorstep or very close to home, when it seems that sometimes 'terrorism' is the only way to define it. In the end though, I often have to simply go on my 'feel' for what is going on and resort to those terms which have become convenient shorthand.

A diplomatic correspondent for the BBC similarly pointed to such difficulties when reporting Northern Ireland, and in describing how he had typically constructed it in the past said:

> You always have to think carefully about the language you use and you have to be able to defend your use of it. If you ask me why I describe certain people as 'terrorists' I would say two things. Firstly, I use the word as a descriptive rather then a pejorative. I'm perfectly aware that people do use it as a pejorative, but the fact is, if you use violence without discriminating targets and the aim of the

violence is to bring about fear and a climate for political change then that is terrorism to me. I've had meetings with Loyalists who have described themselves as 'terrorists' so this suggests that the word is not a pejorative to a lot of people. It's a functional word; it describes what they do. I don't use the term terrorist with the aim of communicating some moral message, I use it to describe the type of violence they're engaged in. One of the things you have to do when reporting Northern Ireland is to describe whether it's a war or a conflict and that affects your language. A lot of definitions come from your understanding of the situation. The conflict and the resulting violence tends to be seen by government as crime and is investigated by the security services who specialise in combating crime, so your choice of language tends to follow that decision.

However, the potential for misrepresentation by adherence to the terrorism paradigm was particularly emphasised by one freelance BBC journalist, who viewed consensus reporting as inappropriate for articulating the political and social divisions of Northern Ireland. She argued:

> When Northern Ireland has been covered, the effort has been to depict terrorism as a thing bred in and conducted by the extremes, as though this society consists solely of a majority centre ground and two bands of diametrically opposed extremists. The truth is that the centre is riven with extremism, where mean and hardline attitudes which are not amenable to compromise pervade. So to suggest that terrorism was some kind of violent activity which existed only on the margins of society was always a lie and indeed missed the point, which was that the whole place was based on two incompatible and violently opposed political philosophies, both of which bred extremism. The word extremist is generally taken to mean masked men with guns in their hands, but if you ask most journalists here who are the most extreme people they have interviewed over the years, the first people they will mention will not be gunmen, but mainstream politicians.

Political Pressure

The question of just how much influence sources exert over news is a particularly contentious one for journalists, since agreement to political management and control of news does not sit easily with notions of autonomy, which journalists impress is necessary for their credibility as information-providers. In relation to this study this is also an important area of consideration since it will provide useful material by which to evaluate whether news tends to adopt a more or less supportive role towards dominant political aims. In relation to Northern Ireland, politics has historically placed a number of pressures on journalists and affected how they have represented acts of political violence. Conventionally, journalists are expected to take a critical stance towards terrorism and tend to do that by reinforcing the condemnations and reactions of those diametrically opposed to it. A BBC political affairs correspondent made clear the expected position which journalists have taken towards Northern Ireland, when in interview he said

> With Northern Ireland the benefit of the doubt with most journalists would be with the government's side, not Sinn Fein's side – that's the starting point. The news media tends to be with the forces of security of the country and that's an historical position. Most journalists would have more contacts and better contacts with the state, the police and the security forces than with the other side.

Noting how pressure can be applied to journalists to adhere to a dominant line, the correspondent went on

> The minister concerned challenged me at the press briefing in front of the other journalists present and said 'You have to decide which side you're on. Are you on the side of law and order or not?' I was asking him a question on Northern Ireland and he said 'People like you have got to decide. Are you on the side of law and order?, do you want to come to the lobby briefings?, do you want to be accorded the facilities of the state?' You also need to consider that the BBC has a responsibility to reflect the news as it is seen by the majority of people in the country who pay the license fee. If we were ignoring Sinn Fein or failing to give them coverage at all, well then I would feel in a guilty position, but we don't. We also do try and test the government, but working as a political journalist for the BBC I have to work as everybody else does. For those working within the system there are responsibilities which go with working in that system. One of the problems with working in the lobby is that you are told operational material which in today's current sensitive political security state you should not reveal. You know for example where politicians will be in 24 hours but for operational and security information purposes you can't always reveal that, so you're compromised. You either work within the system or you don't work within the system.

Another reporter working as a diplomatic affairs correspondent, had a different view on the extent of political news management and saw it this way:

> I don't have a gut view about how far the government is able to get its message across. You generally try to include what you consider interesting, be it from

talking to ministers, Sinn Fein or whoever. Often politicians do go on to attack and just give you party lines, but since we realise that no politician is going to make policy on television we accept that some repetition is inevitable. But my basic criteria for inclusion would be how interesting is it? Having said that you do try and make it clear to the public that you are showing a view from one side and using another view as protection against bias. You try and flag the fact that the information you are using does represent the interests of one group or another. You do try and signpost information.

A view which compares markedly with that of a Channel 4 reporter, who had strong views on political control and how that control is exercised. As he put it:

I think political pressure affects what journalists do very considerably. Ministerial pressure is very great but it's difficult to isolate Northern Ireland on this question from everything else. Foreign news is basically straightforward and no problem with odd exceptions, but news on Northern Ireland like most national news is susceptible to political pressures and editors do take knighthoods. The honours system moves in mysterious ways and there is a very cosy relationship between certain individuals within broadcasting organisations and ministers and prime ministers. If it is sold to the editor that a particular line would be destructive then sometimes it is acted upon. None of these things are easy to nail because they have all happened behind closed doors and in clubs where the establishment operates. Sometimes there is a very collegiate way of arriving at decisions by editors, but occasionally that is discomforted by what appears to be a strange intransigence or insistence that something is covered or isn't covered. That can happen for a number of reasons, from a boredom with Ireland, or lack of interest with the event, or it could be because the editor met Michael Howard the night before who impressed it would be helpful if we could desist from X or whatever. The lines of communication are permanently open with government even if one does not know how effective they actually are. Having said that it if they weren't effective then it's surprising they continue, because they compromise the organisation.

The extent of political pressure exerted on news organisations and its probable influence on the content of reports, is disputed among the different organisations where journalists express varying degrees of freedom and autonomy. For example, a BBC Ireland correspondent, in contrast to the critical comments of the Channel 4 reporter, argued that he had considerable individual control over output even when working within a broad organisational consensus. As he expressed it:

If you've been a BBC journalist for a long time you kind of live and breathe the way things are reported. You don't initially go in saying things that are going to rock the boat, but you will if you've got the evidence to say something. But, there's no person ringing up saying you'd better do this. It doesn't work like that and if it did it would be counterproductive. I'm quite free to chase anything I want really. The only pressure is that London might see something one way and might be keen to pursue a certain agenda which I may or may not disagree with, but even then, I've got considerable power to argue back and have succeeded in getting things changed.

Reporting Peace and Negotiations

The changing political landscape of Northern Ireland from a process of conflict to one of conflict resolution signified a number of changes in the nature of news representations, perhaps the most notable being the absorption of paramilitary representatives into news discourse. As the peace process gained credibility as a formal and deliberative political process, so those who were seen as pivotal to peace were integrated into news reports and became central to the developing story. A BBC Ireland correspondent used the example of Sinn Fein in news stories as indicative of this change

> Adams was getting into news more and more because he was key to changing political events. Adams and those he represents became central to the story. He has been on more and more because Sinn Fein had changed position and become key to events and change in a largely non-changing situation.

However, for some journalists, the peace process meant more than incorporating representatives into news discourse who had previously been largely excluded. It meant structural changes in news construction and a reinterpretation of the conflict through the emerging paradigm of peace. For one freelance BBC journalist working in Northern Ireland, journalists

> have in a real sense helped to put faith in the peace process as a good thing and that has meant to an extent playing down doubts about it. Journalists have put their faith in something good happening and put forward the broad conclusion that something extremely positive is going to result from what is going on. They have led that expectation. But the wrong conclusion they seem to have drawn is that the whole of Northern Ireland has gone through a change of heart. Certainly from my perception, Northern Ireland is not exhausted with the conflict.

Furthermore, argued the journalist, the peace process brought new considerations into coverage which impacted directly on the format of local programming and produced a qualitative shift in content:

> You had within the BBC locally a decision to revamp news. The Head of Programming spoke of 'the post-ceasefire news agenda'. I was in discussions with people who were saying that in this particular climate of peace we should not be concentrating on stories which have a potential to raise sectarian tension. The situation was very much that now we've got peace, don't undermine it. So what we got was a change in production teams to reflect a revamping of news. A new reportage to correspond to a changing society, with a new character and feel to the programming. But what you got was a focus on stories like the one about a dog who wouldn't let a family go near a tumble dryer for example, or a dog that played football, so that news programming would become more like *That's Life*.
>
> The irony was that the Wapping bomb came days before the launch so what you got was a focus on the resumption of IRA violence and the reinforcement of an increasingly dark atmosphere in Belfast as people grew more afraid of what might be coming, and this was taking place against a news programme where political interviews might last a minute and more time would be given to ducks crossing a road. So you had a re-characterisation of local news which was much softer and not actually amenable to political interrogation, although it has now changed again and come back to a tighter political format. The BBC made a mistake thinking about a post- conflict form of reportage when conflict was still going on.

But at a national level, and for other journalists, the peace process represented an opportunity to examine some of the underlying tensions of the conflict which had previously remained neglected. As a Channel 4 reporter saw it:

> The change of circumstances has curiously reopened some of the issues that were being explored in 1969–70, about rights and balance and opportunity. I think some people are quite shocked to discover the imbalance and the injustices which still exist in the province, so from that point of view it's been a positive period.

The opening of discourse to allow for the political representatives of paramilitarism to engage in discussion also opened up the possibilities for such representatives to manage news and shape dialogue. As a freelance reporter observed:

> Paramilitaries have considerable power. They are very secretive and can choose when to make an impact, which they tend to do in two very important ways. They can create what is called 'a spectacular' [a bombing], which can create

international media coverage, and secondly, they are able to control who does and who does not get interviewed. If you talk to Sinn Fein about a bombing for instance, they will say don't talk to us, but when they want an interview placed they will place it and they will be given the opportunity to be interviewed.

This potential to place an interview or response, may not also translate into a propensity to develop constructive dialogue, however. For, even though political representatives of paramilitarism have become central to the peace process (since any eventual resolution to conflict necessarily requires the support of such groupings), there still exists a tendency within news to consider developments by their more conflictive and oppositional elements, which for paramilitary representatives, means positioning their responses against mainstream political articulations. Moreover, because of a tendency to concentrate on rather fixed oppositions and antagonisms which are especially prominent between republicans and unionists, marginal groups working to facilitate tolerance and reconciliation are largely ignored. As a BBC journalist based in Northern Ireland noted on this point:

> Generally, the media seek out and exploit the more contentious positions and not the grassroots opinion which may not be so crudely fixed. There are a range of cross – community groups who have tirelessly worked to bring about peace, but they are never offered a platform in news. News does nothing for an opening of debate. Rather it closes debate down by simplistically presenting things as best understood by two positions, each of which is in opposition to the other. Hardly a basis for helping agreement or peace. The main dynamic does seem to be to get two people in front of a microphone or camera and let them pour scorn over each other and that makes good television, but it's also the beginning and end of constructive dialogue. Television is primarily concerned with drama and conflict. They are the driving forces of most stories.

This was also echoed by a Channel 4 political correspondent, who highlighted how news tends to reinforce intransigence by maintaining an emphasis on the more conflictive positions:

> The one side versus the other representation is a huge problem. You're not likely to end up informing people one jot, because really you're giving them a ping-pong between two views. We do try at times to overcome that by bringing in a third view, or a view at a tangent, or some context, but even then, you still have this ping-pong problem which tends to give people the impression that there is no truth. It actually contributes to political fatigue because it's pretty much a fixed convention. Using two views that oppose each other is the route we've all gone down.

And yet, although the convention of conflict in reports is broadly recognised by journalists, when questioned about the negative or obstructive influence of news in relation to the peace process, they appeared somewhat divided. Commenting on how news might assist or obstruct the development of peace and political dialogue between groups, one BBC political correspondent drew on other examples of the news affecting negotiations between groups, before referring to Northern Ireland:

> There's little doubt that the news media do affect political negotiation and dialogue. During the 1980s the big industrial disputes were negotiated to a degree by the news media, where the employers and unions were having their negotiating positions tested, and when we saw a crack or an inconsistency, we would probe that crack or inconsistency to see whether it was a concession of some kind. That was of tremendous significance to employers who would study the words and similarly with regard to Northern Ireland, groups study the words used by other groups to see whether they have moved or shifted in relation to things. The media play an important role in helping to shape movement, and although on the one hand this might not be seen as a help, it does force explanation and allow for an examination of movement or intransigence. What has cost Gerry Adams support in the US is the television pictures and questions put to him about going to the IRA and asking for a ceasefire. That is pressure.
>
> Northern Ireland is a classic example of where the pressure of the news media is forcing representatives to provide a soundbite about what they are doing. In one sense this is counterproductive because it forces black and white answers when the issue is not black and white, but on the other politicians are being forced to say what they mean. You could say that the news media create unfair pressure by always demanding reactions and that enhanced access to the media by politicians has augmented that pressure, but on the other hand we are now demanding much greater precision in the explanations of those involved.

As argued, the growing demands of media pressure do not complement political demands for constructive or, conciliatory dialogue. Increasing requirement for reactions and soundbites leads quite obviously to an increasing number of reactions and soundbites, but does little to help develop the directions of political policy. Indeed, the soundbite reaction can be damaging to the complex and protracted demands of political negotiations and diplomacy. For many of the journalists interviewed who were based in Northern Ireland, the actual likelihood and effectiveness of negotiating through the news media during the early phases of peace, was seen as questionable. To quote one freelance BBC journalist:

The SDLP has tried to avoid negotiating through the media and they have said that. At the time when Hume thought a ceasefire was possible, before it had materialised, he actively called on the media to refrain from comment, because he said that comment would be dangerous and unsettling. Hume is somebody who very much operates behind the scenes. When he speaks on the media he tends to be repetitive. He acts like someone who has planned his strategy years in advance, and for five years he will say the same thing, 'agreement which threatens no section of our divided people'. Ian Paisley uses the media not so much to send signals to his enemies or political rivals, but to reinforce his intransigence, or to disclose information which undermines reconciliation. He has contacts in the police who will tell him things not in the public domain and he will disclose them publicly and make sharp claims. During the ceasefire, Paisley made an announcement that Republican paramilitaries had imported a large quantity of arms from the US and he gave details about what the quantity of arms contained. Paisley tends to fight his position pretty much through the media, but overall, there is very little negotiation through the media by the parties involved because there are no gains to be made for example by Paisley whether publicly, politically or electorally, by showing any kind of consideration for problems which the SDLP might have, and vice versa. There are just no votes to be gained by conceding ground through the media. No Unionist is going to make the step forward to get a Nationalist vote, especially when that vote isn't there for him anyway.

Expanding on why it was unlikely that the news media played an important role in developing negotiations during the formative stages of peace, a Channel 4 political correspondent contributed:

Clearly, there are intermediaries between groups and there are a range of ways by which politicians acquire information; feelers are put out and responses are made. I remember how the Reverend Roy Magee was used a lot early on and was clearly instrumental in communicating with loyalist prisoners. He would communicate with a number of groups and would report back to a higher political level. So television news is not particularly important as a means of communication. Indeed, often politicians will refuse to use your programme as a means to talk to whoever. They will merely say if so and so wants to talk to me, then he can pick up a phone. I would think that since the Peter Brooke days there are some sophisticated and well tried communication routes other than the media, now well developed.

The notion that communications between the respective parties in the peace process is more effective when conducted through channels other than the news media, received further endorsement by another freelance journalist working in Belfast, who when asked about whether republicans and loyalists engage in dialogue through the media because of not meeting directly responded:

> They don't need to use the media as a conduit because there are all kinds of other channels available. We now know that for some five or six years the UVF was in secret contact with the IRA through various priests and ministers in west Belfast, they didn't need the media to do that. If David Ervine responds to some comment made in the media by Gerry Adams that's little different than the British Labour Party responding to Conservative thinking which they might read about in the Daily Telegraph. There have always been conduits between republican paramilitaries and loyalist paramilitaries and conduits between paramilitaries and the rest of society, including government. I wouldn't put too much stall on the media having any important function to play in helping to drive negotiations and dialogue. If anything it tends to do the opposite.

Other journalists take a different line on the possibilities of the news media being used to develop communications and dialogue. Giving an instance of where he thought the news media could be seen to be operating as a conduit, a freelance journalist based in Belfast commented:

> Clearly in such a divided society as Northern Ireland one of the crosscutting phenomenon is the media. If someone wanted to send a signal to the other side then one of the ways of doing that would be to use the media. Moreover, the lack of interrogation by the media would be a plus because it allows statements to be made more deliberately, without interference. An instance would be recently, when the issue was floated of whether there should be an election and some kind of forum. Mitchel McLaughlin [Sinn Fein] gave an interview on television news where he said that republicans didn't like the size of the elected body (some 90 members), so the implication was that maybe the principal of an elected body wasn't a stumbling block as long as republican concerns could be met in other ways. That was picked up and widely assessed as a kind of signal. As it happened, Gerry Adams quickly responded with a counter-statement attacking the idea of elections and the forum and Martin McGuiness subsequently went on RTV to say absolutely no way. That was an instance of what might have happened if there were no movement on the issue and movement had been made available because space was found in the media to accommodate both the moderate and more hardline versions of republican thinking on the matter. Clearly these differences signalled the scope for movement.

In contrast to the premise that the news media have little influence on negotiations, a BBC journalist working in Belfast argued the importance of the news media's function as a channel of communication between opposing sides, allowing positions to be staked out and giving access to voices largely excluded from the corridors of power. As the journalist put it:

> The politicians do use the media as a conduit, especially when they're not talking to each other. Gerry Adams speech at Sinn Fein's annual conference is always crafted as a statement of positions which the media duly promote. Certainly, when Martin McGuiness goes on *Newsnight*, every single word is analysed to see what he has said by the other side. Unionists do closely read statements made by republicans in the media and we know that television is seen by all sides as a very important part of their communications strategy. Furthermore, the fringe parties who can't get direct access to Downing Street can still make known their positions through television. Sinn Fein also only allow certain representatives to appear on programmes like Newsnight, when they know that the interviewer will be very sharp and invariably watched by those who make important political decisions and have power to influence the direction of the peace process. If it weren't for the power and potential of news to affect political pressure and movement then it's unlikely that groups would be so careful in who they select to speak for them. If one slip up in interview can have significant political repercussions then doesn't this suggest that news can affect the political process? For me, that's what politicians strive for in news, to make the opponent slip up, or appear ineffective, and this can have tremendous impact on the promotion of political ideas and initiatives.

The ability of the news media to facilitate dialogue, can be seen to derive from the way journalists move between sources in order to develop a story. As Strentz (1989: 12) reminds us:

> A far less dramatic but more pervasive role of the reporter as informant occurs as the reporter constructs a dialogue between news sources. Indeed, this role is so common that reporters and news sources accept it often with only a passing thought about the risks and trust that it entails. In this relationship the reporter gets information from one news source and later asks another news source to respond to the first source's comments. Typically such dialogues are constructed by the reporter on controversial and relatively fast-breaking stories. The reporter may work back and forth between sources or involve third and fourth sources in the discussion, again with none of the sources talking directly with one another.

The writer also continues:

> Reporters must at times share information with news sources – educate them, if you will – to get a more informed response to questions that should be answered

for the news audience. The reporter is not a mere transmission belt, taking information from one source and passing it along to another, but a participant in an important and complex communication process. To the extent the reporter is sensitive to how he or she influences what happens in that process, the news audience will be better served (ibid.: 15).

What Strentz implies in his assertion, is that journalists impact directly on the process of political communications by forcing them to take place. But, facilitating and influencing communications is different from facilitating and influencing the actions which result from them. It is clear enough that a number of journalists who have reported the peace process see news as a key component in the communications process, but what is less clear is whether news causes the peace process to move one way or the other. That is, whether it actually affects the process of peace in some tangible way. For a *Newsnight* correspondent this seemed unlikely:

> My hunch is that television news won't have had that much effect, because under most circumstances, TV journalism does not have much influence on the actors it interacts with, or the events it portrays. There are events and circumstances where it has had an affect, as in the Gulf War, where CNN was being used by Saddam and the Americans to communicate with one another very quickly; with interviews and briefings all going out live each day. In that case, to some extent, diplomacy had transferred itself to the media. Clearly, CNN acted as a conduit between those forces, and in certain respects it probably had some impact on policy towards Bosnia, where some of the early reports and coverage of massacres helped to create a public atmosphere where some form of western action was necessary. But, even here, you're into the problem of whether it was the actual massacres, or how those massacres were shown, which created action. However, there is no comparable instance, as far as I'm aware, with the peace process. Essentially this has been about political posturing and a staking of positions, which have not, it seems to me, changed much regardless of coverage.

The ability of news to maintain communications by bringing together comments and contentions into a field of discourse, can however, create a momentum which has political ramifications. As a freelance journalist based in Belfast perceived it:

> There is a tendency for the media to treat an important signal as a 'reaction story'. The traditional way a story moves on in coverage in Northern Ireland, within the conventional routine, is for the first bulletin to report it as a story, and the next bulletin to report the reaction to the story. So, if in the first story it's

'IRA said that', then by the next bulletin, it's 'IRA's statement condemned by whoever', and you might get a further development, where there's a reaction to the reaction. That's also a good instance of how a story which in some sense exists in the 'real world', without the media initially at least, becomes more and more of a construction and less and less rooted in political reality. There may be cases where this process can force reactions to political intransigence and create movement, but from my experience, it tends to perpetuate antagonisms and reduces trust between the sides.

Routines, Constraints and Procedures

The repetitive nature of how journalists work means that what they produce is subject to repetition. News production is structured and achieved through patterns of working which are heavily routinised and from a professional point of view, rather predictable. This predictability is not derived from the events covered, which are different, but from how they are covered; consistent and in notably familiar ways. This similarity is reinforced and conventionalised through the processes of selecting and constructing responses, which are shared and agreed upon by journalists before being produced as reports. Journalistic practice therefore, provides us with simplified and repetitive versions of events. As one freelance journalist in Northern Ireland depicted this routine:

> Journalists certainly tend to hunt in packs and often, just after an interview with a minister, they will get together to check with each other that they've got the right quotes and they do that by comparing what they've got. Quite often journalists will also rely on clippings for background information, so if there's a mistake in the original clippings they tend to perpetuate it and they do that principally because there isn't enough time to reinterrogate them. Invariably, there is always a perceived wisdom as well as a dominant version of a story and how best to cover it and the hunting in packs element is symptomatic of that mentality. There tends to be agreement amongst most news organisations on most days about what the story is and what to do if for example the Secretary of State is set to make a speech. In that instance, you can guarantee that all the correspondents will be there to buttonhole him and aim to get a soundbite out of him about what the story is concerned with, and that whatever news network you tune in to, that's the story you will get. So the tendency towards conventionalism is the tendency to flatten out diversity in coverage itself.

The occupational practice of working in groups and using each other's information was also endorsed by a Channel 4 political correspondent, who in pointing to the repetitive and narrow interpretations offered by news, said:

> Journalists regularly use each other's information. Yes, hugely. In the lobby [Westminster] there is huge tendency for journalists to hunt as a pack. Say there's a statement on Northern Ireland and as usual we're all sitting in the gallery, we will check with each other on the technical nuances of the language and whether something new is being said, or whether it has been said before. So, you check with your colleagues and confer on what was said and this does serve to focus you all on the same issues and problems.

Reinforcing this perception even further, a BBC political correspondent observed:

> Other journalists are a great influence. We do roam in packs and that is also the case with Northern Ireland. If for example, journalists go to the Sinn Fein office for an announcement, or to chase a story, they would tend to go as a group and depart as a group. In doing so, they would inevitably discuss what they have heard and this allows you to find out how other journalists are interpreting the story. So the flow of information from journalist to journalist is very helpful for checking whether you are going along the right lines. It will also allow me to see how the story is perceived from different angles and this will give me a wider realisation of what is going on.

The close contact which journalists have with other journalists and the way they tend to reiterate similar features and priorities in a story, is indicative of the formulaic and procedural nature of news production. It also indicates how such procedures restrain the possibilities for interpreting a story beyond the conventions applied. Notably, the restraining pressures of time and demands for a narrative which summarise issues in a simple fashion, also poses problems for incorporating a range of viewpoints. Highlighting how demands for a precise narrative and time pressures affect the structure and content of reports, a BBC political correspondent asserted:

> You tend to deliver information in formulaic ways and you tend to stick to those formulas and the style of reporting they produce. Often we are seen to just parrot things because of the time restraint. With Northern Ireland, you have to try and condense the horrifying complexities which might for the republican movement annoy a lot of people, in the sense that it's not acknowledging the difficulties they face in getting their position across, or answering questions. We are quick to report that Sinn Fein has not delivered what John Major asked them to deliver, but do not give background or historical reasons on why it is

difficult for them to do so. However, having said that, I wouldn't say that it's made the peace process more difficult. I would of said that it has helped to concentrate minds. It has also helped Sinn Fein. They have been forced to react and move in developing the political parameters and will have to respond to questions like the government. All sides get tested.

Discussing the standard procedures adopted when compiling a report and the typical narrative format used, a Channel 4 correspondent recited the following example:

Let's say that the story is about what differences exist between the unionist parties in relation to the peace process. You would start with a headline such as 'Unionists divided', or 'Unionists more split than ever', and you would be establishing by this what you will be exploring in the piece. So you will give a signpost at the beginning about what you are going to do and you would aim to draw a conclusion at the end, based clearly on what is happening and what affect that may have.

If you're dispatched off to do a report, it will usually be after some discussion with the programme producer, the programme editor and the news editor, who will help you arrange the coverage, and you will come up with a range of elements that you know you've got to get in. Such as: a summation of what is happening, some interviews to explain what is happening and action footage which gives the story an importance and underlines its credibility as news. After that, you're pretty much left to your own devices. You will decide on your own interviews and contacts and you will decide if other contacts or informants are needed. By the time that you make the feed between 6.30 pm–6.45 pm from Belfast, from UTV, there's precious little they can do if they don't like it. Having said that, the time pressures are a major determinant on what we do. You make your calls in the car on the carphone; you talk to people when you get there; you're continually juggling, what's my opening picture?, what am I going to say over it?, can somebody get me a library picture?, is the editor set up?, what time are we feeding?, what if we need to feed earlier than we thought?, what if somebody comes forward with a more interesting comment at the last minute?, how will that affect the piece?, etc. These are major concerns and because they impact on all journalists, it's not surprising that journalists behave in similar ways and produce similar reports.

Journalists view the time factor as a key influence on what they do, and many note how the limitations of time affect scope for explanation, producing simplifications about the issues and events being covered. Journalists are clearly able to apply a degree of autonomy in their daily activities, but this autonomy is notably contained within patterns of working which demand specific and repetitive duties. Moreover, although journalists are able to construct and initiate dialogue between sources, that dialogue is conventionally expressed as conflict. Journalists have their regular sources of information and use that information in regular ways, but the end result is ostensibly an expression of difference and what separates rather than brings together the inherent sides. Or, as one freelance journalist based in Belfast concluded:

> There are universal rules for relations between journalists and politicians which don't have a specific application with regard to Northern Ireland, so the relationship that journalists build up with individual politicians are governed by the same considerations as they are in Westminster, or Washington. The politician chooses the outlet and he will choose the journalist according to trust, or confidence. But, always go for the dissidents in any organisation, because that's where the story is.

Conclusion

Journalistic perspectives on reporting the peace process reveal a number of points about the relationship between politics and news which warrant summarising. Firstly, control of the environment where information is distributed by sources has an impact on the way information is received and conveyed by journalists. Politicians who are able to control the environment where comment is given are seen to be more in control of the news media, as opposed to being in situations where journalists are able to determine the extent of questioning and have some control over what politicians can talk about. The doorstep interview is seen to be much less effective in terms of critical questioning than the news conference, when politicians are expected to answer questions which may subject them to greater scrutiny and difficulty. But, an important part of acquiring background information is the 'off-the - record' interview, when journalists can establish confidential information about developments which can be of significance to future events. This interview also operates as an exchange, where politicians can find out from journalists how other politicians are thinking and planning, as well as vice versa. It indicates that a trust of sorts exists between journalists and their sources and that each benefits from confidential exchanges. The release of leaks and private political information is regularly obtained by journalists through this process, just as politicians are able to acquire significant information about opponents from journalists. The public world of news reports is thus shaped and influenced to an extent by the private activities of information-gathering and this was especially the case during the early stages of the peace process when confidentiality was seen as essential for developing talks and negotiations by politicians. In that instance, when politicians were far less inclined to appear before the media, journalists were particularly reliant on 'off-the-record' interviews and leaks for their stories.

The use of language, phrases and expressions used by dominant political groups and reproduced in news, was recognised as an important factor in describing the peace process by many journalists, but those based in Northern Ireland were especially critical of how news reiterated dominant frames of discourse. One journalist, who in 1996 presented a paper at a conference in Derry on the media and its reporting of the peace process, summarised the contention thus:

> The peace process also introduced a distortion of language which was reminiscent of the language of the cold war. Both Gerry Adams and John Major might talk of 'moving the situation forward'. There is no possibility that the two would be working to the same objective, but a vague use of language was able to suggest that the two men had the same investment in peace. But if somebody wanted to move things forward, that was good enough for many reporters and commentators.
>
> Peace is a good thing like 'democracy' or 'the free world'.
>
> The media allowed itself to use meaningless words and phrases to convey the notion of progress when all that was happening was that entrenched positions were becoming more confident in their opposition to each other.
>
> The very term peace process was itself such a deception. It implied that all the people who were in disagreement with each other were moving closer to agreement, or at least that some of them were moving towards creating the conditions in which all would find agreement. This clearly was not happening, yet the language of journalism, as of politics, implied every day that it was happening (O'Doherty 1996: 3).

On the one hand, O'Doherty emphasises the media's propensity to try and reinforce the notion of a developing peace, but on the other, he suggests that this makes little or, no difference to the development of peace itself. In a way, this is reflective of a general uncertainty amongst journalists of the impact news has on politics. Many are critical of the consensus language which is used in reporting Northern Ireland and note its inability to explain a situation where consensus does not exist. They also note that since language cannot reflect the interests of all sides, it is seen by the population in Northern Ireland as invariably gravitating toward unionist or nationalist articulations.

And yet, although journalists recognise this shortcoming, they seem unable to offer an alternative way of articulating developments. Journalists exhibit a clear recognition that certain forms of language and terminology are subject to repetition and also recognise the problems of defining events and developments in this way. But, so used are they to using such language and terminology, that most are unable to consider explaining things differently. This would appear to suggest that the language of explaining peace is largely the absorption and reproduction of language provided by elites; not a dissemination of that language to reveal the political implications of it. The term peace process, for example, is a phrase which is conventionally used by elites and journalists to define the negotiations and talks in Northern Ireland. However, the peace process is not one process, but a number, subject to contentions and disagreement, which is not referred to by the phrase itself.

The use of dominant language thus reflects associations between journalists and those in positions of power. However, as some journalists revealed, considerable pressures can be brought to bear on those who do not promote a particular line. Journalists are expected to be especially critical of those groups who are seen to be affiliated to, or representative of, those who conduct political violence, and although they may exhibit some autonomy in the explanations they use, there is a clear expectation that they reinforce articulations of the state and where possible, legitimise state policy.

The question of whether news affects the negotiation of peace generated a rather divided response from those interviewed. Although some indicated the importance of groups using news to communicate responses and directions, others indicated that this is better achieved through other channels, appearing to present news as largely ineffectual for the development of dialogue. Moreover, given the importance of drama, conflict and negativity in news, it was seen as unlikely that news could play any facilitative role in helping to create peace. Having said that, journalists do play an intermediary role in communications, carrying responses and comments between sources, and this process takes on a greater importance for those groups who do not use direct political communication channels.

The routinised manner in which journalists operate has a significant affect on what they produce. The repetitive nature of constructing reports and the fact that they tend to work together, also mitigates against the possibility of broad analysis and for some, is a central reason for why news is unable to fully represent the complexity of political life in Northern Ireland. Given this practice of working, there is little chance that news will be able to examine the nuances of a developing peace any more than it examined the nuances of conflict. As Wilson reminds us:

> the hunting-in-packs style of the international media – an ironically homogenising consequence of intensified market competition – has exacerbated the very strict focus on the small number of men in suits who are cynically seen as the 'main players'. And what might be called CNN culture-strong visuals (especially handshakes) plus a soundbite – has only added to the flattening of complexity and suppression of the nuance so crucial to understanding the Northern Ireland story well (Wilson 1996: 28).

Time pressures, a demand for conflictive stories, the repetitive nature of construction in terms of emphasis, language and tone, cumulatively make it difficult for news to help promote constructive dialogue. Clearly journalists engage in the communication of politics and operate within a political environment, but what they produce is not always consistent with political aims, and with regard to the communication of peace, this appears especially so.

What the interview material in this chapter brings to light is that the practices and methods of reporting take precedent over the fragilities or difficulties of the political process being reported. Furthermore, though journalists recognise that they rely on dominant articulations and tend to reiterate dominant language and terminology, they dispute the suggestion that this also means supporting dominant political positions or objectives. A juxtaposition of competing viewpoints and arguments in news can create problems for elites, and other viewpoints incorporated into reports can create representations which undermine the credibility of elite positions. News values, the daily routines of news gathering and the conventions of report compilation are stressed as key factors in determining journalistic output. Support for political power is not.

To carry this analysis further, I shall now seek the views and comments of editors to see if any structural change was introduced into reporting Northern Ireland as a result of the peace process. In attempting to find out if coverage was managed differently because of the changing political climate, this study will now assess how news managers dealt with problems which may have been created by the transition from conflict to conflict resolution. Extending the analysis of reporting which has been gathered from journalistic perceptions, my intention is to see if editors perceived news as having a role to play in the promotion of peace and to find out whether there was any deliberative effort to shape coverage so as to help assist the search for peace. That is, to question if editors also saw the values and routines of news production as more important for reporting peace than the political forces which shaped it.

5 Editorial Perceptions of Reporting and the Peace Process

Introduction

Having outlined how journalists perceived their role within the peace process and how they worked with the politics of that process, I now intend to investigate how television news coverage of peace was decided and managed. Based on interviews with news editors (see Appendix 1), I aim to identify the selective processes and practices used to influence reports, and try to establish whether the peace process paradigm created new problems for editors when producing reports about the developing peace. I want to see if the peace process produced any significant change in the decision-making priorities of editors and to find out how they perceived their role in relation to the politics of peace. Overall, this part of the study will interrogate how news operations are managed in the context of the peace process.

Like the interviews conducted with journalists, this chapter is concerned with how news selects and constructs representations of the peace process, but unlike the previous section, those questions will here relate to the managerial procedures applied by editors. To do this, it will examine the issues and concerns emphasised by editors as especially important in the construction of news and although there are evident distinctions between the aims and objectives of editors working in Northern Ireland compared to those working in London, there nevertheless exist broad similarities in terms of operational duties and gatekeeping priorities, which are seen as key factors when producing news reports.

Like the previous chapter, the interview material gathered from editors covered a broad range of issues and concerns, which has also been categorised in this instance under five headings. Those headings are: (1) the problem of broadcasting Northern Ireland and the search for balance; (2) the representation of conflict; (3) from violence to peace; (4) routines, time and the political process; and (5) tasks and responsibilities.

The primary intention of this part of the study then, is to investigate whether the peace process affected a noticeable change in how editors determine the structure and content of news, and how they react when dealing with Northern Ireland as a news subject. In examining how decision-making is carried out and how the interaction between politics and news is perceived, this chapter provides a valuable insight into how news coverage about Northern Ireland is managed and will contribute to the overriding discussion in this book which is concerned with the role of news in the communication and negotiation of peace. Moreover, by providing an examination of the relationship between news and politics from editorial perspectives, this interview material not only contributes to understanding how news and political power interact, but seeks to question if the changing political climate from conflict to peace produced any noticeable shift in approach to the reporting of Northern Ireland. Consistent with the previous two chapters, this part of the study further investigates problems and concerns associated with controlling news, and its relationship with the politics of peace.

The Problem of Broadcasting Northern Ireland and the Search for Balance

For editors working in Northern Ireland, the process of news is significantly influenced by the problematic of broadcasting to a divided community. This problematic creates particular difficulties for the neutrality of news when each 'side' of the community is sensitive to what might be seen as the promotion of an oppositional ideology which constitutes bias and favouritism by the broadcasters. The absence of a political consensus in Northern Ireland produces coverage which is also without consensus, where each issue and event is contended and argued by the opposing sides and where political division and community fragmentation is emphasised. Summing up the difficulties of reporting in Northern Ireland, one former BBC NI Controller said:

> The difficulties of broadcasting to a divided community are many because the polarisation in Northern Ireland is such that people tend to adhere to one point of view and don't listen to the other argument, irrespective of how that argument is advanced. It's reasonable to talk of two sides because there are distinctly two sides in the Northern Ireland situation. As one side makes the running in terms of news, the other side will accuse you of giving too much publicity to that side and being in favour of them. Let me give you an example of that, albeit historical.

The Hunger Strike – Bobby Sands and nine of his fellow hunger strikers were to die protesting as they saw it for the legitimacy of political status. They made the running, lots of publicity. The Protestants thought we were on their side simply because of the weight of coverage. I don't think they stopped to consider an anti-hunger strike line being advocated from Margaret Thatcher down. Instead, they saw the preponderance of coverage as indicating that the BBC were in favour of the strike. Similarly, the Ulster Workers Council strike in 1974, which sought to bring down the power-sharing executive and the Sunningdale Agreement – the preponderance of the reportage of that was the Ulster Worker Council's actions against that agreement and the power-sharing executive. They made the running and the preponderance was that the Ulster Worker's Council was being supported by the BBC. That is the difficulty of reporting to a divided society. You will tend to please one side and displease the other.

The impossibility of reporting Northern Ireland in a neutral fashion, essentially derives from the staunchly divided political constituencies which exist there. Those constituencies tend to be articulated and constructed along lines of clear ideological and political difference and have combined to obstruct the emergence of a definable middle ground. As the former BBC Controller put it:

When there were organisations – political or non-political – which attempted to walk a middle road, those organisations never cut any ice, because they were ultimately driven to the wall in having to declare themselves on one side, or the other. The arguments of the two extremes always dominate over any attempt to reconcile them. The Alliance Party have not really over the years, made any huge inroads into those two extremes, nor has the Peace Movement.

Describing this polarity in another way, a former Head of News in Northern Ireland noted:

You have to remember that there is a particular difference with Northern Ireland as opposed to the rest of the United Kingdom. Yorkshire isn't probably in any doubt of where it stands in relation to England and there is no great divergence of view between one Yorkshire man or woman about being English. In Northern Ireland, that position does not exist. Identity, geography and politics are heavily disputed. There is no consensus on any of them. There is only dissensus and we as broadcasters have the unenviable task of trying to reflect that.

Elaborating further on the antagonisms and disagreements between the respective communities and how the tensions impact on the broadcasters, the former Head of News went on:

Covering Northern Ireland is like covering a general election every day of the week. There are always cries of foul from one party or the other, complaining of favouritism and bias, demanding a right of reply and more balanced viewpoints etc. It's like that here all the time. We have audiences here who are particularly sensitive to the interviewing of certain persons and who always demand to know why we have interviewed so and so. They will also ask, for example, 'Why did you say that the dead man was Catholic, but not say that the dead politician was Protestant?' I've had a lot of correspondence and discussion about such issues over the years and I understand it. People feel personally involved in what's going on around them here, in not quite the same way as they do in the rest of the UK, ultimately because people feel that their identity is being challenged, or called into question in some way.

Concomitant with the need for accuracy in reporting and indicating the problems of broadcasting to the divided communities in Northern Ireland, a Home News Editor based in London reinforced the above comments by stating:

Although you should always be aware of the possible implications of what you are saying in news, this is especially so with Northern Ireland. Northern Ireland is a place where people watch television with a greater degree of involvement and knowledge than probably anywhere else in the UK. There is a communal knowledge about the situation there and what is broadcast that you tend not to find anywhere else. So, your credibility can be badly damaged by getting things wrong, even if it's a mispronunciation. People in Northern Ireland are onto that like a shot, so it creates a real pressure to get things right.

The assertion by editors that accuracy is crucial in reporting Northern Ireland because of the divergent interests and ideologies of the communities which reside there, also runs parallel with a need for balance and impartiality in coverage. All the editors interviewed for this study stressed the importance of this, though some preferred the word 'fairness' to impartiality. The imperative of balance was determined to be a central concern given the potentially volatile and unstable atmosphere of Northern Ireland and was expressed as inherently necessary in order not to aggravate tensions, or assist those seeking to further polarise sections of the community. As the former Controller of News in Northern Ireland said on the impartiality question:

Using two sides of the argument is important to strike the notion of balance in reportage because there are two fundamentally opposed points of view which drive the situation here. One is that there are people in Northern Ireland who wish to remain part of the UK and these are the Unionists and they are in the majority. And the second is a sizable minority which believes that we should not be part of that union, but part of a Nationalist constituency which leads to an all – Ireland republic. Now to report that decently, honestly and fairly, you've got to balance your reportage of that and I cannot think of too many aspects of that situation where the word balance does not come into play. However, there's a bigger word which comes into play and that's fairness. If you can manifestly show that you have tried to be fair, then you're probably doing a decent job.

The idea of being fair and balanced in coverage is especially problematic, given the opposed positions of Nationalists/Republicans and Unionists/ Loyalists. Each is liable to critically scrutinise news reporting more in terms of what it appears to be offering the opposition, rather than the potential benefits or propaganda gains for one's own side. Quantifying this problem another way, a Deputy Home News Editor based in London noted:

It's the old adage that if you're getting roughly equal complaints from either side, then you've got it about right. It's very difficult to walk a middle line when reporting Northern Ireland and that problem has a long history. At the start of 'The Troubles', many Unionists could not understand why we were reporting in a fair-minded and fair-handed way what was going on in the Nationalist community, because they expected us to support the side of the government. And over the years we've had accusations from the other side about supporting the government at the expense of Nationalists. I would say that such accusations of bias from either side shows that in the main, we've tried to be fair and evenhanded. But, ultimately, it's a no-win situation.

A Home News Editor also based in London, reiterated the importance of trying to achieve impartiality, but going further, also brought into question the possibility of remaining impartial in the wake of a murder or bombing:

Impartiality is something that you have to be aware of when you're dealing with political parties and spokesmen. You simply cannot get away with reporting things in a highly politically charged atmosphere which are unbalanced. The object of the exercise is to be objective. It would however, be difficult to be impartial about the Holocaust, so there are degrees of impartiality. I think with Northern Ireland, the aim is to be as objectively representative of all the opinions as you can be. Phrases and words which lead to a bias against understanding are not useful.

When pressed on what objectivity meant in actuality and how it worked, the Home News Editor was less clear however, presenting it as an instinctive feature of the organisational culture of news. As such, her definition of objectivity was based on the organisational aims of news production rather than any philosophical or coherent articulation of its meaning and intentions:

> It's really difficult to explain to those who aren't here all the time, about the culture of objectivity. It's not something you think about on a minute- by- minute basis. It's just something that's so much part of this culture that you kind of absorb it when you enter the door and it stays with you.

Notions of objectivity, impartiality and balance tended to be used interchangeably by editors when describing the priorities of covering different events and situations, implying that the application for example, of impartiality, depends to a great extent on the moral connotations of that being reported. Echoing the remarks of the Home News Editor, a Senior News Editor put it in the following terms:

> There are times when it's difficult to be impartial and sometimes you shouldn't. How you interview people also depends on how they stand in relation to a particular events at a particular moment in time. Sometimes the best way to interview people is to be sympathetic and drag things out of them and other times, people should be given a hard time. When someone has been murdered you must reflect the problems and horribleness associated with that. In such cases, you can't be impartial.

Offering a more precise attempt to explain how the notion of objectivity operates at editorial level, a Senior News Editor summarised his efforts to apply the concept in this way:

> You don't and indeed shouldn't always try to go down the middle of a line on a particular story.
> Sometimes it's quite clear how, with regard to an event, that someone is right and someone is wrong and you need to judge your piece in that way. But, I think the bottom line is that you need to be as clear as you can in your own mind that you have weighed up the facts, the innuendoes, the different nuances and other elements which affect developing stories, and rule out bias as far as possible. Once you've done all that, then you can probably say that you've been as objective as you can be. You can only be as objective as the information at your disposal allows you to be.

The editor stressed the importance of fairness as a given in news production, but at the same time illustrated the difficulties involved in trying to manage this imperative against the often emotional connotations which derive from particular television images. As the editor expressed it:

> Accuracy and fairness are the most important journalistic guidelines and to make sure that the various sides of an issue are developed. That doesn't mean that each report must have equal balance, but over a period one should have addressed a range of viewpoints. The licensing laws also state that we should strive to be impartial and fair. Unlike newspapers which can be guided by one direction or another, we must be seen to avoid that position. In seeking to uphold these guidelines, ITN has its own way of working which is passed down from editor to editor about how things should be done. If you've got some horrific explosion and you've got some television pictures which are stronger than the written word for emotional content, then this does pose difficulties for balance, because there is always a balance to be struck between showing the horror of an event and not being voyeuristic about it, so you tend to stress to reporters about the need to be sensitive. Normally they do it in their own right, but occasionally you need to reinforce that.

Clearly then, it is the coverage of violence in Northern Ireland which make the aim of impartiality so evasive.

As a number of editors made clear, the imagery of particular acts of violence necessitates a partial rather than impartial response. One might also argue here, that because coverage of Northern Ireland over the years has so concerned itself with covering violence, that this has also contributed to making impartiality less attainable. Or, to put it another way, one could suggest that the media's obsession with the effects of violence has inhibited the potential for impartiality or balance. To illustrate the point, it is worth quoting a former Head of News in Northern Ireland, who said:

> There have been too many occasions when horrific acts of violence have been committed where it's almost impossible to be impartial and we have to be realistic about that. When you get a bombing like Shankill or Enniskillen, those are dreadful events by any stretch of the imagination that no sane person could approve of. The broadcaster has the advantage in many ways of not having to conjure up description him or herself, because seeing and hearing somebody like Gordon Wilson for example, you don't have to do anything else than to put that man on screen and let him speak for himself. Hearing people talk about what has happened to them will leave people to make up their own minds as to how they feel about it. You don't need purple prose form journalists to embellish that.

The Representation of Conflict

It has been suggested that as news coverage of Northern Ireland has concerned itself mainly with acts of violence and terrorism which tend to incite moral condemnation and partial responses, so impartiality becomes less likely in reporting. For many editors, reporting terrorism presented a number of dilemmas principally concerning definitions and language, but the question of whether terrorism had been reported impartiality was rarely confronted directly. Rather, it was impressed that reporting terrorism demanded a partial response precisely because of the illegality of the act. Indeed, it was precisely this illegality which to a large extent removed the burden of impartiality or balance, or at least eased the pressure of applying it. Highlighting how coverage of terrorism was interpreted and explained by the broadcasters in this context, the former Controller of News in Northern Ireland went on:

> The main problem in covering terrorism is: on which side of the argument do you stand and this is where you can get yourself into huge difficulty. I think that people who stand outside the law should be treated differently from those who uphold the law. One of the problems this creates is: when do you talk to the men of violence? The answer should in my view be, sparingly. They should not be afforded the same democratic right as those who espouse democracy and practice democracy. That is why the BBC has a very strict rule that any potential or planned interview with the PIRA or UVF has to be commended in argument to the Director-General and he will decide if such an interview takes place. You must also remember that in Northern Ireland the reporting of terrorism is being presented to the communities which are suffering it and it can sometimes make a bad situation worse. It's a very sensitive and problematical area.

But, even though most editors saw little problem with representing terrorism in a partial way, there was still apparent concern about how violence should be explained, interpreted and articulated. The problem of discourse and its centrality within the conflict was understood by all those interviewed, and indicated the absence of any consensus discourse acceptable to all sides. On the subject of language and explanation, the former NI Controller stressed:

> You cannot be too careful about language and the moment you get blaze about language with a lack of thought, you're in trouble. It is an important issue, although the most important editorial policy about what you're trying to achieve is a fairness and an understanding; a decency of reportage. But, of course, at the centre of this objective is language and how language is deployed. By not recognising that fact you are making editorial policy unviable.

For the former Head of News in Northern Ireland, the use of language is key to gaining public credibility and trust in broadcasting and as he pointed out:

> There are only a limited number of phrases you can use without apparently swinging the pendulum of favouritism to one side or the other. You can give the wrong weight or emphasis by using the wrong word or phrase, and even the terms 'killers', or 'murderers' must be thought about long and hard before use. There was a long discussion much earlier in 'The Troubles' as to whether we were right to call the Protestant terrorists 'Loyalists' because they didn't have the support of the whole Loyalist community. But, once such a term has entered the public consciousness because it's being used by everybody else, then actually the BBC will begin to look out of place with how people interpret and understand others. If you start to use different terms then you have to start to explain why you're using different terms and it starts to cloud the issue.

Underling the assertion that language is central to understanding and articulating the nuances of conflict and those engaged within it, a London based Senior News Editor stated:

> Language is vital with regard to Northern Ireland. Unionist, Loyalist, Republican and Nationalist are very emotive words and journalists must be absolutely correct in how they use those terms, although you can also use them in a pejorative sense. You might say that someone is a Unionist or Loyalist politician and people in England might not see much difference, but in Northern Ireland, there is a huge difference. For anyone who is running a campaign of violence against another part of the community, or the government, we would tend to avoid terrorist and use more 'gunman', 'bombers', 'men of violence', or paramilitaries. We stopped using words like ' The IRA or the UDA claim responsibility' some years ago because it gave a kind of kudos to those organisations and made it sound as if what they had done was almost a proper thing to do. So we now say 'So and so now say they did it'. That is a calmer way of doing it.

Another London based Home News Editor although working for a different news organisation reiterated a similar stance, emphasising the importance of precise wording and a specific definitional picture:

> The use of language in the context of Northern Ireland is incredibly important. It's especially important to those who you are broadcasting to in Northern Ireland. The careful use of Republican/Nationalist, Loyalist/Unionist is important to those who understand it, but I'm not sure those differentiations are so understood this side of the water. They are absolutely clear to people in Northern Ireland.

Terrorism is something which tends to happen in 'democratic countries', with 'democratic institutions' and tends to be carried out against 'democratic structures', or civilians. But the debate about whether something is terrorism or isn't terrorism is an ongoing one. The use of the right language in terms of defining the political divisions is vital in the case of Northern Ireland.

From Violence to Peace

The question of whether language is as vital for articulating the transition from war to peace required a little more elaboration, since it involved addressing how the political climate had shifted in Northern Ireland and whether this shift had affected the priorities of reporting. Commenting on the developing peace and its possible impact on reporting, the former Head of News in Northern Ireland said:

> Some people now say that the violence is over and the story of Northern Ireland will go away, but that is not going to happen. Over the past few years (with particular exceptions) when there was an atrocity there was very much an international interest by the media and there has been an increasing involvement by that media. Northern Ireland is also now a big European story and receives considerable European funding and interest. It is also a big issue in the United States with Clinton taking a close interest in what happens and has never been higher on the agenda of a British prime minister. Even though violence has dominated coverage over the years, the transition to peace will be an equally big news story.

Continuing by discussing the development of peace and its potential influences on the nature of reporting, he went on:

> One thing which is important since the ceasefires is to reflect the changing mood in the communities. It is as important for us to report on the changing mood as it is on political developments and the absence of violence allows us to concentrate more on such issues as education, health and the environment, which of course preoccupy people here as much as in the rest of the UK, but which have been elbowed off the news agenda by the violence. I think there has now arisen an opportunity for us to explore political change and what might happen, for example if there is a united Ireland, or all-Ireland structures? Similarly other questions emerge such as what will happen to the RUC?, what form will the Assembly take?, will there be a new alliance of the parties? and is there a new emerging system of values previously absent? Those concerns will clearly need

to be at the forefront of what we're doing. Having said that, people expect to be guided by news. They expect to hear knowledgeable conversation and informed discussion and debate. We have always said that we have provided the only platform for debate since Stormont disappeared. There is no other really and we will try to maintain that. But, to give you some idea of how things have changed, before the peace process if we did an interview with Gerry Adams on television we would get calls from people demanding that he be removed from the screen. That doesn't happen now. In a large measure that is related to the absence of violence and killing, so there isn't the same degree of anger. Reflecting this change, we did a programme towards the end of 1994 which would have been unthinkable a year before, which was a discussion between Mitchel McLaughlin of Sinn Fein with a former moderator of the Presbyterian church and one or two others of the Protestant community. It was a measured discussion about Sinn Fein's objectives and the way ahead. For once this generated heat rather than light and we had a huge audience response asking for more of it. It was an exploration of positions rather than a conflict of positions and the more we can follow that example the better it will be for facilitating tolerance and understanding.

For a London based Deputy Home News Editor, this transition presented a significant change in terms of how Northern Ireland was now being reported. Effectively, signifying a shift from focusing on violence to the discourse of politics and negotiations, the editor explained:

> Certainly in television news it's going to be a little more difficult to construct packages given that you don't now have the funerals, or the aftermath of bombs etc. So, we're going to have to look for increasingly different ways of getting television pictures. But, now the ceasefires are in place, the story will be largely a political one.

A Senior News Editor based in London further identified how the development of peace now meant news reports had to concentrate more on the discourse of politics rather than violence. As he saw it:

> Coverage is definitely now oriented towards the 'search for peace' story. However, there is always a danger of overreacting to this scenario and depicting peace as inevitable given the direction of events. Once 90 per cent of coverage was about bombs, deaths, murders, now it's about possible political structures and negotiations. The aftermath of a bomb is spectacular from a picture point of view, but there are ways of making stories about diplomatic relations interesting by juxtaposing the comments of people to represent visually what is being discussed. There are times when, even when you think that there's nothing left

to say where you must keep trying because things are still happening. As was the case with the IRA ceasefire which was preceded by months of speculation. We did a number of stories about the possibility of a ceasefire for weeks beforehand and had to keep coming up with ways of covering what was essentially speculation. Nothing visually was happening yet we had to find ways of making news packages and this is a problem which we will clearly have to get used to if peace continues to develop.

Routines, Time and the Political Process

An important question to consider in the context of the changing political landscape in Northern Ireland is whether the new emphasis on political discourse rather than violence led to a change in how editors handled news stories? Or, to put it another way, did the peace process impact on editorial decision-making and therefore affect the construction of news reports? In order to address this question, editors were asked to outline how they decided on the construction and order of news and the organisational priorities which determine time and content. For some editors the basis of gatekeeping is cultural and instinctive rather than precise or objective, or as the former Controller of News in Northern Ireland expressed it,

> Editorial decisions derive form an instinct born out of an experience. This instinct consists of trying to put yourself into the shoes of ordinary viewers and listeners, because that is your constituency as a broadcaster. Also, it means actually saying to yourself, I find that interesting, important and significant and I must extrapolate it to make it equally interesting, important and significant to this community I am part of.

But, for the former Head of News in Northern Ireland, the selection process which comes into play when deciding the order and structure of news was described as a more complex process. As he saw it:

> It is our responsibility to make sure that complex and important issues are explained to the public, but time is an enemy in many respects for doing that. There isn't really any time to ponder or consider the nuances and complexities of an event or document, so it's very difficult to explain such things properly. On the other hand, it can also concentrate the mind when you have to explain the main points quickly. Inevitably, things get left out and things included get simplified. But, simplifying complex issues is part of the job. The job is not just to hand the contents of a document to the audience verbatim, but to read it,

interpret it and to tell the audience the gist of what is in it, to provide guidance about what is important about it and what isn't. Invariably, that involves reduction and condensing and simplifying and for most people, that's helpful and useful.

Continuing with this emphasis, a Deputy Home News Editor in London stressed how:

> In terms of television news, you're dealing with a short span of time. The standard rule of thumb that we use, is that effectively, the amount of material we can convey to people in a 27 or 29 minute bulletin is about the equivalent of the information you would get on the front page of any broadsheet newspaper. Obviously then, there's not much time and you've got to reduce things. Ultimately, that comes down to journalistic and editorial knowledge, where you put the most interesting and the most important facts into the one or two minutes, so that you leave the viewer or listener with as much information about the story as you can tell them in the time available. This problem has been made all the more difficult by the fact that for the last 12 years after the advent of electronic newsgathering, there has been no such thing as a deadline. You can now broadcast 'live' from virtually any corner of the world and with 24 hour rolling news this puts even greater pressure on us to get news out quickly. That inevitably impacts on our ability to examine and explain and possibly, if anything leads to more simplification and this of course, can be a disadvantage.

According to a Senior News Editor, time pressures are one of the key determinants for news and have a considerable impact on what is explained and how it is explained. He explained it in the following way:

> Given the pressures caused by time, it's surprising that new is as objective as it is. The training that most journalists go through means that many will do things by instinct and most are objective. There is always the problem that things will get missed on occasions when you're not aware of something, but the role of editors is to help reporters to get access to as much information as possible. Editors are supposed to keep reports as far as possible on an even keel. Complicated and emotive stories like Northern Ireland are especially difficult and we do keep a close eye on it, particularly if we're sending a journalist to cover a story there who is inexperienced. Then, I try to guide reporters on the need for a careful use of terminology.
>
> However, the content of reports is based on news judgments and all sorts of things come into play when those judgments are made, such as the length of the piece, which of course, determines what goes in and what doesn't. The principal judgment is time and how long we've got to get the story across. We would tell journalists at the beginning of the day if we're aiming at 4–5 minutes, or

whatever, and as the day goes on that can be refined and changed. Sometimes the story gets less important as the day goes on, or conversely, it might get more important. Generally, the length of the piece will determine how much filming you need and the amount of resources needed to be put into it. By and large the time we give to a story is decided by the perceived significance of that particular story on a particular day.

However, for many editors there appears to be no objectively discernible way of allocating time and structure to news reports. Most saw this process as resulting from years of experience in interpreting and making news. They neither indicated outside pressure as an influence over what appears as important on any given day, nor did they see decision-making in any precise way. What they seem to overwhelmingly draw on to impose time and order in bulletins, is the cultural values of the news organisation they represent and these values are invariably instinctive. When describing how editors determine the order and content of news, one Head of News said:

> You learn your craft and you make mistakes and people do it in different ways and judgments will differ legitimately between individuals. There is rarely a right answer to the question 'What story should lead a news programme?' Occasionally, there is an obvious lead, but there isn't a formula, because if there was you would have to pay journalists a lot of money to edit programmes. It's a combination of judgment, insight, feeling, knowledge of what's been reported before on your programme, recently on your programme, judgment between you and your colleagues about whether, for example, this is the start of a real peace process that is going to build, or whether it is just a flash in the pan.

Reinforcing this perception of editorial practice and the institutional pressures of time, one Home News Editor based in London noted how content and structure are

> Largely shaped by how long you've got to do a report, which in turn is shaped by the amount of what is deemed newsworthy on any one day. The object of the exercise is to tell people what is going on, so you include things which go most directly to the issue, both in terms of pictures and actuality. It's a place between the amount of context which you need to make people understand what's going on and the amount of context which you can put in a finite amount of time. I suppose it's also a series of procedures, but it's a series of procedures that you don't think about in step by step terms, because they are things you take as read. So when you go to an incident there is a process you go through to try and get a range of perspectives on the story and the process you go through to get that is

fairly ingrained in people. The Northern Ireland situation may be a bit more stressful, but a journalist would go through the same kinds of procedure with Northern Ireland as most other stories. The processes are very similar.

Yet, important though time and order are in deciding the content and structure of news on any one day, there are other factors which affect news production, such as the political process being reported. A range of responses derived from questions about political pressures, political communications and the politics of peace in Northern Ireland. Although most tended to talk about political influences in general rather than specific terms, there was nevertheless a firm belief in professional autonomy and detachment from politics and the political process. But, on the question of whether politicians sought to use the news media to communicate messages to their political opponents, the responses were somewhat varied. The former Controller of Northern Ireland argued strongly that negotiation through the media is a deliberative process, continuing:

> If you look down the years of strife in Northern Ireland, there are many occasions when broadcasting organisations provide the only platform of debate in Northern Ireland. There have been occasions when there wasn't a Local Assembly, or a Local Deputy Chamber and the BBC actually found itself being one of the few forms for debate. Politicians attempt to do two things: (1) they attempt to communicate with each other, and (2) they attempt to use the media, particularly the electronic media which has a certain potency. I don't personally have problem with politicians trying to bully the media or, trying to intimidate the media. After all, it's their business to get their message across. But, it's certainly the responsibility of the broadcaster to resist and desist intimidation and bullying of the politician.

For a Head of News working in London however, using the media to develop politics proved to be a more contentious question. On this issue, he went on to say:

> I think it's questionable how news impacts on the political process, ultimately because it's unquantifiable. It would be impossible to say, and perhaps inaccurate to say that media coverage doesn't have an affect on the way politics is played out, whether it's political parties, or paramilitary groups. All parties and all paramilitary groups have an eye to a public relations strategy and to the extent to which that strategy is succeeding or not. That success or lack of success is likely to affect the way they conduct themselves and reassess the strategy, so it's likely to have an affect, although my feeling is, it's not a direct affect. There

are occasions when parties to the peace process may well have deliberately expressed views through the media in an attempt to exert pressure on the other parties in the process. I can think of an example a few months ago when John Bruton delivered an impassioned and apparently spontaneous outburst of criticism on the 9 o'clock news against Downing Street and by and large, politicians of Mr Bruton's experience do not spontaneously lose their temper on television. Rather they decide that the time has come to lose their temper on television for some political affect and this would probably have been seen by most parties in Northern Ireland as an effort by Dublin to influence some change in London. Having said that, politicians hardly adopt a sophisticated approach to the media. I don's see much of a sign that any of the parties involved in the peace process have a really strategic view of how to present a case through the media. I think most of them have a public relations strategy but, it's all very short term and reactive and it's largely crisis management – as much as with the government as the paramilitary side. Clearly, there are some pretty intelligent people on all sides trying to make use of the media and some of them doing it quite well. But, all in all I think that the media is not knocked off course by the politicians and the politicians are not particularly knocked off course by the media, so the impact of each on the other seems to me to remain highly questionable.

Adding to the discussion of whether politicians try to use the media as a conduit for conducting negotiations with political opponents, the Head of News stated:

I don't think the media is used as a conduit where the intricacies and details of developments and issues can be discussed. Even during the 1970s there were means by which Loyalists and Nationalists could communicate if they needed to. The people who were driving the strategies could communicate when they wanted to by means far more reliable than the media. I think that politicians do use the media to send out messages to their own supporters and rival supporters to try and force one another into public positions, but there have always been more effective routes for messages and that is when messages are delivered privately. A public message has a quite different intention and affect than a private one and it's the private messages which are most important for political development. Public messages are more about trying to force opponents into positions from which it's difficult to withdraw. Whereas private messages are much more about exploration, discussion and examination. So you might say that private and public messages have almost opposite affects.

The Head of News did illustrate a dichotomy about the ability of news to impede or shape the political process, however. Underlining the main emphasis of journalism as being an interrogation of, rather than an influence on politics, he then went on to clearly illustrate how politicians change positions and articulations when dealing with the media. This would suggest that even if broadcasters attempt to not affect or intervene in politics, they still do so and act as a considerable influence on how politics is presented and constructed. As he put it:

> We absolutely don't have a purpose or role to affect the political process. We get publicly funded for one reason only and that is to try and tell people as honestly, fairly and clearly as we can about what it is in happening in the world. If we were just giving airtime to political theatre which departed from what politicians were telling us off-air, then we would be little more than a mouthpiece for politicians and just part of the process of theatre. There isn't a doubt that politicians say one thing on the floor of the House of Commons, say a marginally different thing on camera and create another spin for the public audience different from that in the House of Commons. Furthermore, as soon as the camera has stopped running they will often say something diametrically opposite to what they have said on camera, and that is most of them. This is not a daily event. It's a minute by minute event. A politician will tell you the truth perhaps until the cameras roll and then will say completely the opposite when the camera starts filming. Politicians tend to say one thing in private and another thing in public. It's a charade. We do try and shift more towards telling the public about what politicians are saying in private because by and large that is nearer to the truth. Sometimes a politician will give us a scurrilous piece of information with the expectation that we will use it and then when we do use it, that same politician will complain to the BBC about how scandalous it was of us to use such information. Yet revealing that person as the source risks jeopardising the lobby information process and undermines the confidentiality of the journalist-source relationship.

Responding as to the whether the media should adopt a deliberate role in attempting to facilitate political negotiations and dialogue, the Head of News stated:

> It isn't our job to try and influence peace negotiations and if we do do that, then it should be incidental, not deliberate. Once journalists think they have a responsibility to affect the political process, then their political views risk starting to influence what they're broadcasting. We should be governed by one thing – broadcasting the truth as far as we can get at it. Politicians and the electorate should determine the political process. Having said that, television is obviously a very powerful medium for conveying politics and some people are more effective at conveying political positions and developments than others. John

Hume, for example, who is incapable of dissembling, conveys his emotions very strongly and directly through television. When he shows anger, it isn't artificial. From time to time when he has lost his patience with what he has seen as stalling by the British government, his anger on television has been so palpable that if I were a Northern Ireland official, or a Foreign Commonwealth Office official, or an official in Downing Street, I would realise that he is not playacting, but a man who can see that the peace process is on the verge of collapse. Sometimes therefore, I think that the media can get across a greater depth of feeling than a Whitehall memo. A written briefing to the Prime Minister about what John Hume thinks doesn't have the same impact. However, having said that, politicians do tend to take their cue from diplomats rather than the performance of politicians on television. The guts of a political argument or problem, is rarely if ever served or moved by television.

A Home News Editor based in London further reinforced the journalistic imperative of detachment from political imperatives, as well as signalling the political importance of the media by noting:

There's not one politician I'm aware of who isn't switched on to how they might be able to use the media for their own advantage. The media's duty is to be aware of this potential manipulation and to expose it where possible. With Northern Ireland, politicians who are involved with the peace process are not quite as skilled with handling the media as other politicians are with other political issues, which is not surprising given the history of the place. Coverage of violence and terrorism has hardly been an environment conducive to sophisticated political communications. But, generally speaking, all politicians are seeking to use the media and develop their positions through the media. I don't think Northern Ireland is any different from other news stories in that journalists are still confronted with asking the right questions and striving to prevent politicians merely using the media for their own ends.

When editors were asked to explain further how politicians tried to influence political events by using the media, a number referred to the use of leaks as often effective in causing disruption to political processes. Though leaks were not depicted as capable of derailing political processes, they were still seen as a powerful destabilising device which could impact on the conduct of political actions. To quote the Head of News from London:

It's true of almost every area of public policy controversy that one party or another to the controversy will indulge in deliberate calculated leaks. Sometimes leaks are of genuine material, other times a leak will not be as authentic as it seems. It would be easy to take a high-minded view to that and say that journalists should never regard leaks from interested parties. However, lots of leaks from interested parties are genuine – in fact, most are genuine – and are of major public interest. The journalist should always be sensitive to the motives of the leaker however and should always take into account the potential benefits and disadvantages to be acquired by using leaks.

Further enforcing the need to critically examine the motives of those who provide leaked information, a Senior News Editor in London argued:

> The thing to remember with sources is that you need to remember what their agenda is. When a source provides information, there's usually something in it for them and journalists need to bear that in mind with whoever they're talking to. By and large assessment of a source's authenticity and reasoning is a matter of instinct. If it comes form someone who you've used before, you tend to use them again. But, there may come a time when what a source is telling you is so contradictory with what others are saying that you may need to further question the accuracy of the information you've been given. There is a danger of getting too close to sources, but ironically it's only by getting close to people that they become a source.

A former Head of News in Northern Ireland stressed how the timing of leaks is central to their effectiveness and drawing on experience said:

> Sunday is always a day for leaks. Sunday is the day for politicians to plant stories they may want to see develop during the course of the week. Politicians will always try to time their messages to deliver maximum impact, so timing is crucial. The Prime Minister can time his emergence from Number 10 just as the 1 o'clock news goes on air in order to make it unavoidable that a story about him will be top of the news agenda. Meetings are often timed to coincide with news programmes. We have to be wary about being used of course, just as we have to be vigilant that our values don't get twisted because of the availability of someone, but the business of political manipulation and news management is a considerable and ongoing problem.

That leaking information can affect the interplay of politics and indeed undermine sensitive political negotiations is a point referred to by Chairman of the Northern Ireland talks, George Mitchell in his recollection of the negotiations surrounding the Good Friday Agreement. As Mitchell explained it:

> I quickly learned that leaks were an integral part of this negotiating process. All of the participants sought to advance their negotiating positions by manipulating

the press outside. Whatever the result from the standpoint of the parties, it made the process of negotiation much more difficult. Countless hours were to be consumed by attacks and counterattacks, accusations and recriminations, over what had appeared in the morning newspapers. It didn't just take up a lot of time, it poisoned the atmosphere, creating and exacerbating hostility among the participants (Mitchell 1999: 62).

Arguing that the use of leaks obstructed political development, Mitchell draws attention to the destabilising affect which media coverage of confidential information can have. Although critical of those leaking information rather than those reporting it, Mitchell is nevertheless clear about the damage which leaks can cause to sensitive negotiations and illustrates how using coverage was seen as an essential part of manipulating the talks process:

> The rules of procedure imposed upon all the participants a rule of confidentiality. The negotiations were private and were supposed to stay private. The reality was just the opposite. There was usually a large contingent of media just outside the gate, and every day while we were in session many of the participants walked out to the gate to hold press conferences. It quickly became a regular part of the process. In addition, virtually every document prepared during the negotiations was immediately leaked to the media (ibid.: 75).

Taking a slightly more sympathetic line towards the media (which may have become less sympathetic when the Labour Party gained power in 1997), the then Shadow Northern Ireland Secretary Mo Mowlam also raised the issue of leaks and the media in an address to students at Harvard University on 11 March 1996, saying:

> Since so much of this process operates semi-confidentially the politicians and officials managing the process are very powerful influences of the news agenda. Accusations of leaking sensitive information fly out from all offices. In all probability all are equally guilty of that. Some would say it's an important aspect of news management. Sometimes it helps to smooth the passage of knowledge and to avoid knee-jerk reactions. Sometimes – as with the leaking of parts of the Joint Framework document in February 1995 it can be harmful. On that occasion, the Northern Ireland Secretary was obliged to make a statement in the House of Commons to respond to signals sent out by the leak (Mowlam 1996: 2).

That leaks and what they produce can be seen as an example of how the news media can affect politics in ways undesirable for the continuation and practice of political domination, indicates an obvious distance between those who exert power and the broadcasters. On the subject of political influence over broadcasting and whether politicians are able to apply some controlling power over what is reported, nearly all the editors were quite adamant that this does not happen, stressing an independence between reporting and the political environment which news draws from and reproduces. For a Deputy Home News Editor in London:

> Political pressure does not really affect coverage. Editors, producers and correspondents do get a lot of phone calls about lobbying from the different sides, mainly about accusations of bias and not giving particular respondents enough time to speak. But overall it doesn't affect changes to reports.

Finding consistency with this position, a Senior News Editor from another channel also London based went on:

> Outside pressure doesn't affect us at all really. Occasionally we will get people from the respective political parties complaining that they should have been better treated. But, if they ask us for an explanation for why we reported them in the way we did, we normally oblige in providing them with one and can justify ourselves.

The Head of News in one organisation saw it this way:

> If it were true that we tend to serve the interests of those in power then why is it that the bulk of complaints about reporting come from those very people and much more so than from those in opposition? Although I agree that we tend to regurgitate the liberal approach of the chattering classes and that network journalism is clearly of London South East mindset, we are not pressured to do that. There is a strong sense of autonomy and we strongly resist attempts at exertions of political control.

A viewpoint similarly shared by a Senior Editor/ Director at ITN, who commented:

> I've never been told by anyone that things had to be done in a particular way or that coverage should change because of political pressure being applied. Of the many, many editorial meetings I've attended over the years, there has never been the suggestion of doing things in order not to upset the government, or that things had to be done in a way so as to minimise any potential trouble which certain political representatives might cause.

Tasks and Duties

Elaborating on what are perceived as other direct pressures on and requirements of editors, it emerged that the logistics of planning and resourcing news play a significant role in the daily routines of editors. As a Senior Editor for ITN explained it:

> If there were a major explosion with a large loss of life, I would recommend sending someone from here with all the back up equipment so events could be covered on the ground there and then. That is how we would react to a fast breaking news event. The alternative to that of course, is that we know some things are going to happen, such as a big press conference or a prime minister's visit and in that case, if it were a story which warranted a reporter and crew being sent I would brief a reporter and producer and make sure a camera crew was on hand (generally hired locally) and we would make sure that the arrangements for travel are made accordingly. The logistics of getting all the right people into the right place at the right time can be a nightmare. My job is to organise the logistics and make the journalism possible.

Underlining how the monitoring of journalistic output also comes under the responsibility of editors, the same editor concluded:

> I always keep a supervisory eye on the report and even though most of the time I tend to leave the content to reporters, I might examine the script closely and say 'Look you should really get this or that in', or 'what that person said was important and it should go in'. By and large, if I tell them to do something they do it. I'm quite happy to have a debate with them, especially when they're in Belfast and they know or can see things which I can't from London. On other occasions, you need to be further away from a problem to see it more clearly, so it works both ways.

An interviewee also working for ITN, as Senior Director, spoke about the use and introduction of technological effects as a key part of his role and stressed:

> In order to clarify what the reporter is saying and to enhance what they're saying, we would incorporate maps and statistics, for example, to improve the package. There are many news packages which don't need any graphic work or visual enhancement, but both of these do tend to help people understand information, and help the reporter to introduce information which would otherwise be bland and boring. The firepower which we've got in computer equipment at ITN is

phenomenal. We've got thousands of pounds worth of technological equipment which we don't use to it's full potential at the moment, mainly because it would be pure gimmickry. You've got to get a balance between presenting a hard news story and enhancing it. We could go much further than we do and make Star Wars films if we wanted to. By enhance, I mean to get over the point of the story and to leave people in no doubt about what the story is and to enhance the journalistic values of the story. To do this, I attend a meeting in the morning and decide how we are going to allocate the resources to get the stories on air. To put it simply, my job is to help translate the written word into television. We have scripts given to us and whilst reporters and camera crews are out shooting it, I take the paper side of it, what they've written and decide where the graphics will go and where the statistics will go. So, I pull it all together and organise the resources for that.

A Home News Editor for the BBC further reinforced the planning requirements for news production and highlighted how much of news is determined in advance of an expected event. As she explained it:

> We had a plan with the teams in Belfast on the types of package which we wanted to produce on the day of the IRA ceasefire and the kind of things we wanted to look at, one of which would be a 'How we got here' analysis which looked at the political manoeuvring. Then we wanted to look at the cost of 25 years of 'The Troubles' in human terms, and then a look at the places and reactions where you could see an immediate effect. So the next day we went down to a couple of border towns and looked at them. That had to be fairly carefully planned in advance and a lot of pre-shooting arranged in anticipation of the final package. I would organise the report and would tell the journalist/ correspondent that we need this or that. Today for example, we will be covering the Peace and Reconciliation Forum and I will converse with journalists about what is needed and where that story will fit in the running order. Sometimes, I will tell a journalist that something needs to go in or something needs to be omitted, but most decisions like that are quite apparent and self-selecting.

Conclusion

What emerges from the interview material gathered from editors tends to be a picture of general editorial practice as much as an insight into the specific editorial dilemmas or problems which arise as a result of covering Northern Ireland as a subject. Certainly, and as one would expect, there is a keen awareness of the difficulties of reporting Northern Ireland from those editors with experience of working there, but this is not to say that London based editors have not also provided a number of instructive and useful comments about the problem of constructing reports about Northern Ireland. Notably, most of those interviewed were receptive to the problem of maintaining balanced coverage, but, given the conflicting communities and accusations of bias from those communities it is not surprising that many editors preferred to talk in terms of fairness in coverage. All were aware of the importance of language and placed considerable emphasis on the need for accuracy when describing events or defining particular groups and individuals. Impartiality was stressed as a desirable aim, but most were also mindful of the expectation that in the light of an atrocity, partiality is called for. This partiality is epitomised by defining certain acts of violence as terrorism, the definition itself reflective of a partial ideological position. Editors made no apology for describing and explaining certain events and acts as terrorist, although they also impressed how important it is to avoid inflammatory language and how journalists are expected to be careful in how they convey violence, knowing that language and definitions have potential for sustaining political division and antagonism.

The transition from violence to peace in Northern Ireland did not apparently incite any radical change in the way editors work. Clearly, many understood how the peace process had attracted international interest and that peace negotiations had necessitated an examination of political structures and discourse which had been largely absent during 'The Troubles'. But, this had not impacted on their decision-making in any prominent fashion and the shift from violence to peace still involved many of the sensitive considerations about language and definitions as before. Also, as before, editors were up against the same problems with regard to time, simplification and the reflexive nature of newsgathering in relation to events. The peace process may not have created the same emotive and dramatic images as had arisen during the violence, but editors still emphasised the need for images and the search for ways of visually explaining the peace process and maintaining it as an ongoing news story.

On the question of whether news provided a means of communication between politicians or affected policy, the responses were more complex. For some editors, news was seen as a lever for exerting pressure on political opponents and affective for debating positions and potential directions, but for others the news media was seen as having little effect on the nuances and developments of policy which were driven privately, not publicly. However, the very fact that it was made clear that what politicians say off camera is often opposite to what they say on camera illustrates that the media has a significant affect on how politicians communicate. This affect is also indicated by the very different outcome which public messages are seen to have in comparison to private ones. Indeed, these affects are almost diametrically opposed to each other, where the prospect for wrecking peace is more likely to be enhanced by what is said to the media, rather what is said in confidence behind closed doors. The significance of using the media to obstruct rather than facilitate the path of peace was seen to derive from leaked information, which as some politicians made clear, caused considerable problems for maintaining momentum and gaining confidence. Nevertheless, even though it was recognised that the media are central to communicating the peace process, they are seen as less central for shaping and influencing the development of negotiations, which are conducted in confidence away from the media and often through intermediaries. It may be true that the television news media play an important role in terms of allowing political debate about the peace process to take place, but what appears less certain is how that debate impacts on the direction of policy. Moreover, the communication of the peace process through news acts as an attempt to legitimise or delegitimise developments which have generally already been tabled or are being discussed, so in that sense, news performs a facilitative function more than a mediative one.

When editors were questioned about the impact of political pressure on what they do, all were quick to insist that politics generally had a negligible affect on routines and decision-making. The autonomy of news organisations was strongly emphasised and editors were quick to point out how political efforts to influence coverage through coercion were nearly always unsuccessful. This independence from political control was also indicated by the argument that complaints came more from those occupying power than those in opposition. The inference being that this very fact illustrated a level of detachment from politics and an ability to criticise those in powerful positions.

Since most editors are preoccupied with the day to day pressures of resourcing and planning for news reports, it is perhaps not surprising that they did not present a picture of any real structural or cultural change in reporting the changing environment of Northern Ireland. Editors proved to be very aware of the recurrent difficulties of covering Northern Ireland and had a firm appreciation of what the peace process meant in political terms. They were also fully aware of what that meant in terms of changes to news content. However, the routine practice of allocating reporters, cameramen, time, visual effects and reacting to events as they happen (whether in a reflexive or predetermined way) proved to be very much the dominant concerns of editors and in that sense underlined how editorial policy and objectives had shifted little with regard to reporting the peace process in comparison to before. The daily conventions of constructing news and maintaining the cultural values of the organisations they work for are the main concerns of editors, not producing reports to assist, or facilitate, the development of conflict resolution in Northern Ireland (as morally desirable as that may be). Or, to put it another way, what editors do is driven more by the imperatives of news production than those of the political process.

The interview material in this chapter therefore reveals that editors regarded news stories about the peace process in much the same way as they did many other news stories. They viewed the primary role of news as challenging rather than supporting the political process, and their comments were broadly consistent with those of journalists in highlighting that the changing climate towards peace created problems for politicians principally because of a disparity between news values and reporting styles, and politics concerned with reconciliation and agreement which conflicted with those values and styles.

In order to test the comments and perceptions of politicians, journalists and editors, and to see if coverage functioned in ways which these groups have described, I will now look at television coverage of the IRA ceasefire of August 1994. By looking at news reports surrounding a key event in the peace process, I intend to see if news demonstrated an approach to reporting peace which underlines the views and experiences of those interviewed. By addressing how news made sense of the IRA ceasefire and represented that event within the peace process, we can see if it created problems for politicians and examine how reports constructed what was a major step towards peace.

6 A Study of News Content: the IRA Ceasefire of August 1994

Introduction

The purpose of this chapter is to examine television news coverage which surrounded the IRA ceasefire of August 1994 and to compare the implications of that coverage in relation to views expressed about reporting by politicians, journalists and editors. The value of this comparison is that it helps to test the validity of the interview material through actual examples of reporting, and provides primary evidence by which to assess the role of news in the political discourse(s) of the peace process.

A content analysis of 17 news reports which surrounded the Provisional IRA ceasefire of August 1994, from the earliest speculation about a possible ceasefire on 24 July 1994, to the ceasefire announcement itself on 31 August 1994 (Appendix 2), will provide useful information about how an important story in the peace process developed, and will enable us to further investigate the central concerns of this study, which are to do with the role of news in the development of negotiations, its representations of the peace process and the events within it, and whether news tended to support or obstruct political objectives concerned with promoting peace. By analysing how news represented the ceasefire story and how it constructed that development within the context of the peace process, this chapter will help to evaluate the comments of the three interview groups by considering them against evidence of news discourse and reporting styles. The central aim here, is therefore to see if the perceptions drawn from the interview material can be witnessed in the flow of news reports over a period of time, and to try and determine whether news functioned towards negotiations in ways which reflect the experiences of those interviewed.

Another aim of this chapter is to see if coverage of the ceasefire symbolised a paradigmatic shift in reporting and a clear rupture of confidence with the terrorism paradigm, or whether because of an inability to comprehend the extent of change going on, journalists merely portrayed the ceasefire as a tactical manoeuvre by the IRA, and so an extension of their war aims by other means. Or, to put it another way, to see if coverage of the ceasefire was constructed in ways consistent with the conflict paradigm of previous years, or whether it signalled a shift in reporting emphasis consistent with the emerging climate of peace.

Since the IRA ceasefire was a primary objective for those involved in the peace process, it seems relevant to see if news provided coverage which was helpful to that objective, or whether by constructing a ceasefire negatively, it was obstructive or unhelpful. Moreover, by seeking to evaluate how speculation about a ceasefire was conveyed as a series of messages which moved between the respective parties, this case study will highlight the role of the journalist as an intermediary in political communications, and enable us to further interrogate the political problem of negotiating peace through news.

In relation to the central concerns of this book then, this content analysis will provide discussion about the media's role within the peace process and its part in shaping communications around a key event in that process.

Speculation and Representation

Television news speculation of a possible IRA ceasefire which was eventually announced on 31 August 1994, emerged in news as early as 25 July, when it was reported that *if* a ceasefire were to be called, it would be short term, lasting approximately three months and would probably occur sometime in the autumn of 1994 (ITN 17.40, 25 July 1994). A firmer basis was given to this speculation a few weeks later when Sir Hugh Annersley, then Head of the RUC in Northern Ireland, publicly stated at a news conference that if a ceasefire were to happen, there would be a reduction in army and police patrols (BBC1 21.00, 11 August 1994). Annersley's comment which were seen by a number of Unionist MPs as a capitulation to IRA demands, was also evidence that a ceasefire was being discussed and represented a signal to Republicans that 'confidence-building' measures were being seriously considered by state forces as a response to the changing climate.

Anticipations of a likely ceasefire intensified during August, but articulations were ostensibly provided by government and Unionist commentators (Republicans downplayed the possibility of a ceasefire) who tended to interpret a ceasefire in terms of the problems, rather than the advantages, it might create. This frame of interpretation dominated in coverage up to and beyond the ceasefire announcement, couching the development in negative, rather than positive terms. Moreover, considering a possible ceasefire through the difficulties it might bring, reduced scope for a Republican propaganda victory by drawing attention away from the work being done by Republican leaders. Caution it seemed, was more appropriate than optimism at this time, thus when leaks were released to the media that an IRA ceasefire was imminent, the British government was said to have 'reacted cautiously', insisting that there 'would have to be a permanent renunciation and cessation of violence before talks could begin with Sinn Fein' (BBC1 21.00, 21 August 1994).

The demand for a 'permanent' end to violence, became a central concern in the ceasefire coverage, being emphasised by government officials as a minimum requirement for Sinn Fein's entry to political talks. As Northern Ireland Minister Michael Ancram put it, 'We are not prepared to enter into any form of dialogue, including the explanatory dialogue, with those who support violence, until there has been a permanent renunciation and cessation of violence on a credible basis' (BBC1 21.00, 21 August 1994). Any disparity between what constituted a permanent cessation of violence and a cessation of violence on a credible basis was ignored in coverage however, although the statement clearly signalled two messages, one giving scope for manoeuvre, aimed at the Nationalist community, and the other giving none and aimed at the Unionist community. Such joint expressions would regularly appear in responses to the media during the peace process and would be essential for supporting the attention of both communities, but the importance of joint messages remained largely unexamined by the media, whose interest resided more in the tone of comment rather than its content and implications.

During late August, the speculation about a ceasefire was subject to a number of conflicting messages. On 22 August, the IRA planted three packages in Regent Street, London. Two of those packages were said to be 'harmless', and a third was defused by the police. An ITN report stressed that the police had defused a 'bomb' (as opposed to an 'explosive device') which consisted of one and a half pounds of Semtex and expressed 'the IRA's warning was vague and had put at risk the lives of shoppers and tourists who had packed the West End's famous shopping area'. Anti-terrorist officers stressed that 'had it detonated, shoppers would have suffered terrible shrapnel injuries'. Whilst not stopping to question how police had come to discover the exact bin where the bomb was located on the basis of a vague warning, nor considering why the IRA was concentrating more on hitting key economic areas in England as part of an ongoing campaign, the news report underlined the conventional image of terrorist violence as being, pathological, ruthless and criminal. An image which contradicted speculation that the IRA were moving away from violence and which added weight to the concluding remark in the report that 'the police are warning against complacency, saying talk of an IRA ceasefire is just that – speculation. They say that the IRA demonstrated their true intentions in the centre of a tourist packed London' (ITN 17.40, 22 August 1998).

The Regent Street incident placed doubt on the notion that a ceasefire was being planned. The focus of the report on the possibilities of the damage and destruction which might have occurred, did not sit well with the idea that violence was coming to an end. In a real sense, this also demonstrated the inability of television news to consider developments which are on the face of it, inconsistent with each other. News could not present the fact that behind the surface of the violence, major changes and developments were taking place which were on the verge of bringing terrorism to an end. These two apparently conflicting notions, merely serve to underline how news cannot grasp political complexity and how it is especially unable to assess developments which are incremental, or slow. Thus after speculation about a ceasefire had been built up, it was now dashed and the picture turned to gloom. The gloom was reinforced by President of Sinn Fein, Gerry Adams who, in response to the Regent Street incident had unsurprisingly 'dismissed suggestions that the IRA is about to call a ceasefire', later saying that talk about a ceasefire 'was news to him and unhelpful'. Further contributing to the expectation that a ceasefire was incompatible with a campaign of ongoing violence, a BBC reporter saw the event as 'one part of Irish Republicanism's twofold message', this being 'that their campaign of violence continues and that they are able to attack when they want' (BBC1 21.00, 22 August 1994). In short, reporting emphasised the depravity of the perpetrators and maintained the myth that terrorism was motivated by criminal rather than political intentions (Latter 1988). It also demonstrated the propensity of journalists to arbitrate, create and amplify the rhetoric of condemnation (Alali and Odasuo and Eke 1991).

The reception of a possible ceasefire in negative terms was not only affirmed by the Regent Street bomb, but also by the prospect that it could lead to an intensification in Loyalist violence: 'real fear in the Unionist community that an IRA cessation will mean that they've secretly been sold out, and that Loyalist paramilitaries will as a result increase their violence' (BBC1 18.00, 22 August 1994). Thus it would be important, argued John Alderice leader of the Alliance Party, 'to think for a while before they [the government] make any response, and see if there is anything that any of us can do without simply caving in to terrorism' (BBC1 18.00, 22 August 1994). Channel 4's report of the same day took a broader view of events, but still underlined that a ceasefire was likely and that the likelihood of a cessation rested on whether 'Internal Republican debate has centred on whether the IRA should announce a fixed period ceasefire, or an open-ended one'. Reiterating the insistence of British and Irish governments that a ceasefire needed to be permanent, the report also included the words of former Northern Ireland Secretary Peter Brooke, who a few years previous had stated that 'Britain is committed to responding imaginatively to a cessation of violence' and positioned those words against those of Sir Hugh Annersley, who a few days earlier had announced that there would be 'a reduction in the level of army support and coverage' if a ceasefire were to be 'prolonged'. Raising questions about political reaction to a ceasefire not worded as permanent, the report broadcast the view of SDLP leader John Hume who stressed that 'the British government must respond to a ceasefire declaration even if it is not permanent, if the province is to have any chance of breaking out of the cycle of violence'. This was followed by the comments of SDLP chairman Mark Durkan, who remarked that 'if the threat of violence does not obtain', then 'security arrangements should be revisited' and a 'demilitarisation agenda should be positively explored and implemented during any prolonged ceasefire'. The statements given by the two SDLP members suggested that there was no great distance between the language of Sinn Fein and the SDLP, since Republicans had been talking for some time in terms of a need for 'demilitarisation' in Northern Ireland. However, the real significance of what Hume and Durkan had said lay in the fact that both were acknowledging the possibility of a forthcoming IRA ceasefire and this was recognised in the general thrust of the report, which concluded that 'there are signs from the Republican camp that any ceasefire announcement might be timed to coincide with a meeting' to be held later that week. Accordingly, stated the Channel 4 report, 'sources in both the British and Dublin governments are signalling that an IRA ceasefire is possible' (Channel 4 19.00, 22 August 1994).

Newsnight (BBC2 22.30, 22 August 1994) focused not so much on whether a ceasefire was possible, but whether it would be declared as permanent, thus implying that it was inevitable. The report stressed how 'one British–Irish all party group wrote to Mr Clinton warning him of the possibility of what it called a beguiling, but dangerous declaration by the IRA of an indefinite rather than a permanent ceasefire'. The 'peace group' mentioned was of course, merely a reiteration of how the government had conceived peace and not a reflection of Nationalist sentiment as expressed in the Channel 4 report. The definition of the peace group as 'all-party' constructed a notion of consensus which was misleading and which underplayed the contentions taking place. Most notable in the report was the negative representation of Republicanism, epitomised by Catholics living on the Falls Road in Belfast, where 'the majority of people who live there hold hardline Republican views' and 'most vote Sinn Fein and may have in the past lent their tacit support to the IRA's campaign of violence'. In the report, Catholics are bounded within a tight geographical location which reflects their apparently restrictive 'hardline' support for the IRA. As such, the identity of Catholics is constructed as an entity without explanation, context or contradiction. As a group, those of the Falls Road are categorised as supporters of violence, who condone and believe in the IRA's programme of violence and see it in largely acceptable terms. However, 'even here' continues the report, 'after 25 years, people are weary. They want peace and the word on the street is that an IRA ceasefire is imminent'. The implication being that war-weariness has set in even amongst those who are 'hardline' and that community support is eroding for the IRA's campaign which has been so fervently supported. The report does not ask the fundamental question of why support might be waning, neither does it address what has changed to bring this about. Rather, the IRA is depicted in a position of weakness by way of fading community support. This suggests that if a ceasefire occurs it will arise not because the IRA finds itself in a position of strength, but because it is in a position of vulnerability and deficiency.

In continuing to develop the point that if a ceasefire were to materialise it would do so out of dwindling support for Republican resistance, the *Newsnight* report focused on Sinn Fein's objections to the wording and layout of The Joint Declaration from a month beforehand, at Sinn Fein's annual conference. Interpreting that the conference (which is taken as a key indicator of Republican thinking) was badly handled by Sinn Fein and that objections to the declaration amounted 'to no more than a cynical fudge', the report stressed that Sinn Fein's credibility had 'sank to a new low' and had left them 'still needing to prove that they were serious about peace'. The claim was given further credence by academic Paul Arthur of Ulster University, who saw the Sinn Fein conference as 'yet another public relations disaster'. Arthur viewed the statements delivered by Sinn Fein as essentially appealing to two audiences, one being the Dublin government and the other the Republican movement itself. Yet appealing to both such audiences had according to Arthur created problems of clarity, made worse by Sinn Fein's inability to successfully manage its own image under the media spotlight. Overlooking any deliberate political desire by Sinn Fein to use a number of alternative statements so as to give scope for manoeuvre in negotiations, Arthur impressed the need for a ceasefire decision and noted the ambiguity surrounding the issue as a sign of uncertainty and weakness: 'There has been so much equivocation, there has been so much perhaps we will perhaps we won't, that they know they can't go on for much longer' (BBC2 22.30, 22 August 1994).

Newsnight also went on to suggest that a ceasefire rather than being a positive step toward peace, might even lead to an increase in violence from Loyalist groups, since such groups might reasonably interpret a ceasefire as evidence of a deal having been done with the British government and that 'the IRA are obviously only prepared to end their campaign albeit temporary, if they're seen to be given something in return'. In other words, a ceasefire runs the risk of making matters worse, creating a 'fear of what Protestants see as a British sell-out', something which 'is causing confusion and suspicion on the staunchly Protestant Shankhill Road'. Note here the proposition that Protestant supporters are 'staunch' as opposed to Republican supporters who are 'hardline', and that the possibility of a ceasefire is destabilising the community into 'fear', which risks moving from 'confusion and suspicion' into escalated violence. Reinforcing the idea that a step towards peace could increase violence, Ulster Unionist Party MP Martin Smyth further noted how there would be problems in the Protestant community 'If they believe there's been a further sell-out to IRA violence', leading to a situation where 'Loyalist paramilitaries would tighten the screw themselves'. We would also be wise to remember, that 'Republican paramilitaries are anxious to remind all that they are capable of instilling violence whenever they want', and that 'people in Northern Ireland and in Britain will need some convincing that an IRA ceasefire, if and when it does come, will be a genuine attempt at peace than merely a cynical ploy'.

Although explanation and comment appears to emphasise the views of government and supportive groups, it did however also contain signals which would have been of interest to Republicans. Following the reported assessment that an IRA ceasefire would in all probability produce negative consequences, there was a studio debate which included Niall O'Dowd, a representative from a US delegation due to visit Sinn Fein later that week, Sir Giles Shaw MP, Vice Chairman of the British and Irish Parliamentary Body, Greg Dyke, Conservative MP and Dr Ian Paisley of the Ulster Unionists. The debate sought to establish what kind of ceasefire would be acceptable and tried to map out how things would proceed if the necessary criteria were to be met. When at the beginning of the debate Sir Giles Shaw was asked what kind of ceasefire the IRA would have to announce in order to meet government demands and so gain Sinn Fein access to talks, he interestingly did not insist that a cessation had to be permanent, stipulating that 'Only a ceasefire which was (a) lasting and (b) credible and led to a renunciation of violence, would have the effect of triggering the offer, and the genuine offer has been made, that the Sinn Fein should become part of talks about constitutional progress in Northern Ireland'. This comment by Shaw was then modified into a more extreme set of demands, when in the next sentence he impressed 'the offer on the table made in the Downing Street Declaration must be accepted if there's to be any hope of a lasting – and the word lasting must be underlined – peace in the province'. Furthermore, before Sinn Fein were to be granted entry to talks, they must convince the IRA 'to actually renounce violence and renounce that violence permanently', a precondition which was 'not a bargaining counter', but actually 'a fact'.

Shaw's rather conflicting interpretation of how a ceasefire needed to be presented was then positioned alongside a more flexible response by Greg Dyke, who emphasised a 'wait- and see' approach. In effect, Dyke's approach also served to make pronounced the obstructive and resistant line of Ian Paisley. Paisley's intention to underline that the possibility of a ceasefire was evidence enough that the British government had capitulated to IRA demands, was in the context of the debate presented as an extreme position in contrast to Shaw and Dyke who were talking in terms of how a ceasefire should be received rather than what it signified at a political level. The positions of Shaw and Dyke (and the fact that both were used) illustrated how British responses were aimed at both Protestant and Nationalist communities, with each appearing to hold something of interest to a respective side. Shaw's apparently unyielding approach appealing to the more authoritarian elements of the Conservative Party and Unionist groups, and Dyke's softer, liberal line appealing more to Nationalist and Republican groups and moderates within the Conservative Party. Dyke's comments in particular, highlighted the scope for movement and offered broader interpretive possibilities for political movement if a ceasefire were called: 'The great thing is that now everyone has to be flexible, that's the point ... now is the chance for some forward movement, and I am quite optimistic there may be some interesting and significant steps in coming months and weeks' (*Newsnight* 22.30, 22 August 1994).

O'Dowd's input was oriented toward articulating the position of the American delegation rather than addressing how a ceasefire should be received by the British government. But the line of questioning by news anchor Peter Snow still attempted to see how similar the American position was in relation to that of Shaw (and not Dyke). O'Dowd's 'wait- and-see' response reinforced the need for pragmatism and suggested that America was more concerned with bringing the violence to a close, rather than stipulating conditions for how it should be brought to a close.

The questions of whether a ceasefire would lead to an upsurge in Loyalist violence and whether if announced, it would be declared as permanent, continued to dominate in coverage. On 26 August, an ITN report confirmed that an IRA ceasefire was impending, stating that 'senior sources in the intelligence services and in the Republican movement have told ITN a decision has been taken, and it's now a question of timing' (ITN 17.40, 26 August 1994). The imminence of a ceasefire was also covered at some length by Channel 4 news on the same day, which included an interview with Gerry Adams (Channel 4 19.00, 26 August 1994). Although Adams maintained that an IRA ceasefire remained 'continuing speculation', he did not flatly reject the possibility and this was taken as a key signal that it was being discussed. A further remark from Adams that there existed 'an historic opportunity to end the bloodshed' and that he 'did not distance himself from the speculation as he did recently', enhanced the credibility of the speculation and the likeliness of a forthcoming announcement. However, ignoring that the IRA and the British government had been communicating on a regular basis since 1989 (Bevins, Mallie and Holland 1993) and had been talking formally throughout 1993 (Adams 1995; McKittrick 1994), the report continued to emphasise the permanence issue and concluded: 'A ceasefire represents a big risk politically and militarily, and they're aware [the IRA] that even an open-ended ceasefire won't get them to the negotiating table with the British government. Only a full cessation of violence says London will do that.'

Attempting to critically represent the involvement of the American delegation in the peace process, Arthur Aughey of Ulster University appeared to assert that the main function of the delegation was 'more to do with the mood music of the Sinn Fein orchestrated peace process, rather than any substantial detail', apparently ignoring the extent of American involvement at that time (Coogan 1995) and failing to anticipate the extent of future involvement (O'Clery 1996; Mitchell 1999). Aughey's contribution also concentrated on what he saw as 'the growing resentment within the SDLP that Sinn Fein is now presenting itself as the leading force in Irish nationalism', an assertion which neglected to examine the long period of consultation between Gerry Adams and John Hume and how an emerging consensus between Sinn Fein and the SDLP would augment the chances of constitutional change (Adams 1995).

Adams in his interview emphasised a need for 'a demilitarisation of the situation', which would see 'all the armed groups ceasing their activity'. He stressed how 'a negotiated settlement' would also lead to 'democratic resolution of the conflict' which, given that it would be 'an inclusive, all embrasive process', would not alienate Unionists, who would be best served by an F. W. De Klerk like leader (the correlative implication being that he was an equivalent Nelson Mandela figure). The likelihood of this position finding agreement within the Unionist fraternity was quickly dashed however, when the report turned from the statements of Adams to William Ross MP, Chief Whip for the Ulster Unionist Party. According to Ross, the peace process would be more aptly named as 'the murder process', where the British government would have to meet continuing IRA 'demands' in order for any ceasefire to be maintained. In effect, the report underlined the disparity of Unionist and Republican positions and indicated how movement would be more likely to favour Nationalists than Unionists.

The position taken by Adams in the Channel 4 report was largely echoed by Sinn Fein Chief Executive Martin McGuiness, who appeared in *Newsnight* and also called for a 'total demilitarisation of the situation', which would incorporate 'the British military, the British intelligence services and the Loyalist death squads'. Bypassing the suggestion that an IRA ceasefire might be a 'cynical ploy', McGuiness focused on the need for 'an inclusive peace process' and noted that there were 'grounds for optimism' to 'move the peace process forward'. The report concentrated not so much on whether a ceasefire would occur (this was now largely excepted as highly likely), but 'the much talked about peace dividend'; in other words, what had Republicans been offered in return for a cessation of violence? That such a line of enquiry may have legitimised Unionist fears by implying that a deal had been done between Republicans and the British government, indicates the obstructive role played by news in relation to early moves towards peace. Indeed, it illustrates that if anything, news played a destabilising function by provoking fears and antagonisms, which could have been downplayed if attention had been given to the potentially positive or beneficial affects of a ceasefire, rather than the potentially negative and harmful affects.

The Provisional IRA Ceasefire – 31 August 1994

News speculation about a possible ceasefire proved to be well founded, when the Provisional IRA announced one on 31 August 1994. However, rather than examining what a significant gesture this was and how important it was for the development of peace, the news media tended to concentrate on the fact that it had not been worded as being permanent. As one ITN report put it, the IRA may have announced a 'complete ceasefire', but 'one word was missing

– permanent'. Furthermore, 'Downing Street insisted that without that word, talks could not take place with Sinn Fein'. For the news media the ceasefire was simplistically represented an end to the violence, as if it were entirely the responsibility of the IRA, i.e. 'after 25 years of violence, countless deaths and immense tragedy, the IRA's campaign is over'. This stereotypical portrayal also contained inaccuracies which tend to reinforce ignorance rather than understanding about Northern Ireland. For example, the deaths which have resulted there through violence are not 'countless', but, well documented (Sutton 1994), just as the number of killings by the IRA was exceeded by Loyalist groups from 1990 onwards.

These important details were neglected and deemed irrelevant however, as the attention was turned to dominant political responses and the permanence issue. Unionist reaction was led by William Ross MP who stressed 'I think that they've left out the word permanent leads me to view the whole thing with grave suspicion'. This emphasis on what the ceasefire was not (i.e. permanent) rather than what it was (a highly significant move towards peace), was indicative of the general tone of the ITN report and its tendency to reinforce dominant interpretations of the ceasefire announcement. The Downing Street response to the ceasefire, for example, was 'markedly cautious' rather than obstructive, and legitimately so given that 'the wording of the IRA announcement did not go far enough', or was not 'clear that this is indeed intended to be a permanent renunciation of violence'. Ulster Unionist leader James Molyneaux similarly noted that although there had been 'a halt to the killing', the problem still had to be faced that 'those who have influence with the IRA will now be able to persuade them to take the next decisive step and make the halt permanent'. Labour leader Tony Blair saw the ceasefire as a positive step but tempered the possibility of overreaction by stating how 'we would be foolish if we weren't cautious' or reduced pressure on insisting that violence 'ceases permanently' (ITN 17.40 31 August 1994).

The reaction of the Irish government to the ceasefire not being declared as permanent, highlighted a different attitude towards the announcement and was more in keeping Nationalist articulations and concerns. The Irish Prime Minister Albert Reynolds for example, reinforcing the line taken by SDLP leader John Hume that the omission of the word permanent was quite irrelevant, impressed 'We have a cessation of military operations, and the context of the whole statement makes it quite clear where the direction is. The direction is towards talks and negotiations'. The more positive reception provided by the Irish government and the apparent intention to appeal to Nationalist and Republican audiences, was nevertheless given negligible attention in comparison to the coverage given to the British government and supporting voices. All the major networks also carried a live interview with John Major about the government's interpretation of the ceasefire which consisted largely of open questioning and allowed the government to regain the public relations initiative which had been taken by Republicans through the ceasefire announcement.

The BBC took a similar view of the ceasefire as ITN and continued to portray the Republican movement in a negative light. As one Northern Ireland correspondent observed: 'Republican supporters at least, greeted the end of physical force as a political tactic, like a victory', a position apparently underlined by the reception given to Gerry Adams at a news conference in West Belfast, where he was 'greeted like a victor', and subsequently provided a statement 'with military language' (BBC1 18.00, 31 August 1994). Stating how Gerry Adams had 'listed things he wanted in return for this IRA cessation', the report then went on to broadcast Adams commenting 'We are demanding of Mr Major's government that he takes decisive steps now to move the situation forward in a fundamental way, and that means a demilitarisation of the situation, it means our prisoners home from England.' Such demands were represented as quite unacceptable given that the ceasefire did not amount to a permanent renunciation of violence, and it was because of this omission that understandably 'there was a careful cautious mood in Downing Street'.

The fact that both ITN and the BBC put major emphasis on the permanence issue and described the government's response as 'cautious' indicated a tendency to reproduce dominant expressions and concerns about the ceasefire which clearly proved more advantageous to the government's perception of how the ceasefire should be received and dealt with. Yet within the BBC report there existed an important signal to Republicans which suggested that the permanence issue was a matter of interpretation, rather than some absolute precondition. Or as Northern Ireland Secretary, Sir Patrick Mayhew put it: 'Once there is permanent renunciation of the use of violence and a permanent renunciation of the justification or support for violence, then within three months, the British government will be prepared to enter into preliminary discussions on three topics. How they can be brought into a democratic process, how they can ultimately come into the talks process, matters of that kind' (BBC1 18.00, 31 August 1994). The report did not question where a time period of three months had come from, or assess whether a ceasefire would be deemed to be permanent after three months regardless of whether it had been declared permanent by Republicans or not. What Mayhew's comment suggested is that ultimately, the acceptability of a ceasefire would be determined by government and that the permanence issue was in fact an attempt to regain the propaganda initiative. John Major in a live interview from Downing Street reinforced the stance taken by Mayhew, also presenting the permanence demand as something which would be decided by government when an acceptable time period of nonviolence had passed. To quote Major, 'Once we have a permanent renunciation of violence, a large number of options are open. We will consider those when we're clear we have permanent renunciation' (BBC1 18.00, 31 August 1994).

Rather than examine what Major meant by a 'large number of options' becoming open after a time frame had passed without violence, the BBC report then went on to focus on whether the ceasefire would lead to an escalation of Loyalist violence. This possibility was made more likely because that morning 'a 37 year old Catholic man was shot dead outside Antrim', and 'appeared to be a sectarian killing', according to police sources. The killing was followed by a statement 'from an umbrella group representing the Loyalist paramilitaries', who 'said they would not be dancing to the pan-Nationalist tune'. The suggestion in the report was that the killing had been a response to the ceasefire announcement, when in fact it occurred prior to the announcement, made just before midday (ITN 17.40, 31 August 1994). The BBC report implied a direct association between the two events however, legitimising the consideration that the ceasefire would lead to an increase in Loyalist violence and make the situation in Northern Ireland worse rather than better. The report then moved on to remind us of a statement released by 'the combined Loyalist terrorist leadership' made in July 1994 which said that if Republicans ceased their hostilities then Loyalists 'would respond to accommodate dialogue'. But, such dialogue would also depend on the guarantee of 'no diminution of the Northern Ireland position with the United Kingdom', where the 'people of Northern Ireland alone should determine the province's future', and where there would be 'no interference in internal jurisdiction in Northern Ireland'. Yet although this statement contradicted the assumption that an IRA ceasefire might exacerbate Loyalist hostilities, the report continued to view the ceasefire as a problem, which could lead to 'the very real threat of an escalation in Loyalist violence'; a prospect which apparently 'looms large'.

In attempting to broaden the consideration of Loyalist violence increasing as a result of the ceasefire, the report then looked at the 'siege mentality' which 'lingers in the Waterside', where Protestants 'fear the IRA ceasefire is the proof that it's winning and the union is being sold out'. Moreover, 'If peace is to follow this ceasefire, Protestants need convincing and fast that the price for it has not been the union with Britain and that the IRA hasn't won'.

In one sense, this could be viewed as an example of news being used to pressure concessions from political leaders to appease Protestant fears, but what is more certain, is that coverage represented the IRA ceasefire in ways highly unfavourable to the Republican position; not as an important, or useful step towards peace, but as a significant danger which could obstruct or undermine peace, by instigating further violence. Given this point of view, ' The penalty for raising false hopes in Northern Ireland has always been increased bloodshed' and in this case, if Protestant 'suspicions of betrayal prove correct, another opportunity for lasting peace would disintegrate' (BBC1 18.00, 31 August 1994). This emphasis was not related to the fact that the IRA had not declared their ceasefire permanent, but was a subject of concern because it represented a story about fear, conflict and speculation. And yet, to try and give some basis for this assertion, the report returned to the absence of permanent from the ceasefire statement to indicate that fears of an increase in violence were understandable given the apparent confusion about the IRA's commitment to peace.

For some journalists, if the ceasefire were permanent then the IRA could not be viewed as terrorists. Or, to put it another way, if a ceasefire were not worded as permanent then those who announce it remain terrorists. As one political correspondent summed it up, 'The Prime Minister is making it quite clear, they're not [the government] prepared to negotiate under duress, that's the point. If you remember, for years they have said they would not negotiate with terrorists, so what's the definition of a terrorist? Well obviously, if the IRA renounce violence permanently then they can be considered to be no longer terrorists and therefore negotiations can start up' (BBC1 18.00, 31 August 1994). Largely reaffirming the government line about the permanence wording as a precondition for negotiations, reports downplayed the fact that the government had been involved in negotiations with the Republican movement for years (*Setting The Record Straight*, 1994), thus effectively minimising critical appraisal of government responses to the ceasefire statement, and helping to legitimise government concerns.

Conclusion

Although this analysis highlights that television news referred overwhelmingly to elites for their views and comments on the IRA ceasefire and therefore tended to rely on dominant discourse, it also indicates that news did not portray the ceasefire in a manner which was particularly helpful towards the political objectives of those elites. Clearly, if the main desire of the British government was to get the IRA to relinquish violence and news depicted this move as quite dangerous and a threat to peace, then reporting cannot be seen as being obviously supportive towards political aims. However, this tendency also reflected an inability to fully comprehend changes in the political climate and an inclination to read the new political environment as a continuation of the old one. Because of this inability, the ceasefire though clearly desired by dominant groups, was interpreted by the news media, as an event with little background context and political significance (the ceasefire resulted from dialogues which began in 1988), and more of a tactical manoeuvre by the IRA to disrupt the peace process.

There is little doubt that the bulk of interpretation and comment about an IRA ceasefire was provided by groups opposed to Republicanism, who viewed a ceasefire in cautious or critical terms, but what news tended to do (in conflict with political aims) was to construct the ceasefire as something which would undermine rather than assist peace by leading to an increase rather than a decrease, in the level of violence in Northern Ireland. Moreover, although speculation within reports about the likelihood of a ceasefire announcement proved justified, the speculation about an upsurge in Loyalist violence did not. On the one hand, though this could be seen as part of a British government strategy to regain the propaganda initiative from Republicans by representing any move they might make towards peace as a problem, and so negatively. But, this should not detract from the overriding emphasis given in reports that the ceasefire was a move consistent with motives which were more to do with past conflict than future peace. As such, the IRA ceasefire was presented not so much as a key step in the development of the peace process, but as something designed to obstruct that peace. Conventional representations of Republican motivations (which meant associations with terrorism) were clearly adopted in reports surrounding the ceasefire of 1994, which notably meant referring to developments through the conflict paradigm rather than the peace process paradigm.

Having said that, what this analysis also brings to light is that news can be more than a mouthpiece for the British government and its supporting voices, offering other possibilities for communicating the development of peace. For example, although there was a clear dominant emphasis within reports, there was also a secondary emphasis allowing for a promotion of positions different from the dominant line, which signified scope for interpretation, discussion and perhaps most importantly, movement. There are instances in this analysis which illustrate how news can be used to promote different positions and nuances which appeal to correspondingly different audiences and groups. These tend to oscillate around harder, fixed reactions and softer, more flexible ones. In turn, each represents something of interest to Unionist and Nationalist denominations and sends a signal to each side (as well as both) with potential for development. Republicans for example, would be more receptive and interested in the idea that a ceasefire should facilitate an imaginative and flexible response from the British government, whilst Unionists would, in general, be more keen to emphasise stringent preconditions which restrict the chances of development, or movement.

Furthermore, whilst Nationalists would find themselves agreeing more with the emphasis given to the ceasefire statement given by the Irish government, Unionists would be more prone to support the British government's explicit demands and preconditions, designed to exact maximum pressure on the IRA and limit the extent of manoeuvre they might have. It thus appears to be the case, that although news served to ostensibly promote the views and opinions of the British government with regard to a ceasefire, it also at times gave scope for more flexible articulations which seemed designed to appeal to Nationalist and Republican groups. Given this tendency, it could be argued that news can operate as a communicative device which has implications for diplomatic activity, or what Miller has referred to as 'megaphone diplomacy' (Miller 1994: 283–4).

Overall, the news media concentrated much more heavily on the potential disadvantages which might derive from a ceasefire rather than the potential advantages. Reports tended to reiterate similar concerns about suggested deals, growing unrest between Protestant and Nationalist communities, a war-weariness amongst the Republican grassroots support, threats of retaliation in response to a possible 'sell-out' by the British government and doubts about a commitment to nonviolence because the ceasefire announcement made no reference to being permanent. Given the consideration and emphasis of such problems, it is not surprising that news tended to obstruct or hinder, rather than facilitate constructive dialogue, promoting negative more than positive reaction. Moreover, whether the speculation helped to bring about the ceasefire is most unlikely. Indeed, as interview material in this study reveals, if anything, the speculation hindered the ceasefire by creating an expectation for its announcement that Republicans may have preferred to resist.

Using this analysis to consider how news constructed a key event in the early stages of peace, it seems apparent that the peace process paradigm took some time to take hold in reporting. In the case of the IRA ceasefire of 1994, reporting generally failed to make sense of how the political landscape had shifted in Northern Ireland, or how Republicanism had changed within the developing climate of peace. However, even though, as during the conflict paradigm, news tended to promote the interests and concerns of dominant political groups (and at times overwhelmingly so), it also contained other nuances and communicative signals which offered a different trajectory from that emphasised by the central message, and in that sense reflected a shift. But, it is hard to conclude from this study that coverage helped to facilitate a ceasefire. If anything, reporting appeared to undermine the credibility of a ceasefire by representing it as a move which could inflame tensions and so undermine peace. A prospect which seemed to be in opposition with the thinking of dominant political groups who had striven to bring it about.

This chapter tends to confirm rather than dispute the interview comments of politicians, journalists and editors and their experiences of the news within the peace process. It underlines how news maintained a preoccupation with values concerned with conflictual scenarios, negativity and simplistic interpretation and how these conventions of reporting were prioritised over examination of the political change and negotiation which was going on. Unable to fully comprehend or explain the significance of the ceasefire and how the political climate has shifted to bring it about, reporting failed to locate and examine this considerable step towards peace within the complex political context from which it derived, or represent it in ways which were consistent with dominant political objectives.

The findings of this research have theoretical implications for understanding the role of television news in politics and moments of political change. To highlight those implications and how they contribute to knowledge about the impact of news on the political process, this study will now consider three important theories which address the relationship between news and politics, the impact of reporting during a climate of political change, and the media's role within political conflict and peace. It will use those theories to point out what are seen as central arguments in debates about the interaction between news and politics, and evaluate those arguments in the light of the research findings from this study. Although the content of the theories used here varies in approach and orientation, they nevertheless investigate issues and concerns which have been central to this study and which need revisiting, given what has been discovered from this research.

7   News, Politics and Conflict

Introduction

The purpose of this chapter is to look at three theories which address the relationship between news, politics and conflict and to consider those theories in relation to the research material used in this study. The research findings of this study have implications for thinking about the impact of news on politics and reference to established theories such as those used in this chapter will help to make pronounced those implications and highlight the significance of this study as a contribution to media theory. Each of the theories is concerned with how politics and news interact and the role of news in relation to conflict, the political process and peace.

My main intention here is to outline the key points and arguments of each theory and to take into account critiques which have engaged within debates which the theories have stimulated, before then considering those points and arguments in relation to the research evidence from this study. Based on what has been discovered from the interview data, I will then offer some recommendations for thinking about the limitations of such theories. This will not only indicate potential shortcomings in how the arguments they offer grasp the complexities of interaction between news and political objectives, but will also help to make apparent the need for a more complex appreciation of the dynamic which exists between news and politics, as demonstrated by the role of news in peace negotiations. I conclude this chapter by calling for a need to continue further empirical studies on the role of news within political processes, which will help to develop the progressive and detailed analysis needed in order to understand the complex role played by news in modern political affairs.

In the first of those theories, Stuart Hall's structuralist conceptualisation of politico-media relations depicts journalism as a largely subordinate practice, which reproduces and reinforces dominant articulations about social order and conflict. Hall reaches this conclusion by focusing on the political representations used in news which construct a 'primary definition' of problems and responses and which invite expectant solutions that elites tend to benefit from. From this perspective, news is an extension of political power and a means of legitimising political order.

In the second theory being looked at, Daniel Hallin's analysis of how the news media covered the Vietnam war on the other hand, is concerned with how coverage amplified political frictions and contributed to a rupture of political unity about the war. In that sense, and in contrast to Hall, Hallin emphasises the affect of news on politics as well as the other way round and draws our attention to the potentially destabilising impact which news can have on politics. Though Hallin, like Hall, acknowledges the reproductive tendencies of news in relation to dominant discourse, he nevertheless highlights that political reporting is an interactive process which cannot always be easily controlled by those who represent the political process.

In the third theory being examined, Gadi Wolfsfeld takes this path of enquiry further, by depicting the media environment as the principal arena for political debate and formulation and views news coverage as central to the development of political discourse and political contestation. Although Wolfsfeld, like Hall and Hallin, recognises that news relies on political articulations of problems and tends to reiterate those articulations in reports, he nevertheless brings our attention to the constructed nature of political discourse in news and highlights the mediative role played by news in political decision-making.

Particularly interesting in the work of Wolfsfeld is his study of how news engages with and promotes peace (interesting in the sense that this study is also concerned with similar questions). Wolfsfeld finds here that even though dominant political articulations may emphasise the need for peace and reconciliation in a peace process, such articulations may not necessarily be supported by news, which is more concerned with conflict, antagonism and crisis. In a real sense, this throws open new questions about the role of the news media in politics and challenges the notion that news is a subordinate practice. Rather, it suggests that news can sometimes undermine political activity, or at least create problems for it and that it does so especially when political aims do not 'fit' with the conventions of news construction.

The theories of Hall, Hallin and Wolfsfeld have been used here because they provide three conceptualisations about how the news media engage with politics which together form a broad appreciation for how news operates in relation to political power. Furthermore, they raise different but equally important questions about the ability of politicians to control the media which have relevance for the purposes of this study. Political efforts to control the media are clearly subject to contestation between political groups and this is to some extent acknowledged by Hall, but ultimately underestimated. Hallin addresses this deficiency by looking at how news can amplify dissensus and division between politicians and how this is especially pronounced during a of a period of political change. This perspective is then taken further by Wolfsfeld who views news as the central arena for political conflicts to be played out today, and it is because of this tendency to emphasise conflict he argues, that news tends to be more obstructive than helpful for the promotion of peace.

Primary Definition and News as Hegemony

Stuart Hall's essay 'The Social Production of News' (1978) raises important questions about the news media's role in reproducing and legitimising political discourse and power. It also has particular relevance for understanding interactions between politics and news, and still holds as an important theoretical perspective on the sociology of journalism (Schlesinger and Tumber 1994: 17–21). For Hall, political elites are able to create a 'primary definition' of problems which shape public perceptions and this defining process is structured through the news media which ideologically reproduces the comments and viewpoints of those elites. Hall argues that it is because of a close relationship with political power that the media, 'play a crucial secondary role in *reproducing* the definitions of those who have privileged access, as of right, to the media as "accredited sources"'. From this point of view, 'in the moment of news production, the media stand in a position of structured subordination to the primary definers' (Hall 1978: 59). In emphasising how the media reproduce dominant strands of discourse when reporting deviance, Hall's analysis also has implications for considering coverage of Northern Ireland, where news constructions of terrorism have conventionally provided a consensual picture emanating from dominant political viewpoints (Elliott 1977; Butler 1995; Rolston and Miller 1996).

Referring in particular to how dominant discourse is carried in reports and how such discourse helps to construct a 'preferred reading' of events, Hall draws attention to the 'structured relationship' between journalists and elites, which, 'permits the institutional definers to establish the initial definition or *primary definition* of the topic in question. This interpretation then "commands the field" in all subsequent treatment and sets the terms of reference within which all further coverage or debate takes place' (Hall 1978: 58). For Hall, it is precisely because of the 'systematically structured over-accessing to the media of those in powerful and privileged institutional positions', that the media are seen as an extension of political control, which operates 'faithfully and impartially, to reproduce symbolically the existing structures of power in society's institutional order' (ibid.: 58).

Drawing on Gramsci's concept of hegemony in order to explain how the media shape social consensus, where values and ideas about society and its structures are represented in common sense fashion, Hall notes how messages about social order construct 'the distinction between those who are fundamentally *of* society and those who are *outside* of it' (ibid.: 68), and views this representation as indicative of how the media 'serve to "frame" events within dominant interpretive paradigms' (ibid.: 65). To put it simply, Hall is arguing that since the news media rely on powerful groups and elites for information and comment, they also prioritise the viewpoints and opinions of those groups and invite the rest of us to share similar positions. For Hall, the media's main function is 'to reproduce the ideological field of society in such a way as to reproduce, also its structure of domination' (ibid.: 346),

This consensus model also receives attention in the work of Ericson, Baranek and Chan, who in examining the media's construction of deviance also emphasise its hegemonic tendencies. In their study *Visualising Deviance* (1987), the authors underline the reproductive nature of the media in relation to dominant discourse, viewing its main purpose as 'producing common social knowledge and cultural values' (Ericson et al. 1987: 17). The importance of the news media for the stability of the political system is seen to result from cultural and social classifications which are shaped by political institutions, and it is through the close and routinised interactions of the news media with those institutions which allow dominant ideologies to be reproduced. Like Hall, the authors emphasise the access of elites to the media and a predisposition toward ideological positions articulated by those elites, highlighting that the news media itself is political in orientation to the subjects it reports and that 'As part of politics, the news media have the characteristics of politics and contribute to the political process' (ibid.: 39). Underlining how the news media function as a mechanism of social control and serve as agents of control in the process, the authors note:

> Journalists are central agents in the social construction of reality about deviance and control. They shape the moral boundaries and contours of social order, providing an ongoing articulation of our senses of propriety and impropriety, stability and change, order and crisis. They underpin the authority of certain other control, agencies and agents, offering them preferred access and framing issues and events in their terms. They are control agents themselves, using their

power of imprinting reality in the public culture to police what is being done in the microcultures of bureaucratic life, including especially the activities of other control agencies (ibid.: 356).

Hall's reading of the ideological effects of news discourse and its clear influence on the work of Baranek at al. is questionable on a number of fronts. Schlesinger and Tumber for example, raise six highly pertinent criticisms. First, note the authors, the totalising conceptualisation offered 'does not take account of contention between official sources, in trying to influence the construction of a story' (Schlesinger and Tumber 1994: 18). Second, Hall's argument 'fails to register the well established fact that official sources often attempt to influence the construction of a story by using '"off-the-record" briefings – in which case the primary definers do not appear directly as such, in unveiled and attributable form' (ibid.). Third, there is no explanation of why the boundaries of 'primary definition' shift, or why access to 'recognised "representative" voices' is unequal. That is, 'There is nothing in the formulation of primary defining that permits us to deal with such inequalities of access amongst the privileged themselves' (ibid.). Fourth, there is no real consideration of how shifts within the power structure occur, or how new forces emerge. 'Thus, the media are characterised as a subordinate site for the reproduction of the ideological field; in effect, they are conceived as "secondary definers"' (ibid.: 19). Fifth, Hall tends 'to overstate the passivity of the media as recipients of information from news sources: the flow of definitions is seen as moving uniformly from the centres of power to the media'. From this position 'there is no space to account for the occasions on which the media may themselves take the initiative in the definitional process by challenging the so-called primary definers and forcing them to respond' (ibid.). And sixth, Hall's argument 'renders largely invisible the activities of sources that attempt to generate "counter-definitions". This rules out any analysis of the process of *negotiation* about policy questions between power-holders and their opponents that may occur prior to the issuing of what are assumed to be primary definitions' (ibid.: 20). In their conclusion on the weaknesses of Hall's argument, Schlesinger and Tumber sum up:

> The key point is that because the conception of 'primary definition' resolves the question of source power on the basis of structuralist assumptions, it closes off any engagement with the dynamic processes of contestation in a given field of discourse. It has the signal advantage of directing our attention to the exercise of definitional power in society, but it offers no account of how this is achieved as the outcome of strategies pursued by political actors. That is because 'primary

definers' are seen as simply guaranteed access to the news media in virtue of their structural position. To sum up: 'primary definition', which ought to be an empirically ascertainable outcome, is held instead to be a priori effect of privileged access (ibid.: 21).

The issue of contestation between groups who compete for definitional advantage over a problem is also highlighted by Miller in his consideration of 'primary definition' and the Northern Ireland situation. Although Miller notes that 'On the face of it, there can be few issues in British politics where it is more likely that "primary definition" could be secured than the issue of the conflict in Ireland' (Miller 1993: 386), he identifies three areas which make questionable the ability of official sources to gain definitional advantage. These he lists as, 'divisions within organisations (for example, personal, professional or political); 'the effect of different levels of competition and co-operation between organisations'; and 'the impact of news values' (ibid.: 386–7). Even here, against a broad political consensus on terrorism and the Northern Ireland problem, Miller outlines competing tensions between sources and indicates a considerable weakness in the 'primary definition' argument. It is worth quoting at length Miller's concluding remarks on this issue:

> the ability of any source to gain definitional advantage is related to active negotiation and contestation. To put it in a less media-centred way, the strategies formulated by organizations to exercise power and influence often involve strategies for definitional advantage. It is important that it is recognized that the massive resources at the disposal of the central institutions of the state give them a significant advantage in struggles for definition, but that there are limits to state attempts at agenda-building. These relate to the cohesiveness of any organization and its abilities to co-ordinate its activities with other organizations in a unified power bloc. They also relate to the ability to formulate strategies with which to compete with the opposition, which itself may be more or less divided or powerful. Finally, the routine operations of media organizations cannot be relied upon to coincide with the presentational requirements of governmental initiatives.
>   When the state is relatively united and actively pursuing a media strategy, then it is rare indeed to find a strong media opposition. However, the relative unity of the state is not affected by pressure from the top but also by pressure from below. That is to say the power to define does not only, or even pre-eminently, rest with the state (ibid.: 401–2).

However, though Hall's hegemonic emphasis assumes that common values or a dominant ideology are necessary for social order when they may not be

(Turner 1990: 245), just as cultural and ideological consensus shared by elites may not become absorbed or necessarily shared by other subordinate groups in society (ibid.: 254), it nevertheless still provides a pertinent (if limited) conceptualisation of relations between the news media and official sources. It is clear enough that a process of contestation between sources goes on and that this illustrates how 'primary definition' neglects the nature of struggle over definition of issues.

News demands for information and the availability of elites to provide that information reinforce the relationship of power between the two and it is through this interaction that some reproduction of dominant discourse becomes inevitable. Underlining Hall's argument and further highlighting how news draws on the interpretations of elites as a matter of convention, Gans observes:

> The means by which sources gain access to journalists, source considerations, and the relationships between reporters and their sources feed into each other to create a cumulative pattern by which journalists are repeatedly brought into contact with a limited number of the same type of sources. Eager and powerful sources which need to appear in the news first become suitable because they can always supply information, and then because they satisfy the source considerations for authoritativeness and productivity. The most regular sources develop an almost institutionalised relationship with the news organisation (ibid.: 144).

Furthermore, though journalists strive for some sense of detachment from the opinions of the sources they rely upon (Gans 1980: 183–90; McNair 1994: 22–38), the extent of this detachment is both limited and shaped by the relationship between journalist and source. Journalists would be unwise to alienate or undermine their relationship with sources (jeopardizing informational contacts), and so tend to not contradict the comments which those sources provide. Given this close interaction and mutual reliance, journalistic autonomy though an aspiration, becomes a balancing act, where 'acceptable' criticism of sources has to be ensured, if the relationship is to continue. As Gans observed when examining this process:

> Sources alone do not determine the news, but they go a long way in focusing the journalists' attention on the social order ... Neither do sources alone determine the values in news, but their values are implicit in the information they provide. Journalists do not, by any means, parrot these values, but being objective and detached, they don't rebut them either (ibid.: 145).

By initiating events which appear to meet criteria for being newsworthy (ibid.: 129–31), sources then provide journalists with information, which it useful and relevant are reproduced in reports. If sources respond to press interest quickly and deliver information in the form required then this also increases the chances of information being used. As Negrine puts it 'By making it easier for reporters to collect information, sources may be better able to ensure that their version of events come to the fore' (Negrine 1996: 27).

But, this process of information collection and distribution by journalists though complex, also indicates the rather mythical nature of the journalist as impartial and objective observer, since news coverage depends ostensibly on reacting to and reproducing structures of discourse determined by the political establishment. Or, as McNair puts it:

> The broadcasters' concept of *impartiality* for example, works to contain political debate within a more or less tightly drawn consensus, which admits only an established political class and marginalises or excludes others. In coverage of politics ... impartiality means giving equal representation (representation proportionate to an organisation's electoral support) to the main political parties, particularly during election campaigns (McNair 1995: 58).

However, as McNair also reminds us, this

> does not mean the reporting of all significant participants to a political debate. In Northern Ireland, 'impartiality' was explicitly withheld from the paramilitary organisations and their political wings, because they operated outside the established democratic structures of the United Kingdom's constitutional system. The broadcasting ban introduced by the Conservative government in 1989 and removed only in 1994, prevented television and radio from airing the voices of some elected Northern Ireland politicians because they were deemed to support those who challenged the legitimacy of the British state (ibid.).

The hegemonic approach adopted by Hall emphasises how journalists rely on official sources and the interpretations they provide. But, what Hall fails to adequately acknowledge is how those official sources contend for ideological and definitional prominence in reports. Gitlin's contribution to the hegemonic debate addresses this problem and presents the contestation process as something 'continually to be renewed, recreated and defended', and which must be 'continually challenged and in certain respects modified' (Gitlin 1980: 257). The modification which Gitlin talks of derives from the competing forces which engage within the dialogue of news discourse. Gitlin underlines that although there is clearly an ideological dominance which comes from news reports and that this dominance reflects elite opinion, this dominance is still subject to oppositional interpretations (however slight) and is not the result of one view leading to the exclusion of all others. Indeed, the dominance of certain viewpoints must be presented as convincing in order to remain dominant and achieves this best by demonstrating the limitations and weaknesses of other viewpoints. As Gitlin puts it, 'the hegemonic ideology of bourgeois culture is extremely complex and absorptive; only by absorbing and domesticating conflicting values, definitions of reality, and demands on it, in fact does it remain hegemonic' (ibid.: 256).

Gitlin's assessment of how news operates to promote ideological dominance recognises the importance of political contestation much more than Hall who tends to overstate the reproductive tendencies of news. However, even Gitlin's analysis does not fully appreciate that news can cause problems for elites precisely because of a propensity to emphasise and amplify conflict. That, I would argue is the central weakness of arguments which favour Hall's hegemonic approach to politics and news. Not only does Hall understate the process of contestation which goes on in news and that news can create problems for dominant groups by representing their arguments as unconvincing just as they can represent them as convincing, but, he fails to consider what happens when political environments change and what problems news can manufacture during that change. As will be argued in the conclusion, Hall's perspective is useful when considering the role of news in relation to subjects which tend to promote consensus and so has particular value when considering news coverage of 'The Troubles' in Northern Ireland when reporting played a supportive function in relation to state objectives and responses. But, the hegemonic approach he outlines is not adequate for explaining the role of news in relation to political change. It is not therefore adequate for explaining how the consensus over terrorism changed to the dissensus over peace or how that change became contested in news. Most importantly, it does not help us to interrogate the problems which news can cause for politicians when the political climate undergoes transition.

From Consensus to Dissensus and the Impact of News on Policy

The issue of contestation between sources and the impact of news during a climate of political change, is given particular attention by Hallin, who, in his study of media coverage of the Vietnam War addressed 'the relatively neglected questions of shifts in news content over time and the functioning of the media as political institutions' (Hallin 1994: 42). Hallin's argument is based on the observation that the news media can shift from reproducing political consensus to accelerating a collapse of that consensus, but importantly, that such a collapse is initiated by the political process under change, rather than through the impetus of coverage. His point being that a paradigm shift in coverage is shaped by the polity and in response to political change, not the other way round.

Examining how the news media reflected the dissensus among elites as the Vietnam War progressed (ibid.: 43). Hallin, utilises a conception of journalism which depicts reporting in terms of three regions which collectively represent the transitional features of moving from consensus to dissensus. Picturing the three regions as concentric spheres, Hallin, explains the spheres thus:

> The province of objectivity is the middle region, which can be called the Sphere of Legitimate Controversy. This is the region of electoral contests and legislative debates, of issues recognized as such by the major established actors of the American political process. The limits of this sphere are defined primarily by the two-party system – by the parameters of debate between and within the Democratic and Republican parties – as well as by the decision-making process in the bureaucracies of the executive branch. Within this region, objectivity and balance reign as the supreme journalistic virtues.
>
> Bounding the Sphere of Legitimate Controversy on one side is what can be called the Sphere of Consensus. This is the region of 'motherhood and apple pie'; it encompasses those social objects not regarded by the journalists and most of the society as controversial. Within this region journalists do not feel compelled either to present opposing views or to remain disinterested observers. On the contrary, the journalist's role is to serve as an advocate or celebrant of consensus values.
>
> And beyond the Sphere of Legitimate Controversy lies the Sphere of Deviance, the realm of those political actors and views which journalists and the political mainstream of the society reject as unworthy of being heard (Hallin 1989: 116–17).

Noting that the boundaries between the spheres are somewhat fuzzy, Hallin nevertheless uses the model to explain how news reporting can move from supporting political consensus to undermining that consensus and how explanation of political positions can shift from the sympathetic to the controversial.

This transition, which according to Hallin developed in coverage of the Vietnam War from mid-1967 and was accelerated by the Tet Offensive (Hallin 1994: 53), is 'best explained as a reflection of and a response to a collapse of consensus – especially of elite consensus – on foreign policy' (ibid.). It is thus an amplification of division which is exaggerated by the emotional emphasis given to stories by television news; a medium able 'to generate much more intense political reactions than other media' (Hallin 1989: 123).

Highlighting the 'media's fluidity and adaptability in the context of a fluid, dynamic political system, governed not by a single ruling class, but by rotating elites drawn from different parties and factions within parties' (McNair 1995: 60), Hallin's conceptualisation argues McNair, underlines how 'adaptability of the media to shifting lines of debate is essential to the retention of their legitimacy as facilitators of political discourse in the public sphere and hence, ultimately, to their "hegemonic" role' (ibid.). On the one hand, although the work of Hallin, brings to attention the potential of the media to disrupt politics, he also argues that this disruption reflects the divisions and disorganisation within the polity to begin with, and that therefore the media reflects rather than drives political dissensus. Hallin notes that constructions of dissensus are not so much 'determined by the dramatic nature of the medium itself', but based on 'the prevailing ideology of society as well as on the particular historical conjuncture, which brings certain elements of that ideology to the fore and pushes others into the background' (Hallin 1989: 124). He points out that even if television news promotes contesting positions within reports as a matter of convention, it will nevertheless tend to emphasise the ideological dominance of certain positions and that this is reflective of the relative dominance such positions occupy within the polity at a particular moment in time. In that sense, the news media follow rather than instigate political trends and movements.

Summarizing his findings on the interpretive shift applied to coverage of the Vietnam War through news, Hallin writes:

> the case of Vietnam suggests that whether the media tend to be supporting or critical of government depends on the degree of consensus those policies enjoy, particularly within the political establishment. In a limited sense, the mirror analogy is correct. News content may not mirror the facts, but the media as institutions, do reflect the prevailing pattern of political debate; when consensus is strong, they tend to stay within the limits of the political discussion it defines; when it begins to break down, coverage becomes increasingly critical and diverse in the viewpoints it represents, and increasingly difficult for parties to control. This does not necessarily imply that the media's role is purely passive or unimportant. It seems likely, on the contrary ... that the media not only reflect but strengthen prevailing political trends, serving in a time of consensus as consensus maintaining institutions, and contributing, when consensus breaks down to a certain point, to an accelerating expansion of the bounds of political debate. If this interpretation is correct, however, the media are clearly intervening and not ... independent variables in the process by which political support is generated or broken down (Hallin 1994: 55).

Therefore, as long as political unity is maintained towards particular issues and situations it would appear that unity is reinforced and underlined by news coverage, but (and perhaps more interestingly), when that unity dissolves into splits/divisions/differences, then the media amplify antagonisms by giving prominent attention and expression to the conflicts involved. The protagonists must then respond to the expression of those conflicts which become absorbed into the political process, so in that sense the news media are able to exert pressure and influence on politics.

However, we should not forget that the continuing tension between news and politics which is built on the contradiction of journalistic attachment towards and detachment from the political process, is always conducted within a political environment and so in that sense, politically influenced. It should also be noted that the extent of journalistic detachment from politics is ultimately affected by its disposition towards the political system within which it operates, and that news reflects rather than determines that process. It was lack of political unity and not a subversive media which contributed to the news media changing its exposition of the Vietnam War. Indicating how a disintegration of political consensus corresponded with a more critical stance in reporting, Williams observed: 'Differences that existed inside the political establishment were exposed as the war progressed and the White House found it increasingly difficult to set the agenda for the media' (Williams 1993: 307). Referring to how the fracture of political consensus was accelerated by news attention which focused on the dissensus arising from that fracture, Williams concludes his analysis (largely echoing the findings of Hallin) thus:

> Elite sources are not always successful in their attempts to dictate the agenda. The political elite is not homogeneous and the divisions are reflected in the media's reporting. For example, in the early days of Vietnam the disagreement over how the war should be fought was a part of the media's agenda. However, such disagreement was within the boundaries of appropriate and responsible debate, in other words a debate between elite sources. The reporting of the Vietnam war did not reflect the growing opposition to the war among the public. As this opposition grew the media coverage, by and large, followed the White House's view of the war being waged successfully and effectively by the United States armed forces. It was only when divisions inside the elite concerning the very nature of the war itself emerged that the media took the cue from their informants and became more critical in their reporting (ibid.: 326).

The findings of Hallin and Williams strongly indicate that the media's ability to create problems for politicians is derived particularly from its ability to amplify divisions and dissensions which already exist in the political arena. But although the amplification of problems may affect political behaviour by stimulating particular kinds of response, these tend to fit more the short term interests of news and less the long term more complex aims of policy-making. Here, it would appear that the main political function of news is to prepare public opinion for policy change and development, rather than initiate that change and development, and that 'The media provide a central nervous system for this constituency-building process' (Rotberg, Weiss 1996: 10). Though there are examples of where it is difficult to see how the news media could not affect political policy (in the case of Northern Ireland we might ask would the British and Irish governments have adopted stronger anti-terrorist legislation if it were not for the harrowing television and press images of the Omagh bombing?) it would seem that overall, the impact of coverage is rather tangential or ineffective on policy decision-making, and that the process of policy-making is driven ostensibly by political interests and intentions (Natsios 1996: 152–9).

Clearly, for Hallin and Williams political coverage is reflective of interactions within the polity and moves in time with changes which occur in that polity, but technological developments coupled with increasing news distribution systems have brought new pressures to bear on politics which centre on speed and response, raising new considerations about the relationship between news and the policy- making process. However, even against these new pressures there are doubts concerning the impact of news on the policy-building process. Rather than shape and incite actual policy decisions, the news media tend to shape the space and time within which decisions are made, therefore 'From a policy-maker's perspective, the omnipresence of the media compresses reaction time for deliberation, and makes contingency planning and readiness more important' (Shattuck 1996: 174). A prominent pressure which television news brings on the policy process derives from the expectations that it creates for action. But, as Rotberg and Weiss observe, this action can have various functions and effects and can operate at different political levels. That is:

> First the media may be employed to project messages within the bureaucracy. A news story can be a 'super interoffice memo'. Second, the media may be used to set an agenda. For example, the media, carefully briefed, helped launch controversial change in food aid policy during the Somalia crisis. Third, the media may be used to build a constituency for action (Rotberg and Weiss 1996: 188).

Though the news media may follow a story in ways which can negatively affect the progression of political action because coverage may develop a momentum and direction of its own with political consequences (Jones 1996), it seems evident that the ability of news to influence foreign policy is highly limited by the dependence of journalists on official groups for information and the political arena from which that information is disseminated. As Merin discovered in his examination of the American television news networks in their reporting of the American intervention in Somalia in 1992, 'television coverage of Somalia in the summer and fall of 1992 did not originate in the independent actions of journalists but in the interaction of journalists engaged in routine newsgathering practices and sources in Washington who made efforts to get Somalia onto the foreign policy agenda' (Merin 1997: 386). Highlighting how the story about American intervention was instigated by political rather than journalistic motivations, Merin notes that 'only when Washington turned its attention to Somalia did ABC, CBS, and NBC deem events there worthy of coverage' (ibid.), and that 'journalists worked closely with governmental sources in deciding when to cover Somalia, how to frame the story, and how much coverage it deserved' (ibid.: 389). Merin also underlines how the risks of American intervention were limited by politically induced articulations of possible counterproductive affects, and that such articulations limited the scope for politically damaging news. That is, 'if ABC influenced American policy in crystallizing and amplifying the political stakes in Somalia, it is American politics – and the situation in Bosnia – that created those stakes in the first place and that is the frame through which ABC interpreted events in Somalia and the U.S. response' (ibid.: 396–7). Although acknowledging that television news coverage of American intervention played an important role in helping to legitimise that intervention, Merin emphasises that foreign policy decisions tend to be made *prior to* rather than *because of* news coverage and concludes his study:

> Television is clearly a player in the foreign policy arena, but the evidence from Somalia is that journalists set the news agenda and frame the stories they report in close collaboration with actors in Washington. In the case of Somalia, television turns out not to be the independent driving force that much of the commentary on its influence would lead one to believe (ibid.: 400).

This position which seems to find support with Hallin's study that the news media amplify political circumstances which already exist, affirms the news media's reproductive role by way of its interaction and expression of those circumstances, as well as its importance in legitimising courses of political action, but tends not to discuss the disadvantageous consequences of coverage. That is, the inference on political domination tends to obscure the inter-relatedness of journalism with politics and how journalism can influence political actions by exacerbating and shaping policy differences and positions (Kurz 1991: 77).

The political consequences of news distribution which has increased and speeded up information flow, has helped to change the course of political communications and the relations which are served by that process. This is a significant shift from the premise outlined by Hall who dramatically under-values the dynamic of contestation between sources and tends to depict news production in largely reproductive and one-dimensional terms. As the work of Hallin and others who more recently have indicated the news media's potential to exacerbate political conflict illustrate, the news media have an ability to impact on the conduct of political life by representing it in conflictive terms, which forces politicians to react in conflictive ways and so fuels political contestation. Although it is clear that such contestation takes place within ideological limits and accepted frames of discourse and structures of power, this process nevertheless highlights the complex nature of the relationship between the news media and politics, as well as the potentially destabilising affect which news coverage can have on the political process.

The value of Hallin's study resides is his recognition of the media's ability to amplify conflict. This is especially pronounced during a process of political change and has notable relevance with regard to coverage of the peace process when the consensus over terrorism shifted to a dissensus over peace and contestations over the shape of that peace. What Hallin's observations tend to point out, along with other contributions here, is that this conflict within news derives foremost from the polity and that therefore news is representing conflict which already exists rather than actually shaping it. As I shall later conclude however, Hallin does not give enough attention to the possibility of news destabilising or obstructing politics, nor does he fully address the possibility of news creating problems for politicians.

News, Political Conflict and Reporting Peace

A more recent and perhaps more complete account of the media's ability to affect political contestation and how that ability impacts on efforts to create peace can be found in the work of Gadi Wolfsfeld. Wolfsfeld's analysis, which looks at news coverage from the Middle East through case studies of the Gulf War, the Intifada and the Oslo accords, notes how the news media have become the central arena for political conflicts today. He argues that in order to understand the role of the modern news media within politics, it is best to view the competition for control over news 'as part of a larger and more significant contest among political antagonists for political control' (Wolfsfeld 1997: 3). Wolfsfeld views the media's ability to create conflict as resulting from an overriding emphasis on political antagonisms and disagreements, but he also provides a broader interpretation of the media's engagement with politics than Hall and Hallin, by acknowledging both the media's propensity to reflect discourses of power and a potential to affect the arena within which those discourses are played out.

The relevance of Wolfsfeld's perceptions about the media and conflict result from the wide ranging model of analysis which he uses and which he labels a 'political contest model'. The model rests on five main strands of argument which together depict the news media as providing an arena within which political conflicts occur.

The first strand of argument is that 'the political process is more likely to have an influence on the news media than the news media on the political process' (ibid.). This is because, the media 'respond to political power, they reflect the political values and norms of their society in which they operate and they react to events produced by political actors' (ibid.: 215-6).

The second strand of argument is that 'the authorities level of control over the political environment is one of the key variables that determine the role of the news media in political conflicts' (ibid.: 4). Here, Wolfsfeld focuses on how political groups compete for control of news and sees this competition as evidence of the media's detachment from politics where 'authorities are rarely able to take full control over the environment' and where ' this provides important opportunities for a greater level of independence for the media' (ibid.: 216–17). In highlighting how political contestation is itself reflective of an inability to exert complete control over news output, Wolfsfeld indicates how news provides a space within which the struggle for political definition and advantage takes place. In that arena 'Political conflicts are characterized by moves and countermoves as each antagonist tries to initiate and control political events, to dominate political discourses about the conflict, and to mobilize as many supporters as possible to their side' (ibid.: 4).

The third strand of argument is that 'the role of the news media in political conflict varies over time and circumstance' and that such variation is affected by 'the political context of the conflict, the resources, skills, and political power of the players involved, the relationship between the press and each antagonist, the state of public opinion, the ability of the journalists to gain access to the conflict events, and last but certainly not least what is happening in the field' (ibid.). Summarising this argument in terms of the organisational imperatives of news agencies working to a different set of imperatives which influence the political sphere, Wolfsfeld also writes:

> The role the news media play in conflicts varies primarily because politics is in a constant state of flux. The ability of the authorities and challengers to create newsworthy events, the willingness and the ability of the news media to become independent of the authorities, and editorial decisions about how to frame political conflicts all vary – and with them, so does the role of the press (ibid.; 217).

In the fourth strand of argument, the author observes that 'those who hope to understand variations in the role of the news media must look at the competition among antagonists along two lines: one structural and the other cultural' (ibid.: 4). Describing the structural dimension of analysis, our attention is drawn to 'the extent of mutual dependence between the antagonists and each news medium to explain the power of each side in the transaction', whereas in the cultural dimension, focus is placed on 'how norms, beliefs, and routines all have an influence on the construction of media frames of conflict' (ibid.). That is, 'The battle over media frames is a cultural struggle over meaning. Although there is a clear overlap between the two dimensions, wearing two sets of glasses brings different parts of the picture into focus', and that 'gaining access to the news media should not be confused with success' (ibid.: 218).

Lastly, the fifth strand of argument asserts that 'while authorities have tremendous advantages over challengers in the quantity and quality of media coverage they receive, many challengers can overcome these obstacles and use the news media as a tool for political influence' (ibid.: 5). This realisation acknowledges the potential for news to undermine political power and hints at the possibility of news destabilising the direction of authoritarian imperatives: 'Challengers can and do compete with the authorities in the news media. Some of these opportunities emerge from the political blunders of the powerful while others can be attributed to outside events' (ibid.). The potential for undermining and challenging political domination prompts the consideration that news can impact on dominant groups in an obstructive fashion, and that it can exert pressures and influences on how those groups behave and respond.

But, if the ability of the news media to exert an obstructive or negative influence on authorities engaged in conflict is possible, it is especially likely when such authorities are involved in efforts to resolve conflict. Wolfsfeld's work on news coverage of the Oslo accords is particularly instructive on this point.

Here, Wolfsfeld, views the news media as an obstacle to peace for three key reasons. Firstly, because of a journalistic tendency to concentrate on events rather than processes; secondly, because of a tendency to represent the dramatic and negative aspects of political developments; and thirdly, because of a propensity to undermine negotiations by concentrating on that which divides rather than that which unites groups. Regarding the first of these, Wolfsfeld writes:

> Government policies, especially those that involve significant amounts of change, take a long time to implement. Journalists, however, are not in the business of waiting. They expect to see results immediately. Leaders who attempt to initiate significant amounts of change run into setbacks and problems. The event – centred orientation of journalists lead them to exaggerate the severity of such problems and to ignore more subtle developments which could, in time, prove more significant (Wolfsfeld 1998: 220).

Concerning the second difficulty which news creates for the promotion of peace, the author looks at the media's inclination to amplify ' the unusual, the dramatic and the conflictual aspects of politics'. Here,

> Citizens are presented with an extremely pessimistic view of how the process is unfolding. When citizens learn only about the unusual – and usually negative – aspects of a particular subject or place, it is natural for them to develop images and opinions based on this perspective. This propensity for drama over substance can be especially dangerous regarding news about peace (ibid.: 221).

In the case of the third problem, Wolfsfeld addresses the obstructive function of the media in relation to peace and its ability to undermine successful negotiations. Indicating how the negotiation process is at odds with reporting conventions, he argues:

> As every diplomat knows, negotiations can succeed only when they are held in private. Leaders and negotiators must constantly defend themselves against charges of 'giving in' to the enemy. Leaks about concessions provide valuable ammunition for opposition forces in their attempts to discredit the government. Concessions, especially costly ones, are seen as failures. Both sides find

themselves spending more time engaging in public posturing than in bridging the gaps that divide them (ibid.).

That the news media may serve as an impediment to the negotiation of peace is of central importance when considering the role of news as part of a peace process, and poses a challenge to the assertion that news discourse principally operates to legitimise dominant positions and intentions. In outlining further why news tends to undermine rather then assist the negotiation of peace, Wolfsfeld brings to attention the disparity between diplomacy and reporting and the potentially negative impact which news can produce on the development of peace, and on this point notes:

> Those who expect quick results from such negotiations are inevitably going to be disappointed. The need to provide daily reports about the negotiations only serves to exacerbate this problem: the constant repetition about lack of progress provides increasing evidence of deadlock. Policy makers take a long range view of such talks and understand that such setbacks are an inevitable stage of the process (ibid.: 224–5).

The ability of news to undermine the promotion of peace derives to a great extent from the immediate informational demands of news organisations which conflict with the slow, deliberate and complex actions of those politically engaged in peace. Indeed, it is because of this discrepancy that confidentiality and secrecy are deemed essential for successful negotiations. As Wolfsfeld explains: 'A peace process is not only long but complicated. Governments also face another difficulty in competing for public attention during such periods. The need to maintain secrecy makes it difficult for spokespeople to provide reporters with any real information' (ibid.: 225). In highlighting how attempts to use the media to develop negotiations can have the affect of destabilising those negotiations, the author continues:

> The fact that negotiators are turning to the media, rather than dealing with each other, may be a *sign* that the talks are failing rather then a cause. The flow of influence, in other words, moves in both directions. The negotiators themselves have a certain amount of control over how much contact they want to have with the press. When the two sides are making progress they are less likely to turn to the news media, especially because they realise the damage such actions can cause (ibid.: 229).

Emphasising how public posturing through the news media can reinforce a hardening of positions which is inimical to compromise, Wolfsfeld brings to light an area of media influence which is neglected within the realms of academic analysis. His work clearly outlines how 'the need to speak to the public conflicts with the need to make compromises. Concessions to the enemy are considered signs of weakness and failure, and the opposition is always ready and willing to seize such opportunities' (ibid.: 230), and thus, indicates an 'inherent conflict between the need to keep the public informed and the need to make progress in negotiations' (ibid.: 231).

Conclusion

I have addressed the theories of Hall, Hallin and Wolfsfeld in this chapter, in order to help identify the theoretical significance of this study and to place it within an analytical context where its contribution to media analysis may be realised. Although the three perspectives looked at here cumulatively provide a broad theoretical framework by which to consider the relationship between news and politics and conflict, they neglect certain problems with this relationship which this research has revealed and which need summarising here.

The model used by Hall establishes journalism as a process of subordination to elite power, where journalists are subject to political control and manipulation. By focusing on the ideological reproduction of news, which draws on and promotes the cultural and ideological classifications provided by those who occupy positions of power and domination, Hall expresses journalistic practice as central to the maintenance of power structures and the social control of elites. However, one of the main problems with this thesis is that it does not adequately deal with the issue of political contestation and how sources compete for control of the news agenda. Neither does it fully acknowledge how the news media can exert pressure on political power, or destabilise the political process.

Hall's perspective has particular validity with regard to the coverage given to Northern Ireland during The Troubles, when reporting helped to reinforce and promote the government consensus against terrorism. As was made clear in chapter 1 of this book, news has throughout the modern period up until the peace process began, continued to legitimise the presence and interests of the British state in Northern Ireland and largely functioned as a public relations arm of the British government in its efforts to contain terrorism. But, as the political climate changed from conflict to conflict resolution, so this paradigm of reportage shifted. The climate of peace opened channels of alternative discourse previously closed and posed new challenges for the political control of news. The consensus over conflict, which helped to support ideological control of its representation, has given way to a dissensus over how that conflict is to be resolved and this dissensus arguably makes it harder to manage the direction and scope of discourse. This change also indicates the shortcomings of Hall's argument. In my study, it is clear that many politicians in senior positions found the media frustrating and at times almost impossible to control. Furthermore, if news functions in a subordinate manner in relation to elites as Hall insists, then why is it that on so many occasions politicians tried to keep communications and developments away from the media?

On the issue of a changing political context and the media's ability to initiate and reinforce the political contestations which develop within that context , Hallin's work on news coverage of Vietnam is useful. Hallin highlights how news can amplify political dissensus in the wake of changing political circumstances and brings to attention how political control over news is more difficult when voices of dissent are absorbed into news discourse. Though he identifies how news discourse reproduces the articulations of political sources and places dissensus within a frame of interpretation which is largely determined by elites, Hallin nevertheless also brings to attention the power of news to exacerbate political disagreement and raises questions about its impact on policy. Though there appears to be some consensus amongst academics about the unlikeliness of news affecting the shape and outcome of policy formulation, there is still nevertheless a recognition of the potential of news to exacerbate and pressure policy decisions. This pressure may indicate a problem with the rather totalising concept that journalism is a subordinate practice as Hall argues, but should not detract from the fact that news is reliant on politicians for information and that political discourse is more influential on news discourse than the other way round. Indeed, as Hallin points out, if the news media are able to amplify political dissensus they are doing little more than reinforcing a political trend which already exists and thus drawing on that which is already manifest in the political process.

Unlike Hall's interpretation which emphasises the reproductive tendencies of news in relation to political discourse, Hallin views news as a political institution in itself, with ability to engage in the communication and contestation of problems. This has considerable relevance to the interview research of this study, where it can been seen that news was seen to cause difficulties for politicians because of a tendency to concentrate on issues which were a distraction or inconvenience in relation what they were trying to do. There is little doubt that the peace process set in motion political contestation which the media served to amplify. But, what is not so considered by Hallin is the possibility that as a political climate changes the media may undermine that change by not making sense of it properly, such is their concern with simplification and conflict. As my case study strongly indicates, during the IRA ceasefire of August 1994 journalists struggled to make sense of what was going on and often structured the speculation as if steps towards peace were a continuation of the war by other means. A tendency to read an IRA ceasefire in terms of how it could make the situation worse rather than better not only ran counter to political efforts which had been designed to bring a ceasefire about, but maintained the stereotypical view of the IRA as a pathological organisation which had not changed. Clearly an inaccurate assessment and one which reflected the media's difficulty in breaking free from the terrorism paradigm. From this and in contrast to Hallin, one might conclude that there are times when the media may be unable to properly interpret or explain political change and that this may create problems for the legitimisation of that change, if not its pace and direction.

The importance of news as an arena for political contestation and its centrality within the process of political conflict is key to the work of Wolfsfeld, which establishes news as the main field where political argument and debate is carried out. Though Wolfsfeld, like Hallin, recognises the ideological significance of news as a channel for dominant discourse and sees politics as a driving force over news rather than vice versa, he mentions a range of elements which impact on the effectiveness of political management such as the context of conflict, the resources applied by source groups, the political power they wield, public consent of political direction and journalistic access to information providers. The importance of such elements for those engaged in the battle for definitional advantage of an issue, also illustrates the complexity of the contestation process and the potential for things to go wrong. The notion of a *struggle* for political control of the news agenda brings to light the possibility that such struggles can at times be more or less successful and that weaknesses can emerge which may be exploited by alternative groups. As Wolfsfeld confirms, a struggle over definition brings with it challenges to definitional authority.

His work on the role of news in a peace process on the other hand, raises a number of other questions about the effectiveness of political control. In the case of conflict resolution, it would appear that political objectives are being pursued which hold little interest for journalists. The ponderous and complex nature of peace negotiations is at odds with journalistic interest in drama, action, negativity and amplification. As Wolfsfeld rightly observes, the study of how news impacts on and influences the development of peace is notably thin in comparison to how it is used to facilitate conflict, even though news is as central to the articulations and definitions of peace as it is conflict.

However, as important though Wolfsfeld's study of news to promote peace is, it neglects to fully examine the interplay between private and public communications or to consider how politicians decide when confidentiality must prevail over media access. The issue of when news is used to promote peace needs to be considered against the question of when it is not appropriate and why? The fact that leading political players in peace processes have strongly emphasised the importance of confidentiality when peace is being discussed (Mitchell 1999: 62, 75; Beilin 1999: 134-5) indicates that political progress and advantage is undermined rather than assisted by news coverage and poses problems for Wolfsfeld's political contest model which emphasises the centrality of news within political processes.

Once a peace process becomes established as a key political process and has gained public acceptance, then confidentiality arguably becomes less of a problem. But, during the early more fragile stages of a peace process news can amplify fears and set back communications because of that propensity. Coverage which is simplistic and focused on the dramatic, can bring accusations against politicians of 'selling out' on their constituencies and create communal fears because of this. Wolfsfeld is right to point out that news values conflict with efforts to create peace, but his study does not give as much attention as it might do to examining the question of what this tells us about the actual affect of news on peace and how the interaction between politics and news is changed or affected during the early stages of conflict resolution.

Clearly, the theories of Hall, Hallin and Wolfsfeld have notable significance for considering the role of news within the political process and they provide much useful material for interrogating this dynamic. However, what this study also reveals in relation to analysing the role of news within peace negotiations, is that they provide a limited and ultimately inadequate framework for understanding the complex interactions which go on at this time. What is called for when considering the role of news in politics is not only a clear recognition of the particular political context which news is operating in, but a broader appreciation of the media's ability to interrupt, obstruct or destabilise the political objectives being pursued. In the search for peace, politicians have often found the news to be less than helpful and this brings into question conventional arguments which stress the importance of news for the legitimisation of political power.

Given the range of political circumstances which the media engage with, there will always be questions about their political role which expansive theories will not be able to accommodate or fully realise. Because of this problem and because of the increasing absorption of the media into political affairs, there is a need to carry out more detailed analysis and more specific case studies. Only by conducting extensive empirical work which examines the role of news in different political processes, will we be able to broadly realise the impact of news reporting on politics, and only then, will we be able to start to fully understand what happens inside the relationship between politics and news.

Conclusion

What this study indicates is that at particular historical moments the role of news reporting can change in relation to political circumstances. It demonstrates this point by highlighting how television news reports of Northern Ireland underwent a paradigmatic shift with the emergence of the peace process, where coverage moved from playing a supportive role in connection to dominant political positions, to playing a more obstructive role towards those positions. This transition merits a need for breaking with past explanations about news coverage of Northern Ireland concerned with conflict and requires reassessing the role of coverage in relation to the new political climate of peace. The primary concern of this study has been to question the role of news as part of this changing climate and to analyse the impact of news on the politics of peace.

At the beginning of this study I highlighted the work of Curtis, Miller and Schlesinger as important contributions for understanding the role of news in the Northern Ireland conflict. These studies bring to attention how news tended to reproduce dominant articulations of the conflict during 'The Troubles' and indicate the centrality of reporting for the legitimisation of state policy in Northern Ireland. Representations which focused on terrorist violence obscured the underlying causes of violence but allowed elites to comment with minimal critical interrogation by the media. But, although studies on this interaction may well be crucial for understanding the media's political role during the process of conflict in Northern Ireland, they are now less appropriate for understanding a role which is concerned with peace. As such, the peace process has changed the interaction between news and political discourse to the extent where the work of Curtis, Miller and Schlesinger is not that helpful if we want to comprehend the current climate of reporting. What is called for now and what this study provides, is a re-evaluation of news within this changing political environment. Or, to put it another way, what is required is examination of the media's role in the politics of peace rather than the politics of conflict.

Though studies of the media's role within the conflict of Northern Ireland provide valuable historical material, they do not recognise the possibility of change in the political climate, and so they do not bring into view the possibility that reporting can shift from supporting to obstructing dominant political discourse. It is precisely because political circumstances tend to change that we should recognise the need for a continuing series of empirical studies about news and political processes, for only then can we build a comprehensive picture of how reporting operates and moves in relation to political activity.

Notably, the peace process presented a fundamental rupture from the previous years of conflict by signalling a process of conflict resolution which sought to confront the causes of division and violence. As such, the Northern Ireland problem moved from a process of criminalisation to one of politicisation and with it, television news began to incorporate a broader range of viewpoints into reports about how peace might develop. This opened space for political contestation and dialogue which before had been largely absent from coverage and created a number of problems for dominant groups who had previously (with few exceptions) found the news media quite supportive and amenable.

As political wings of paramilitary groups were absorbed into the workings of mainstream politics, they became subject to greater media scrutiny and were thus able to inject perspectives and comments which challenged dominant official viewpoints. This posed a number of difficulties for dominant groups trying to use news as a means for communicating the direction of peace and given the growing contestations over this direction, the media's role became less orientated towards any dominant consensus about peace and more oriented towards emphasising disputes and dissensus. Or, to put it another way, the news media were now more concerned with promoting contestation than consensus.

Because of this tendency for news to promote contestation, politicians found it difficult to use news to communicate reconciliation and agreement. Such was the unhelpful nature of reporting towards efforts at promoting peace that confidentiality became a key political objective for making progress, with intermediaries regularly used to carry communications and dialogue between opposing groups instead of the media. The ability of television news to destabilise negotiations was further reinforced by a propensity to emphasise conflict and antagonism and represent complex negotiation in a dramatic and simplified fashion.

Politicians interviewed in this study, acknowledge how news tends to reinforce differences and disagreement, making it difficult to generate trust and confidence between opposing sides. They bring to attention the media's tendency to construct the impression of 'winners' and 'losers' and how this often contributes to a hardening of attitudes between groups as each strives to avoid being seen in a position of weakness, often contributing to intransigence. It was particularly because of this inclination by news to reinforce division that privacy became a key feature of the negotiation process, with communications and dialogue preferably conducted away from the glare of media scrutiny. Politicians saw the media as having the potential to undermine or unravel work being done and this placed a question mark over their ability to control or manage the flow of reports. Although television reporting did serve political uses by promoting subjects of discussion and areas of concern, its role during the early stages of peace was regularly seen as unhelpful and in some cases, as obstructive. As coverage of key issues and events such as the IRA ceasefire of 1994, weapons decommissioning and Drumcree indicate.

Furthermore, by regularly and simplistically representing the peace process as lurching from success to failure, the detail and continuity of negotiations became obscured, as the more emotive and problematical aspects of developments became emphasised. Although the peace process was always going to be a process fraught with problems and obstructions, it would appear that for many politicians at least, the news media's obsession with extremes was a hindrance rather than a help. And as with the reporting conventions applied before the peace process, drama and conflict continued to take prominence over analysis and background context.

In one of the few available articles which look at the media's role within the peace negotiations of Northern Ireland and which is referred to in this study, Miller and McLaughlin fail to recognise how relations between news and politics were changed by the development of a peace process (1996). They do not take into account the media's ability to undermine or destabilise negotiations and present a study of negotiation through news which depicts elite groups as being largely supported by coverage. The authors paint a picture of relations between the media and elites which seem largely unaltered by the shifting political climate. Not surprisingly then, the media appear to maintain a reproductive function with regard to dominant political discourse and cause little disturbance to the flow of dominant opinion.

What this study brings into view is a different picture, with elites experiencing considerable difficulty in managing news to complement their objectives. As the politicians interviewed here make clear, if anything, news made the search for peace harder rather than easier. Even in coverage of the IRA ceasefire of 1994 which overwhelmingly emphasised dominant viewpoints, there was a tendency to portray the ceasefire as a significant problem, when for British and Irish governments, as well as most of the other parties involved in peace talks, it was a crucial and necessary step towards peace. Moreover, as interview material with high level respondents involved in brokering the ceasefire underlines, coverage was seen to have obstructed rather than facilitated the ceasefire announcement. By representing an IRA cessation of violence as a move consistent with Republican war aims, news mistakingly read the ceasefire as a continuation of those aims, and not a development which dominant groups had been strenuously working for. Coverage failed to take into account the extent of political change which had brought about the ceasefire and largely ignored how republican thinking had significantly moved in order to bring about such a development.

Responses from journalists and editors about the possibilities of negotiating peace through news tended to support more than contradict the position taken by many politicians. Some of the more well respected and informed journalists working in Northern Ireland saw the negotiating prospects of news as problematic rather than helpful and referred to the use of political intermediaries and other communicative conduits as more effective options for dialogue. They were also only too aware that public announcements and messages are often used to distract attention from actual political developments, raising other questions about the motives and usefulness of negotiating political developments through reports.

What consequences for understanding the relationship between politics and news does this study produce and what do those consequences mean in relation to established theories? In the last chapter, I consider such questions in relation to three important theories which address how news and politics interact. I also highlight that although the theories of Hall, Hallin and Wolfsfeld have importance for thinking about the political uses of news, they also have notable limitations when considered in the light of this research.

The notion that news operates in a reproductive fashion towards political power and dominant articulations as Hall argues, is clearly challenged here. The fact that coverage can obstruct political objectives, report events in ways which are not reflective of political developments, or that politicians can at times try to avoid the media because of a threat which reporting poses to political progress, suggests a complex picture of relations between news and politics which is not adequately explained by Hall.

Hallin's analysis of the media's ability to amplify conflict when political consensus gives way to division and dissensus is very useful for understanding how news can affect politics during a period of change, and has significant uses for thinking about the impact of coverage on politics in Northern Ireland as conflict shifted towards conflict resolution. This research tends to support Hallin's analysis on the media's propensity to amplify conflict. However, as analysis of the IRA ceasefire coverage highlights, in the early stages of political change, news may not always be accurately representing the extent of that change, and this can create potential problems for the politicians shaping it. Hallin's work tends to underline the media's ability to relay dominant articulations even during a period of mounting political dissensus, but as this study reveals, within a peace process the media can be unhelpful towards dominant opinion, to the extent where confidentiality becomes a more preferable option for political progress than using the media.

Wolfsfeld's work on the media and politics emphasises the media as an arena where modern politics is played out and contested. He points to the spaces afforded by news coverage as critical for the legitimisation of politics today and notes that politics is contested and debated increasingly through the media. This sits in contrast to his work on the media's role within the Middle East peace process where he describes how coverage tended to obstruct and hinder negotiations. In the case of peace, it would appear that the media's role (in the early stages at least) can be negative towards political progress and this raises questions about its centrality and importance. Conflict politics may be able to use the media more effectively given that news values are well suited to the expression and emphasis of conflict. But, values which prioritise conflict, negativity, simplification and drama are less complementary to the promotion of peace.

But, even though Wolfsfeld's analysis is extremely useful for grasping how the news media interact with the politics of peace, it does not engage comprehensively enough with the interplay which goes on between public and private communications in a peace process. Questions about confidentiality and why politicians decide when something should and should not remain private are largely ignored by Wolfsfeld. Questions about how reports impact on political efforts at peace and whether initiatives are changed or not because of coverage, are similarly overlooked.

Arguably, what this research brings to light, is the need for a more complex appreciation of the relationship between news and politics. An appreciation which is based not on totalising theorisations about news and politics but on examination of actual and specific political activities and processes. It does not correspond, for example, that because the news media are crucial for conducting peace diplomacy as part of political foreign policy (Holbrooke 1998; Bildt 1998: 218–19) they therefore also play an equally central role in the development of peace at a domestic level. The study of how news reporting impacts on peace is likely to produces different results in relation to different political contexts and objectives being pursued.

I am not disputing the centrality of news in political affairs and the importance of coverage for the legitimisation of political practice. I am saying that different contexts and situations bring different interactions and results. Generally speaking Havel is right when he says:

> Of course a political action cannot serve as a symbol or play an important role unless it is known about. Today, in the era of mass media, it is often true that if a deed lacks adequate coverage, particularly on television, it might as well have remained undone. Even those who doubt the political importance of spatiotemporal architecture or the meaning of political symbols and rituals cannot deny one aspect of theatricality in politics: the dependence of politics on the media (Havel 1997: 254),

but this should not distract us from the realisation that there may be occasions (however rare) when political success also depends on the opposite of this assertion. That is, where politics does not need the media and indeed actively tries to avoid it.

This extent of change, where the media can be considered key for political activity in one context, and obstructive or to be avoided in another, highlights the need for continuous reassessment and empirical work on the media's role in political affairs. It brings into view the need to interrogate relations between political players and news personnel to see what they make of changing political climates and environments and to see how such changes impact on what they do. This study makes a valid contribution to understanding the role of news in the peace process during its early stages, but should not be thought of as any definitive account about the role of television news in peace processes. No doubt, that as the peace process in Northern Ireland moves into different stages (and if it continues) and generates different political institutions, the role of news will change and that if interviews are conducted as those stages emerge they will produce a different set of responses. It is important to bear in mind that when this study was carried out, the peace process was at a sensitive and precarious stage of development and that this had an influence on political reactions, but that such reactions are also perfectly valid for understanding how news and politics interacted at this time.

A tendency for the news media to maintain short-sighted stereotypes about particular groupings in the Northern Ireland peace process, Unionist as well as Republican (Parkinson 1998; Dudley Edwards 1999) has not helped to facilitate the development of peace. Though reporting has come to accept the peace process as a formal political process, it would appear that during the formative stages of peace, news had problems in breaking with the conflict paradigm and continued to interpret (as well as underplay) political change by way of reading events through the conventional representations of conflict. This emphasis on conflict created obstructions for the development of confidence and trust between the opposing sides and hindered constructive dialogue. A tendency for news to represent negotiations as an apparently random mix of breakthroughs and crises, with winners and losers, and a tendency to represent complex negotiations as a combination of simplistic problems and expected solutions leads this study to conclude that television news has been more obstructive than helpful towards the early years of peace in Northern Ireland.

APPENDICES

Appendix 1: Research Methodology

Research Problem and Method of Inquiry

This project is based on extensive qualitative interview data gathered from 15 politicians, 11 journalists and seven editors, who were involved in the politics and reporting of the Northern Ireland peace process from 1994–98. The research problem being addressed is this: How did politicians, journalists and editors interact during the early stages of the peace process and how did reporting affect the politics and development of that process?

To gather empirical data which allowed me to interrogate this problem, I conducted face-to-face interviews with each of the above groups over a period of three years. Given that these interviews were to be done individually and likely to elicit information both personal and confidential, it seemed entirely appropriate to use an interview format which was unstructured (Fielding 1998: 138). I was particularly interested in gathering responses which accurately reflected the personal experiences of those interviewed, so although the interviews followed a set list of questions they were not always asked in the same order, but rather raised at points in the interview when they seemed most relevant and effective. Notably, the interviews were designed to enable the respondents to articulate their experiences and problems in their own words as much as possible. The fluid and more open aspects of the unstructured interview helped to develop a rapport between the interviewer and interviewee which was often conversational and consistent with Fielding's description of the unstructured interview, where although 'interviewers simply have a list of topics which they want the respondent to talk about', they are nevertheless 'free to phrase the questions as they wish, ask them in any order that seems sensible at the time, and even to join in the conversation by discussing what they think of the topics themselves' (ibid.: 136).

This study also follows a set of aims which complement aspects of interactionist theory. According to this approach, as Silverman reminds us, 'interviewees are viewed as experiencing subjects who actively construct their

191

social worlds; the primary issue is to generate data which give an authentic insight into people's experiences' (Silverman 1994: 91). Referring to the unstructured interview as the main methodology of data collection for this purpose, Silverman also uses the work of Denzin to demonstrate the particular validity of interactionism. According to Denzin, three prominent reasons underline the preference for an interactionist approach:

1) It allows respondents to use their 'unique ways of defining the world' (Denzin 1970: 125).
2) It assumes that no fixed sequence of questions is suitable to all respondents.
3) It allows respondents to 'raise important issues not contained in the schedule' (ibid.) (quoted in Silverman 1994: 95),

and it is the case that interviews conducted here were consistent with those reasons. A prime intention of the interviews was to gather evidence about interactions between politicians, journalists and editors which would allow for the discovery of problems and concerns largely unknown. The interview was therefore as Searle puts it 'a *resource* to discover things about events outside the interview situation' (Searle 1998: 215).

Yet, although this study adopts a perspective towards the enquiry which is interactionist, it also indicates another theoretical orientation towards that enquiry which is reflective of grounded theory. This theory 'involves the coding of the interview transcript – and/or other data collected – in terms of key concepts, which are mainly developed during the work itself' (Blaxter et al. 1998: 189). With grounded theory 'As the research process unfolds, winding on and around itself, a clearer identification and understanding of the concepts of relevance is reached' (ibid.). In the case of this research, the theoretical concerns and central arguments were made in the light of the interview material, and not in advance of it being gathered. Concepts, explanations and suppositions came out of the data, highlighting a research design which has a grounded basis. As Punch puts it, the notion of data being grounded points to a design where 'the theory will be generated on the basis of the data; the theory will be therefore grounded in the data' (1998: 163). Grounded theory tends to follow a pattern of research where collection of data is followed by analysis of that data, which then subsequently refines and informs future collection and analysis and so on (ibid.: 167). Or to put it another way, the researcher develops conceptual categories from the data which leads to modification and clarification of those categories, and which in turn bring new observations and refinements to the research (Glaser and Strauss 1967).

In relation to this work, this meant interview responses helping to refine future interview structures and helping to (re)define questions on the basis of the responses as they progressed. It was certainly the case with this study that the process of questioning was informed and improved in relation to the data as it developed and expanded. Here, the experiences of respondents have been used to gather grounded concepts which build into a sensitised, subsequently informed picture of 'reality'.

Those grounded concepts were then used to interrogate key theories concerned with the interactions between news, political power and conflict. By bringing to light potential weaknesses with those theories which derive from a tendency to neglect how interactions can change with political circumstances and environments, this study then goes on to call for an ongoing series of empirical studies which more specifically address the complexities and nuances of relations between news and politics.

Because so many of those interviewed asked not to be named, they have all remained anonymous, identifiable only by the positions they occupied past and present at the time of interview. Those who had worked in a position which they no longer occupied at the time of interview, are referred to as 'former' in the data samples.

A number of politicians stressed the confidential nature of what they were saying and asked me categorically not to identify them as a source for the comments they were providing, and this applied to some news personnel as well. To name some respondents and not others would have given a discontinuity to the responses which could have confused the research, so for this reason, interviewees have been described in the following terms:

Politicians: MPs and ministers, former Irish Prime Minister, former Northern Ireland Secretary, former Shadow Northern Ireland Secretary, Sinn Fein councillor, Progressive Unionist Party MP, Social and Democratic Liberal Party MP, US peace envoy.

Journalists: BBC Ireland correspondent, Channel 4/ITN political correspondent, BBC political correspondent, freelance NI journalist, BBC Foreign Affairs correspondent, BBC correspondent (London based and NI based).

Editors: former Controller of BBC NI, former Head of BBC News NI, Deputy Home News Editor BBC, Senior News Editor Channel 4, Senior News Editor BBC, Senior Director of News ITN, Home News Editor BBC.

Access and Interviews

Individuals were contacted by letter after having appeared in news reports as political spokesmen or reporters. In the case of editors, names were taken from the credits of bulletins. Out of all the politicians contacted, only three declined to be interviewed, For reporters and editors it was two each. Once agreement for interview had been given, arrangements were made for the interview over the telephone and a mutually acceptable time and date for both interviewer and interviewee decided. All the interviews were conducted on a one-to one basis. All political interviews were conducted in offices or places of work, but for the majority of reporters and editors, interviews were carried out in cafes or restaurants This was not so much because they felt able to talk more openly outside of work, but because it far reduced the possibility of disturbance. The daily grind of political life is much more ordered in terms of time and for the bulk of political interviews, I had a fixed time which was rarely disturbed. In most cases, interviews went on for 30–45 minutes, depending on how much time the respondent could give. The interviews themselves were carried out in London, Belfast, Dublin and New York.

Three important conditions were taken into account for the successful completion of the interviews. Those conditions as May explains (1997: 116) are accessibility, cognition and motivation. The condition of accessibility 'refers to whether or not the person answering the questions has access to the information which the interviewer seeks'. With cognition there needs to be 'an understanding by the person being interviewed of what is required of him or her in the role of interviewee', and on the issue of motivation, 'The interviewer must make the subjects feel that their participation and answers are valued, for their cooperation is fundamental to the conduct of the research' (ibid.). With the interviewees I contacted for this research, it was made clear in a letter what the aims of the interview were. In one or two cases, politicians asked for the interview questions in advance, but in all other cases interviewees were happy to answer questions without prior knowledge of them, requiring only a rough outline of my aims at the start of the interview.

I asked all respondents if the interviews could be tape-recorded and all gave their full consent to having the interviews recorded. One of the main advantages to recording interviews is that it allows the interview to flow and enables the interviewer to concentrate on establishing and developing dialogue with the interviewee. Another important advantage with recording interviews is that this process tends to facilitate response categories which make it easier for disseminating and coding information later. Although there can be problems with using recorders which can derive from the respondent feeling inhibited by their comments being taped, or the long and laborious process of transcription, or interviewers substituting their own words for those of the respondent (May 1997: 124–5), the advantages in this case greatly outweighed the disadvantages. Tape-recording the comments of respondents for this study notably assisted the flow of the open interview structure, and they soon became accustomed to the presence of the recorder. Without having to concentrate on transcribing comments as they were made, the interview became conversational and helped to improve the rapport between interviewer and interviewee as a result. The use of a tape-recorder gives the interview flexibility, opportunity for developing eye contact between interviewer and interviewee, and encourages a broader range of responses which help to elicit a comprehensive representation of experiences and attitudes.

These advantages should not obscure the interventions of the interviewer in the interview, however. The interview is clearly a two way process and the interviewer plays a central role in shaping the responses of the interviewee. As May puts it when summing up this interaction

> the data derived from interviews are not simply 'accurate' or 'distorted' pieces of information, but provide the researcher with a means of analysing the ways in which people consider events and relationships and the reasons they offer for doing so. Yet, they are mediated not only by the interviewee, but also by the interviewer. It is their presuppositions in the interpretation of the data that should also be a subject of the analysis. Quite simply, if both the strengths and weaknesses of different methods of interviewing and approaches to their analysis are understood, they can provide us with an essential way of understanding and explaining social events and relations (ibid.: 130–31).

The interviews in this study are also characterised by two conventions which underpin effective interviewing. Those conventions are to do with concerns of equality and comparability (ibid.: 124). In order to gather data which realistically represents the experiences and attitudes of respondents, it is important that the interview material gathered from one interview is of comparable quality, content and duration with the next. Comparisons in response, form the basis of this research and so each is as significant and relevant to the line of enquiry as any other. Fully representative interview samples have significance primarily when they are treated with equal and comparable importance and that has been the case in this study.

Interview Questions and Interpreting the Data

According to Punch, research questions have five essential functions:

- They organise the project and give it direction and coherence
- They limit the project, showing it boundaries
- They keep the researcher focused during the project
- They provide a framework for writing up the project
- They point to the data that is needed (1998: 38).

For this project, the interview questions were designed to address specific areas of concern and oriented towards the overriding problem of finding out about how each respondent interacted with television news coverage of the peace process. Although there were some differences between the questions given to reporters and politicians (and necessarily so given that each works with news differently), the interviews followed a consistent pattern of questioning in relation to investigation of subject areas. This not only served to keep the data focused and limited, but by minimising deviation in the interviews, allowed for data to be categorised and compared more easily.

The list of questions given to political representatives was as follows:

1) In your opinion, has television news played an active part in the peace process?
2) Have you tried to use television news to inject momentum or obstruct momentum in the peace process?
3) Have you used the media to talk to groups who you might not talk to directly?
4) How important is 'megaphone diplomacy' for the peace process?
5) How important is language to the communication of peace?
6) What overriding aims do you tend to follow when talking to news and can you give examples of those aims in action?
7) Has television news helped you to develop the peace process?
8) What problems do you think are associated with using news to promote peace?
9) Has television news affected the direction of the peace process or political policy towards it?
10) Are there occasions when you might try to avoid using the media?
11) How would you summarise your relationship with journalists?
12) What are your thoughts about how television news has covered the peace process?

13) Does media speculation and pressure help to bring about political goals and can you think of how it may or may not have helped the peace process?
14) How important or effective are leaks and what problems do they cause?
15) What are the main problems with communicating peace in Northern Ireland?
16) Do you follow a particular communications strategy over the peace process?
17) What are your thoughts about the peace process and how easy has news made it for you to communicate those thoughts?
18) Are there particular occasions when reporters tend to seek your views?
19) What problems has news created for politicians?
20) How do you see things developing?

For reporters and editors the questions used were:

1) What are the problems and concerns with reporting Northern Ireland and the peace process?
2) Do you think that politicians use television news to communicate with each other?
3) What aims and objectives do you put into practice when covering Northern Ireland?
4) How important is language for reporting the peace process?
5) Is there a tendency for reports to reiterate dominant political comment?
6) Does news create problems for those working to promote peace?
7) How do you see the role of news in relation to the peace process?
8) How does political pressure affect what you do?
9) Can you explain the process of interaction between reporters and sources?
10) How important are leaks for making news?
11) What are the main pressures and concerns when reporting the peace process?
12) Do you try and facilitate 'megaphone diplomacy'?
13) Has news affected the development and direction of the peace process in any way?
14) Has the peace process affected changes in the way you now approach the subject of Northern Ireland?
15) What processes and values influence what you do?
16) How do you try and achieve impartiality when reporting the peace process?

17) What do you think about the communications strategies used by politicians to develop the peace process and do you see some as more effective than others?
18) Do you have any criticisms about the coverage news has provided so far about the peace process?
19) How do you decide what to include in reports and what to leave out?

With the responses to those questions, I adopted an open-coded approach to the data, a process which shapes the material into categories and concepts. As Punch explains, open-coding involves 'a close examination of (some of) the data, identifying conceptual categories implicit or explicit in the data, and the theoretical possibilities the data carry' (1998: 211). Concerned primarily with sorting the data into areas which assist explanation, open-coding 'is about using the data to generate conceptual labels and categories for use in theory-building. Its function is to expose theoretical possibilities in the data' (ibid.: 213). For purposes of this study, coding enabled the data to be grouped into categories which provided for an easier understanding of respondent experiences and which helped to generate ideas for thinking about the subjects and issues under discussion. Those ideas then served the process of explanation and theoretical design.

In evaluating the interview material, two related processes come into play: the management and analysis of data. The management of data is about 'reducing its size and scope, so that you can report upon it adequately and usefully', and the analysis of that data once shaped into a manageable size is about abstracting the material into areas of priority and 'drawing attention to what you think is of particular importance and significance' (Blaxter at al. 1998: 183). In the chapters of the study which are based on interview material, it is made clear in the introduction to those chapters how each is constructed into sections which address specific issues and areas. Such categorisations derive from management and analysis of the data which then enables the presentation of that data to be delivered in a narrative form convenient to the aims and objectives of the work. Of course, this presentation involves selections and interpretations which effectively (re)contextualise the data for reading rather than listening (the oral to the literal) and this change in emphasis reflects the interventions of the researcher in the research process. By placing the comments of one interviewee alongside another, comments become affected and meanings transformed, and this needs to be taken into account. In trying to demonstrate the differences in responses, the juxtaposition of data inevitably leads to certain comments appearing more convincing that others. Although I have tried to show the broadest differences in responses and indicated how perceptions and experiences vary, the presentation of data is ultimately determined by the researcher who by categorising responses also tends to categorise respondents. This places obvious limits on the truth value of the work.

This study applied the technique of non-probability sampling when disseminating the selecting response material. Non-probability sampling involves utilising the material which most conveniently and appropriately addresses the subject of analysis (ibid.: 81). In instances where interviewees have spoken about events, issues and problems which are not considered relevant for the concerns of this study (such as talking about other political activities and the impact of reporting on those activities) they have been excluded from analysis. One of the problems with unstructured interviewing, is that no matter how specific the questioning, the flexible nature of the conversation inevitably leaves room for the interviewee to divert from the subject of interview, and to bring in other considerations which they may see as relevant but which the interviewer may not. Although on occasions such deviations can be productive and provide useful additional material which has a bearing on the subject of enquiry, often they are not, and are deselected from the data when it is transcribed as a result.

Overall, this research provides original data on a neglected area of research. Indeed, it would be no exaggeration to say that at the time of writing there has been no empirical work carried out which examines the role of television news in the peace process of Northern Ireland from the perspectives of politicians and news personnel. As such, it makes a significant contribution to the field of media research and to understanding the role of news within conflict resolution politics.

Appendix 2: News Content Analysis

This case study examined the coverage of 17 television news reports about the IRA ceasefire of August 1994. The study followed coverage from when speculation about a possible ceasefire began (24 July 1994), to the ceasefire announcement itself, which was made on 31 August 1994. The reports analysed were as follows:

1) BBC1, 18.00, 24 July 1994
2) ITN, 17.40, 25 July 1994
3) BBC1, 21.00, 25 July 1994
4) BBC1, 21.00, 11 August 1994
5) BBC1, 18.00, 14 August 1994
6) ITN, 17.40, 14 August 1994
7) BBC1, 21.00, 21 August 1994
8) ITN, 17.40, 22 August 1994
9) BBC1, 18.00, 22 August 1994
10) Channel 4, 19.00, 22 August 1994
11) BBC2, *Newsnight*, 22.30, 22 August 1994
12) BBC1, 18.00, 25 August 1994
13) ITN, 17.40, 26 August 1994
14) Channel 4, 19.00, 26 August 1994
15) BBC2, *Newsnight*, 22.30, 26 August 1994
16) ITN, 17.40, 31 August 1994
17) BBC1, 18.00, 31 August 1994

Appendix 3: Chronology

A Brief Chronology of Key Events in the Northern Ireland Peace Process: 1993–98

1993

7 October: Hume gives document containing broad principles of his agreement with Adams to the Irish First Minister, Dick Spring and Irish Prime Minister, Albert Reynolds.

23 October : 10 people are killed following an IRA bomb at a fish shop on the Shankill Road in Belfast. Gerry Adam's later carries the bomber's coffin.

30 October: seven people killed in UFF gun attack in a bar in Greysteel, Co Derry.

28 November: *The Observer* reveals that a channel of communication has existed between the IRA and the British government for years.

15 December: The Downing Street Declaration published by Reynolds and Major. It includes a commitment that the people of Northern Ireland will decide its future and a demand that the IRA permanently renounces violence.

1994

19 January: the Irish government removes the Section 31 Broadcasting Ban.

18 June: six Catholic men shot dead by Loyalist paramilitaries in a pub in Loughinisland, Co. Derry.

31 August: IRA announces a complete cessation of violence.

6 September: Reynolds, Hume and Adams shake hands on the steps of Government buildings, Dublin.

13 October: the Combined Loyalist Military Command calls a ceasefire.

9 December: first offical meeting between government officials and Sinn Fein. Decommissioning is a stumbling block.

1995

12 January: British army ends daytime patrols in Belfast.

17 June : Sinn Fein pulls out of talks with the government. Four weeks later Gerry Adams tells party rally that the 'IRA has not gone away'.

30 November: President Clinton shakes Adams by hand in Falls Road cafe during his visit to Belfast.

5 December: the head of the International Body on Decommissioning, former US senator George Mitchell, invites submissions on arms decommissioning from all parties.

1996

26 January: the Mitchell Report is published, laying down six principles of nonviolence for entry into all-party talks.

9 February: the IRA ceasefire ends after 16 months with a one tonne bomb in London's Canary Wharf district which kills two people.

30 May: in the Northern Ireland Forum elections to all-party talks, Sinn Fein polls a record vote.

7 June: Jerry McCabe is killed during a post office raid in Adare, Co. Limerick. Hallmarks of an IRA raid.

10 June: Sinn Fein are barred from the opening of inter-party talks.

15 June: a 1.5 tonne van bomb explodes in Manchester city centre.

7 July: a Catholic taxi-driver, Michael McGoldrick, is shot dead near Lurgan, Co. Armagh by the UVF.

13 July: a 1200lb car bomb destroys Killyhevlin Hotel at Enniskillen, Co. Fermanagh, injuring 40 people. This follows a week of rioting after the RUC force an Orange march down the Garvaghy Road in Portadown.

7 October: two IRA bombs explode at British Army's Northern Ireland HQ, Thiepval Barracks in Lisburn, Co. Antrim killing one soldier.

1997

5 April: IRA bomb threats forced the postponement of the Aintree Grand National. A blitz of IRA bomb threats in Britain ensues.

1 May: results in the British General Election put the Labour Party leader, Tony Blair, in 10 Downing Street and returns Gerry Adams and party colleague, Martin McGuiness, to Westminster.

16 May: Blair visits Northern Ireland and gives the go-ahead for exploratory contacts between government officials and Sinn Fein.

16 June: Blair bans further contact between senior civil servants and Sinn Fein following IRA shooting of two RUC men in Lurgan, Co. Armagh.

6 July: violence erupts in Portadown, and later spreads, after RUC move in early hours to seal off Garvaghy Road for Orange march.

20 July: following a request from Gerry Adams, the IRA declares a renewal of its ceasefire.

26 August: international decommissioning body set up to oversee the handover of weapons. The coming months are to see no progress on the arms issue.

29 August: Secretary of State for Northern Ireland, Mo Mowlam, announces IRA ceasefire has been sufficiently well observed for Sinn Fein to enter talks.

9 September: Sinn Fein signs up to the Mitchell Principles and enters all-party talks.

17 September: the Ulster Unionists join the talks. The DUP stays away.

13 October: Adams and McGuiness meet Blair for the first time at Stormont's Castle buildings.

9 December: Adams and McGuiness make their historic visit to Downing Street.

27 December: LVF leader Billy Wright is shot dead in Maze prison. In the following four weeks, seven Catholics and one Protestant are shot dead. The LVF is blamed for most of the murders but mainstream Loyalist involvement is also suspected.

1998

17 January: Sinn Fein reject the British and Irish governments' new proposals for a settlement in Northern Ireland.

19 January: Sinn Fein leaders go to Downing Street for what they describe as an 'urgent'meeting with Tony Blair.

21 January: IRA reject the Anglo-Irish paper.

23 January: UFF admits killing of Catholics.

24 January: Catholic taxi driver is shot dead in Belfast.

26 January: peace talks move to London and the UDP is forced to leave.

29 January: a new inquiry into Bloody Sunday is announced by Tony Blair. The LVF announces it will continue to target republicans.

16 February: peace talks move to Dublin.

20 February: Sinn Fein suspended from talks because of RUC chief constable's assessment of IRA involvement in recent murders.

23 February: Car bomb explodes in Portadown, Co. Armargh.

3 March: a Protestant and a Catholic (both friends) are shot dead by the LVF in Poyntzpass, Co. Armagh.

10 March: a mortar attack is launched on Armargh police station. Dissident Republicans are blamed.

22 March: 1000lb car bomb is discovered by police in Dundalk.

23 March: peace talks resume at Stormont with Sinn Fein reinstated in talks.

7 April: Ulster Unionists reject draft drawn up by talks chairman George Mitchell, plunging talks into trouble 72 hours before a settlement is due.

8 April: Irish prime minister Bertie Ahern arrives at Stormont to try and avert talks crisis.

10 April: historic announcement of the Good Friday Agreement which outlines structures and mechanisms for devolved power to Northern Ireland and a power-sharing executive.

Source: www.ireland.com/special/peace/troubles

References

Adams, Gerry (1995), *Free Ireland: Towards a Lasting Peace*, Brandon.

Adams, Gerry (1997), *An Irish Voice: The Quest For Peace*, Roberts Rinehart.

Alali, A. Odasuo and Eke, Kenoye Kelvin (1991), *Media Coverage of Terrorism*, Sage.

Allen, Tim and Seaton, Jean (1999), *The Media Of Conflict*, Zed Books.

Apter, David E. (1997), 'Political Violence in Analytical Perspective', in Apter, David E. (ed.), *The Legitimization of Violence*, United Nations Research Institute for Social Development.

Bairner, Alan (1996), 'The Media', in Aughey, Arthur and Morrow, Duncan (eds), *Northern Ireland Politics*, Longman.

Baker, Keith (1996), 'Reporting the Conflict', in McLoone, Martin (ed.), *Broadcasting in a Divided Community*, Institute of Irish Studies, The Queen's University of Belfast.

Bantz, Charles R. (1997), 'News Organizations: Conflict as a Crafted Cultural Norm', in Berkowitz, Dan (ed.), *Social Meanings Of News*, Sage.

Beilin, Yossi (1999), *Touching Peace*, Weidenfeld and Nicolson.

Bevins, Antony, Mallie, Eamonn and Holland, Mary, 'Major's secret links with IRA leadership revealed', *The Observer*, 28 November 1993.

Bew, Paul and Gillespie, Gordon (1993), *The Northern Ireland Peace Process 1993-1996*, Serif.

Bew, Paul, Patterson, Henry and Teague, Paul (1997), *Between War and Peace*, Lawrence and Wishart.

Bildt, Carl (1998), *Peace Journey*, Weidenfeld and Nicolson.

Blaxter, Loraine, Hughes, Christina and Tight, Malcolm (1998), *How To Research*, Sage.

Bowyer Bell, J. (1997), *The Secret Army: The IRA*, Transaction Books.

Broomfield, David (1998), *Political Dialogue in Northern Ireland*, Macmillan.

Bruce, Steve (1992), *The Red Hand*, Oxford University Press.

Butler, David (1991), 'Unionism and British Broadcasting Journalism', in Rolston, Bill (ed.), *The Media and Northern Ireland: Covering The Troubles*, Macmillan.

Butler, David (1995), *The Trouble With Reporting Northern Ireland*, Avebury.

Butler, David (1996), 'The Trouble With Reporting Northern Ireland', in McLoone, Martin (ed.), *Broadcasting in a Divided Community*, Institute of Irish Studies, The Queen's University of Belfast.

Cathcart, Rex (1984), *The Most Contrary Region: The BBC in Northern Ireland 1924-1984*, Blackstaff Press.

Clawson, Patrick (1990), 'Why we need more but better coverage of terrorism', in Kegley, Charles W. (ed.), *International Terrorism: Characteristics, Causes, Controls*, Macmillan.

Clutterbuck, Richard (1983), *The Media and Political Violence*, Macmillan.

Cohen, Akiba A., Adoni, Hanna and Bantz, Charles R. (1990), *Social Conflict and Television News*, Sage.

Coogan, Tim Pat (1995), *The Troubles*, Hutchinson.

Curran, James and Seaton, Jean (1995), *Power Without Responsibility*, Routledge.

Curtis, Liz (1984), *Ireland: The Propaganda War*, Pluto Press.

Curtis, Liz and Jempson, Mike (1984), *Interference on the Airwaves: Ireland, The Media and the Broadcasting Ban*, Campaign for Press and Broadcasting Freedom.

Darby, John (1977), *Scorpions in a Bottle*, Minority Rights Press.

Duignan, Sean (1996), *One Spin on the Merry-Go-Round*, Blackwater Press.

Edelmann, Murray (1988), *Constructing the Political Spectacle*, University of Chicago Press.

Edwards, Ruth Dudley (1999), *The Faithful Tribe*, Harper Collins.

Eldridge, John (1995), *Glasgow Media Group Reader, Vol. 1: News Content, Language and Visuals*, Routledge.

Elliott, Philip (1977), 'Reporting Northern Ireland: A Study of News in Great Britain, Northern Ireland and The Republic of Ireland', in UNESCO (ed.), *Media and Ethnicity*, UNESCO.

Ericson, Richard V., Baranek, Patricia M. and Chan, Janet B.L. (1987), *Visualising Deviance*, Open University Press.

Farrell, Michael (1988), *Twenty Years On*, Brandon.

Fielding, Nigel (1998), 'Qualitative Interviewing', in Gilbert, Nigel (ed.), *Researching Social Life*, Sage.

Flackes, W.D. and Elliott, Sydney (1994), *Northern Ireland: A Political Directory 1968–1993*, Blackstaff Press.

Fowler, Roger (1991), *Language in the News*, Routledge.

Frameworks For The Future (1995), HMSO.

Gans, Herbert (1980), *Deciding What's News*, Vintage.

Gearty, Conor (1997), *The Future of Terrorism*, Phoenix.

Gilbert, Paul (1994), *Terrorism, Security and Nationality*, Routledge.

Gilligan, Chris (1997), 'Peace or Pacification Process? A Brief Critique of the Peace Process', in Gilligan, Chris and Tonge, Jon (eds), *Peace or War? Understanding the Peace Process in Northern Ireland*, Ashgate.

Gitlin, Todd (1980), *The Whole World is Watching*, University of California Press.

Glaser, B.G. and Strauss, A.L. (1967), *The Discovery of Grounded Theory: Strategies for Qualitative Research*, Chicago: Aldine.

Gowing, Nic (1994), *Real-Time Television Coverage of Armed Conflicts and Diplomatic Crises: Does it Pressure or Distort Foreign Policy Decisions*, Working Paper 94–1, Joan Shorenstein Barone Center on the Press, Politics and Public Policy, Harvard University.

Hall, Stuart (1978), 'The Social Production of News', in Hall, Stuart and Critcher, Chas and Jefferson, Tony and Clarke, John and Roberts, Brian (eds), *Policing The Crisis: Mugging, the State and Law and Order*, Macmillan.

Hallin, Daniel (1989), *The Uncensored War*, University of California Press.

Hallin, Daniel (1994), *We Keep America on Top of the World*, Routledge.

Havel, Vaclav (1997), *The Art of The Impossible*, Fromm International.

Henderson, Lesley and Miller, David and Reilly, Jaqueline (1990), *Speak No Evil: The British Broadcasting Ban, The Media and The Conflict in Ireland*, Glasgow Media Group.

Hennessey, Thomas (1997), *A History of Northern Ireland 1920–1996*, Macmillan.

Holbrooke, Richard (1998), *To End A War*, Random House.

Jones, Nicholas (1996), *Soundbites and Spin Doctors*, Indigo.

Kurz, Robert J. (1991), 'Congress and the Media. Forces in the Struggle Over Foreign Policy', in Serfaty, Simon (ed.), *The Media and Foreign Policy*, St Martin's Press.

Latter, Richard (1988), *Terrorism and the Media: Ethical and Practical Dilemmas for Government, Journalists and the Public*, Wilton Park Papers 1, Jan. 1988, HMSO.

Mallie, Eamonn and McKittrick, David (1996), *The Fight For Peace*, Heinemann.

Maltese, John Antony (1994), *Spin Control*, The University of North Carolina Press.

May, Tim (1997), *Social Research* (2nd edn), Open University Press.

McGarry, John and O'Leary, Brendan (1995), *Explaining Northern Ireland*, Blackwell.

McGovern, Mark (1997), 'Unity in Diversity? The SDLP and the Peace Process', in Gilligan, Chris and Tonge, Jon (eds), *Peace or War? Understanding the Peace Process in Northern Ireland*, Ashgate.

McKittrick, David (1994), *Endgame*, Blackstaff Press.

McLoone, Martin (1991), 'Inventions and Re-Imaginings: Some Thoughts on Identity and Broadcasting in Ireland', in McLoone, Martin (ed.), *Culture, Identity and Broadcasting in Ireland: Local Issues, Global Perspectives*, Proceedings of the Cultural Traditions Group/Media Studies, U.U.C. Symposium, Institute of Irish Studies, The Queen's University of Belfast.

McNair, Brian (1994), *News and Journalism in the UK*, Routledge.

McNair, Brian (1995), *An Introduction to Political Communication*, Routledge.

Merin, Jonathan (1997), *Television News and American Intervention in Somalia: The Myth of a Media-Driven Foreign Policy*, Political Science Quarterly, Vol. 112, No. 3.

Miller, David (1993), *Official Sources and 'Primary Definition': the case of Northern Ireland*, Media, Culture and Society, Vol. 15, No. 3.

Miller, David (1994), *Don't Mention The War*, Pluto Press.

Miller, David (1995), 'The Media and Northern Ireland: censorship, information management and the broadcasting ban', in Philo, Greg (ed.), *Glasgow Media Group Reader, Vol. 2: Industry, Economy, War and Politics*, Routledge.

Miller, David and McLaughlin, Greg (1996), 'Reporting the Peace in Northern Ireland', in Miller, David and Rolston, Bill (eds), *War and Words*, Beyond the Pale Publications.

Mitchell, George (1999), *Making Peace*, Heinemann.

Moloney, Ed (1988), 'The Media: Asking the Right Questions?', in Farrell, Michael (ed.), *Twenty Years On*, Brandon.

Moloney, Ed (1991), 'Closing Down The Airwaves: The Story of the Broadcasting Ban', in Rolston, Bill (ed.), *The Media and Northern Ireland: Covering the Troubles*, Macmillan.

Morris, Colin (1988), 'Tip-toeing Through the Minefield: Tracking the Truth in Northern Ireland', University of Ulster Convocation Lecture, University of Ulster, Jordanstown, 18 May, Belfast: BBC.

Mowlam, Mo (1996), untitled speech delivered at The Shorenstein Center, Kennedy School of Government, Harvard University, 11 March (courtesy of author).

Mullen, Don (ed.) (1997), *Eyewitness Bloody Sunday*, Wolfhound Press.

Nastios, Andrew (1996), 'Illusions of Influence', in Rotberg, Robert I. and Weiss, Thomas G. (eds), *From Massacres to Genocide*, The World Peace Foundation.

Negrine, Ralph (1996), *The Communication of Politics*, Sage.

Nesbitt, Dermot (1995), *Unionism Restated*, Ulster Unionist Information Centre.

No Comment: Censorship, Secrecy and the Irish Troubles (1989), Article 19.

O'Brien, Brendan (1995), *The Long War*, O'Brien Press.

O'Clery, Conor (1996), *The Greening of The White House*, Gill and Macmillan.

O'Connor, Fionnuala (1993), *In Search of A Catholic State*, Blackstaff Press.

O'Doherty, Malachi (1996), 'The Media and Reporting the Peace Process', paper delivered at Derry conference in Derry, 25 June (courtesy of the author).

O' Malley, Padraig (1997), *The Uncivil Wars*, Beacon Press.

Paletz, David L. and Boiney, John (1992), 'Researchers Perspectives', in Paletz, David L. and Schmid, Alex P. (eds), *Terrorism and the Media*, Sage.

Pollak, Andy (ed.), *A Citizen's Inquiry: The Opsahl Report on Northern Ireland*, Lilliput Press.

Parkinson, Alan (1998), *Ulster Loyalism and the British Media*, Four Courts Press.

Patterson, Henry (1997), T*he Politics of Illusion: A Political History of the IRA*, Serif.

Picard, Robert G. (1991), 'The Journalist's Role in Coverage of Terrorism', in Alali, A. Odasuo and Eke, Kenoye Kelvin (eds), *Media Coverage of Terrorism*, Sage.

Porter, Norman (1996), *Rethinking Unionism*, Blackstaff Press.

Producers Guidelines (1994), BBC.

Punch, Keith F. (1998), *Introduction to Social Research*, Sage.

Report of The International Body (1996), HMSO.

Rolston, Bill and Miller, David (1996), *War and Words*, Beyond The Pale Publications.

Rotberg, Robert I. and Weiss, Thomas G. (1996), *From Massacres To Genocide*, The World Peace Foundation.

Rowan, Brian (1995), *Behind The Lines*, Blackstaff Press.

Ruane, Joseph and Todd, Jennifer (1996), *The Dynamics of Conflict in Northern Ireland*, Cambridge University Press.

Schlesinger, Philip (1979), 'The BBC in Northern Ireland', in *The British Media and Ireland: Truth: The First Casualty*, Information on Ireland.

Schlesinger, Philip (1987), *Putting Reality Together,* Methuen.

Schlesinger, Philip (1991), 'Rethinking the Sociology of Journalism: Source Strategies and the Limits of Media-Centrism', in Ferguson, Marjorie (ed.), *Public Communication: The New Imperatives,* Sage.

Schlesinger, Philip and Elliott, Philip and Murdoch, Graham (1983), *Televising Terrorism: Political Violence in Popular Culture*, Comedia.

Schlesinger, Philip and Tumber, Howard (1994), *Reporting Crime*, Clarendon Press.

Searle, Clive (1998), *Researching Society and Culture*, Sage.

Shattuck, John (1996), 'Human Rights and Humanitarian Crises', in Rotberg, Robert I. and Weiss, Thomas G. (eds), *From Massacres To Genocide*, The World Peace Foundation.

Shirlow, Peter and McGovern, Mark (1997), *Who Are 'The People'?*, Pluto Press.

Silverman, David (1994), *Interpreting Qualitative Data*, Sage.

Sinn Fein (1992), *Towards A Lasting Peace*, Sinn Fein.

Sinn Fein (1994), *Setting The Record Straight: A record of communications between Sinn Fein and the British Government, October 1990–November 1993*, Sinn Fein.

Stevenson, Jonathan (1996), *'We Wrecked The Place': Contemplating an End to the Irish Studies*, Free Press.

Strentz, Herbert (1989), *News Reporters and News Sources*, Iowa State University Press.

Strobel, Warren P. (1997), *Late-Breaking Foreign Policy: The News Media's Influence on Peace Operations*, United States Institute of Peace Press.

Sutton, Malcolm (1994), *'Bear in Mind These Dead': an index of deaths from the conflict in Northern Ireland 1969–1993*, Beyond The Pale Publications.

Tangen Page, Michael von and Schwarz, Kirsten Sparre (1994), 'Peace in Northern Ireland through the journalist channel?', paper presented to the Second European Conference on Peacemaking and Conflict Resolution, Donostia–San Sebastian, 8–12 October, University of Bradford.

Taylor, John (1991), *War Photography*, Routledge.

Taylor, Maxwell and Quayle, Ethel (1994), *Terrorist Lives*, Brassey.

Taylor, Peter (1986), 'The Semantics of Political Violence', in Golding, Peter and Murdock, Graham and Schlesinger, Peter (eds), *Communicating Politics: Mass Communication and the Political Process*, Leicester University Press.

Taylor, Peter (1997), *Provos: The IRA and Sinn Fein*, Bloomsbury.

The Joint Declaration (1993), HMSO.

Thompson, John B. (1995), *The Media and Modernity*, Polity Press.

Turner, Bryan S. (1990), 'Peroration on Ideology', in Abercrombie, Nicholas and Hill, Stephen and Turner, Bryan S. (eds), *Dominant Ideologies*, Unwin Hyman.

Whyte, John (1990), *Interpreting Northern Ireland*, Clarendon Press.

Williams, Kevin (1993), 'The Light at the End of the Tunnel', in Eldridge, John (ed.), *Getting The Message*, The Glasgow Media Group, Routledge.

Wilson, Andrew (1996), 'Survey', in Graham, Paul (ed.), *Troubled Land*, Phaidon.

Wilson, Robin (1996), 'Peace Process by Soundbite', *The Journalists' Handbook*, Jan. 1996, No. 44.

Wolfsfeld, Gadi (1997), *Promoting Peace Through the News Media: Some Initial Lessons From the Oslo Peace Process*, Press/Politics, Vol. 2, No. 4.

Wolfsfeld, Gadi (1997), *Media and Political Conflict*, Cambridge University Press.

Wolfsfeld, Gadi (1998), 'Promoting Peace through the News Media', in Liebes, Tamor and Curran, James (eds), *Media, Ritual and Identity*, Routledge.

Yorke, Ivor (1995), *Television News*, Focal Press.

Zolo, Daniel (1992), *Democracy and Complexity*, Polity Press.